The House on the Hill

Annie Seaton

This book is a work of fiction. Names, characters, places, magazine and incidents are the product of the author's imagination or are used fictitiously. Any resemblance to actual events, locales, or persons, living or dead, is coincidental.

An anthology comprising Beach House (2015) Beach Music, Beach Walk and Beach Dreams (2018).

DEDICATION

This book is dedicated to our much-loved mother who left us. Like Aggie, she was not with us for the last few years of her life, but we knew she still loved us.

ACKNOWLEDGMENTS

A special thank you to my wonderful editor and critique partner, Susanne Bellamy.
You polish my sentences until they shine.

Rosie's story

Beach House

Annie Seaton

Chapter 1

"Friend or family?"

"Sorry?" Rosie Pemberton stared at the usher waiting to direct her to the left or the right side of the small chapel in the aged care facility. His eyes were round and sad, and the tones of his mournful voice blended in with the soft music piping through the small room.

I guess there's a certain look you get working in the funeral industry.

"Friend or family," he repeated gently.

"Oh…oh, friend…I suppose." She smiled up at him and her voice was quiet as she fought back the solid ache in her throat. This was going to be a celebration of Aggie's life; she'd shed all of her tears last week. Her foster mother had slipped away holding her hand as the morning sun cleared the horizon. One gentle sigh was as soft as the lull of the surf on the beach below and Aggie was gone.

A life of joy and giving finished in one soft breath as her spirit left her. Rosie's tears threatened again, and she drew in a deep breath of her own, reaffirming her life. She had loved Aggie as though she had been her birth mother. The usher handed her an order of service and pointed to the left of the small funeral chapel before she could change her mind. The chapel was set in the grounds of the aged care facility overlooking Tamarama Beach and Aggie had been able to sit at the window and look out at her beloved ocean, and across the bay to the house on the hill where she had spent most of her life.

Technically, Rosie *was* a friend and had no blood relationship with Aunt Agatha. No matter that Aggie had taken her in when Rosie was eight years old. No matter that she had loved her like a mother; she wasn't real family. For twelve years, Aggie had looked after her; housed her, fed her, loved her, listened to her teenage woes and sent her off to the local schools where she'd found her confidence, her best friends, and had become a normal teenager. Growing up on the southern beaches of Sydney, she'd been truly blessed. The day the government agency had placed her with Aggie had been the best in Rosie's life.

She could still hear Aggie's voice. "Of course, you're family, sweet pea. My family."

But no, I'm not. She had no claim to family. They had been two lonely souls and they had fitted very well together. Nothing formal. No adoption. Just foster care.

It wouldn't be a big funeral. As she walked to the front pew on the friends' side, Rosie nodded at the familiar faces of the staff from the high care section of the nursing home where Aggie had spent her final months. Since Aggie's stroke and her admission into the aged care facility just after Rosie's twenty-first birthday, Rosie had come to know the staff very well. When Aggie had started to make breaks for the beach at all hours of the day and night, saying she wanted to go for a swim, she'd been admitted to the dementia ward—the lock-up ward, the girls had joked.

You had to joke, or your heart would break. Over the past three years, their roles had reversed, and Rosie had cared for her, making sure that Aggie was settled and happy. As happy as she could be anyway as dementia took a cruel hold of the once vibrant woman who'd taken such good care of a lonely little girl.

Rosie held her fitted red skirt straight as she slid along the polished timber pew. God knows where she'd be now if Aggie hadn't taken her in. The sweet old soul had helped her forget about a father who died in prison and a mother who'd left her when she was three years old. Her birth mother—Rosie could never think of her as Mum—had died from a drug overdose before Rosie's seventh birthday. After a few months in three foster homes where the carers had been more interested in the money from the government than sorting out the emotions of a confused little girl, Aggie came along.

So yes. Rosie lifted her chin and bit her lip to stop it from trembling.

I may not be family, but she was my best friend in the whole world and I will miss her so much.

She turned as a flurry of noise and movement came from the entry, stifling a grin as her two housemates, and colleagues made their usual colourful, dramatic entrance.

And in the friendship stakes, this pair followed a close second to Aggie. Sally and Sonia strode down the narrow aisle and slid into the pew beside her. Sally wore an emerald green suit with a string of pearls gracing her elegant neck, and Sonia was clad in a loose flowing dress striped with every colour of the rainbow. Rosie rolled her eyes. And her feet are bare. Toe rings graced each of Sonia's ten toes.

Sally folded her hands on her lap and sat straight, like one of her yoga positions. She exuded calm as much as her younger sister, Sonia—sorry, Ocean Lily was the name of choice this month—created chaos wherever she went.

Now Ocean Lily leaned across her twin sister and hissed at Rosie. "Psst. Rosie."

"Ssh, the service is about to start." As the music faded away, Rosie folded her hands in her lap too, attempting to absorb some of Sally's calm. She tried to focus on the man tapping the microphone mounted on the lectern at the front of the chapel. She settled her gaze above his head, avoiding the white coffin that was covered in purple flowers. Aggie's favourites; she would have loved them. That damn ache lodged in her throat again.

"I have to tell you." Sonia—Ocean Lily— reached over and grabbed Rosie's hands.

"Tell me what?"

"You will never—never ever in one million years"—Lily was as prone to exaggeration as she was to name changing—"guess who is in the foyer out there."

"Keep your voice down." Rosie frowned at her flamboyant friend.

"Rosie. It's him."

"Who?"

"Taj Brown."

"Taj Brown?" Rosie smiled. "I'm okay, so there's no need to try and cheer me up with a joke, Sonia."

"I'm not Sonia anymore…I'm Ocean Lily." Her friend's plump painted lips settled into a thin line for a moment before she leaned right across the front of her sister and squeezed Rosie's hand. "It *is* him. I heard the usher guy welcome him."

"My Taj Brown? No, not mine." She shook her head. "You know what I mean. No way. Why would he be here?" Rosie's heart picked up a beat and she fought the urge to turn around again.

Stop it. Show some respect to Aggie.

"Maybe he's a rellie of Aggie's. Brown? They share the same last name."

Rosie lowered her voice to a whisper. Holy hell. *Taj Brown?* "Can't be. She had none. No family, I mean."

"Don't be so sure of that. It has to be that. Why else would he be here? Look."

Rosie's eyes followed the direction of Lily's finger and her heart lodged in her throat. "Oh my God." She grabbed Lily's hand and pulled it down to her lap. "Don't be so bloody obvious."

Sure enough, Taj Brown, world champion surfer, was making his way to the front pew on the *family* side. Dressed in an immaculate grey suit, his usual sun-tangled locks were pulled back neatly with a leather tie.

No way. Her heart jumped into her throat. Her romantic hero, the gorgeous surfer on her posters, the hero she had dreamed about for years was in the same room as her.

But blast and damnation, what a horrid occasion to meet him. Not that she'd be meeting him, she'd be too nervous to go anywhere near him.

Her mouth dried. His suit pants were snug over muscular thighs and his suit jacket was a perfect fit over his broad shoulders. Of all the places to see Taj Brown, the heartthrob of her teenage years; absolutely and totally unexpected. As she covertly eyed him, another small group of older people followed him and streamed into the front three rows.

On the family side. How many are there?

"God, look at him…he's gorgeous. Even better looking than on TV." Lily's voice was breathless. "Or on any of your posters."

And yes, those posters still covered Rosie's bedroom wall, even though she was almost twenty-four and way too old for hero worship. She'd never got around to taking them down. The landscapes brought a bit of sunshine—ocean and sky—into her dark room. Had nothing to do with the toned and buff surfer on the surfboard in the middle of each poster.

No way. They just provided a nice scene on her walls.

Sally nudged them both. "Stop gawking and yakking, and show some respect, you pair. You can find out why they are all here after the service."

Rosie turned her gaze to the front, away from the broad shoulders and sun-bleached hair of the man who had filled her lustful fantasies since she was sixteen years old.

Oh my God. Aggie, what didn't you tell me?

Family?

And what did that mean for the house on the hill…and

her future?

Chapter 2

After the brief service, Theodore Alfred James—known to the world as Taj—Brown, stood apart from his assorted aunts, uncles and cousins as they congregated around the large table in the centre of the room adjacent to the small chapel.

The last thing he wanted was a plate loaded with gooey confections that they were hoeing into, just like he didn't want to speak to any of his family. Not that he knew most of them. Amazing how the death of a wealthy relative brought the vultures circling. He assumed these people were family because they'd traipsed down the aisle behind him and sat on the family side of the chapel with him. The only two he recognized were Uncle Jack and Aunt Esther and when he'd shot back a huge grin he'd received the usual frown of disapproval in return. The life of a surfer didn't quite cut it in a business-suited family who worshipped the dollar. The clink of tea cups around him was very civilised and he attempted to keep his emotions just as civilised and in check. He didn't give a toss what they thought of him.

The irony was he'd probably earned more money on the surfing circuit over the past ten years than they had in a lifetime in their boring offices in the city. But they didn't have a clue about him or his life. Aggie had been the only one who'd ever understood his passion for the ocean after his parents had been killed in the car accident. Hell, she'd given him his first boogie board when he was just a little grommet. If he'd had his way, he would have lived with her in the house on the hill but he'd been marched off to a boarding school on the north shore by his guardian.

The music swelled to a crescendo as the service ended and he dragged his thoughts back to the present. The three women who had sat on the other side of the chapel during the service stood together beside the window that overlooked the ocean, and he wondered who they were. The large group who'd sat behind them had disappeared as soon as the music stopped—the pink shirts embroidered with the name of the facility gave them away as staff, as did their hasty exit as soon as the curtains had closed over the coffin after the last words of the officiating minister. The woman in the fire-engine red suit had legs that went forever, a serious-looking woman in a green suit and pearls stood beside her, and the third one wore a dress that looked like a colourful tent. Maybe some of Great Aunt Aggie's strays; he assumed she'd stayed in touch with some of the children she'd fostered over the years.

Taj stared across the room. The woman in the red suit was drop-dead gorgeous. Her jet-black hair was pulled back into a glossy fall that reached almost to her waist. Her pale skin was like porcelain and her almond-shaped eyes were currently focused on the stormy ocean outside. Like him, she looked like she wished she was somewhere else. His eyes lingered on the curve of her back as she reached for a cup resting on the window sill and an inappropriate interest stirred in his groin.

Christ, man. You're at a funeral. Show a bit of class.

He bit back a grin as he recalled a piece of advice that one of his buddies had passed his way when he'd hit town last week.

"There's a great escort service in an old house at the top of the hill at Bondi Beach."

Taj had shaken his head. "If I ever have to resort to that, I'll give the game away, buddy."

"The 'Sisters' something, it's called. Just in case you change your mind."

"No fear of that." Taj had laughed and gone to the bar

for the next shout. The guy on the tour obviously had his cities mixed up. After a while, they all seemed the same. He knew that the house on the hill above North Bondi belonged to his Great Aunt Agatha and he couldn't imagine that she'd become a madam in her twilight years.

Hell, it must be past time for some female company if he was blessed with a hard-on at a funeral service. He forced his gaze past the beautiful woman and watched the break build on the point. The southerly buster that had roared in during the service was whipping up the swell. He'd much rather be out there, free as a bird with salt air filling his lungs rather than here with the cold artificial smell of air conditioning and the cloying aroma of the purple flowers wafting from the adjacent chapel.

As if that's going to happen with my bloody knee. Taj's mood worsened and he glanced down at his Rolex, finally giving in to the impatience that tugged at him as he waited.

Great Aunt Agatha's lawyer, Mr Pepper, had asked him to stay after the service. The elderly solicitor wanted a brief meeting this afternoon, but the damn man had insisted on having a cup of tea first. So the cousins were hovering around, waiting for the kill; they knew something was happening. He wasn't sure who else had been invited to the meeting.

Probably all hoped they'd inherit Aggie's house; the beautiful old mansion that sat on the hill at the northern edge of Bondi Beach. Just above the surf on the rocky point, he was staring at. It was the last house on Ramsgate Avenue and was perched precariously on an acre of land above the rocks at North Bondi.

Prime piece of real estate. Worth millions. Taj watched as the cousins gathered together, whispering and throwing the occasional glance his way and then, strangely, over to the women near the window.

Good luck to them. He didn't want—or need—anything from his family. There were some good memories of staying there with Aggie for a few summers before he'd dropped out of school and hit the world surfing circuit at sixteen; that would do him. He should have kept in touch with her—she'd been a kind old soul— but his career had taken off and he was out of the country more than he was in it. Last time he'd been at her house, just after his thirteenth birthday, she'd had a new foster child, a pretty little girl with black hair called Rosie. God, there'd been a lot of water under the bridge since then.

Or under my board. All over the world. Taj grinned ruefully and stretched his leg, wincing as the ever-present pain tugged at his knee. With it came a little tug of guilt that he'd not visited Aggie once since his early teens. He hadn't even known about her stroke or dementia they'd mentioned in the brief eulogy.

"Ahem." Mr Pepper cleared his throat beside him and pulled Taj's thoughts back to the present. "Theodore? The home has kindly allowed us to use the board room to have our discussion. It won't take long. Follow me…please."

***

Taj Brown. The one and the same Taj Brown in the surfing posters on her bedroom walls in the house on the hill. But the Taj Brown in the posters had kind blue eyes that complimented his rakish grin. Nothing like this cold man who sat across the table from her. She'd looked up and caught him checking her out but not a flicker of emotion had warmed his clinical expression.

Those posters are coming down tonight. Sad how all the teenage dreams turned out to be wrong.

"Thank you for meeting with me, Ms Pemberton. Theodore." The old solicitor looked from one to the other as they sat on one side of the big square table across from the old solicitor. "I presume you are each acquainted with the other?"

Tension radiated off *Theodore* as he held her gaze, and Rosie fought the heat that she knew would stain her fair skin brick-red as it inched up her neck. For all her poring over the surfing magazines and documentaries, she'd never known his real name was Theodore.

She'd lived in a teenage fantasy world.

So what do I say? Do I admit I know who he is? God, the whole world knows who he is.

Before she could answer, Mr Pepper filled the awkward silence. "No? I'm sorry, how remiss of me to make assumptions. Theodore, this is Ms Rosie Pemberton. Ms Pemberton, this is Mr Brown. Theodore is—or rather—he was Agatha's great nephew."

Rosie saw the instant his jaw dropped, and recognition flared in the baby blues, filling them with warmth. And bringing back the sexy crinkles beside them as his lips turned up into a smile.

Okay, so the posters can stay.

"Rosie? Little Rosie, who lived with Aunt Aggie?"

"That's me." To her relief her voice was calm and she'd fought that blasted heat away before she looked like a beetroot. She held out her hand and he took it in his with a gentle squeeze. "But I don't think we've met before?" She straightened her spine and her hand stayed steady in his. Hell, she even impressed herself with her cool, calm voice. Who would ever think she'd get to touch her idol in real life?

My God. Taj Brown is holding my hand. And her nerve endings were going crazy.

"Once…a very long time ago when you were still in pigtails. So, I guess you stayed with her for a while?" His voice was just as sexy as in his news interviews and surfing documentaries. Truly, she had been a Taj Brown tragic.

"If you're still around now, that is?" That voice could still send a ripple or two down her spine. Although now that she was grown up it travelled to places that were best not thought of in a meeting like this. Rosie gave herself a little shake and pulled her hand back.

"Yes, I'm still around." She kept her voice cool. More around than he'd been if he was a relative. Not once had any other person visited Aggie in the aged care facility, or enquired about her wellbeing, and here they were filling three pews at her funeral service.

Not one single visitor. Rosie stiffened her spine a little more and the nervous trembly feeling receded a bit. From everywhere.

She wasn't giving anything away until she knew just what was going on here, but the feeling of impending doom lodged in her chest. It was worse than the flutters that his touch had generated.

Pepper cleared his throat and shuffled the papers in his hand. "I just wanted to let you both know, informally, that I will require you to meet with me in my office next week to discuss the disbursement of Agatha's estate. I preferred to let you each know personally without you reading it in a formal letter." He turned to Rosie and a frown wrinkled his high forehead. "Particularly as the situation may be difficult for you, Rosie."

"Difficult?" The sexy voice of Mr Brown was now cold as were the baby blues turned back to Mr Pepper.

Sheesh. Posters down again.

"Until I read the will, and we discuss the…er…complicated things we have to discuss, I wanted to give you both fair warning, that this may be a difficult process."

"Difficult in what way?" Rosie's voice was still steady, and completely at odds with the nerves that were running rampant inside her. As if it wasn't bad enough that Taj Brown was sitting beside her sending her hormones into a frenzy, things were going to be difficult with the will?

Mr Pepper held up one hand. "I'll read the letter that is in the post to you and then we can discuss the…er…actual situation…in my office next week."

Cold fingers of disbelief crawled up Rosie's spine as Mr Pepper read the document in a sonorous monotone. When he finished reading, he shook his head slowly. "So Rose, my dear, I know that your income is…er…how shall we say, derived from the house on the hill, as is that of your er…partners, and you are going to have to rethink the situation until matters are finalised."

"You still live in Aggie's house at the top of the hill?" If it was possible, Mr Brown's voice was even colder and there was a strange expression fixed on his face. The words came from tight lips.

How did I ever think he had a sexy mouth? Memories of pretending to kiss a poster when she was about fifteen were banished.

"The house that overlooks Bondi Beach?" he said.

"Yes, that's the one. Where I live and work." Rosie nodded at him and stood slowly. "Thank you, Mr Pepper. I'll see you next week, and I'll certainly give the situation some thought before we meet again."

Some thought? She'd be lucky if the 'situation' didn't take over her mind forever.

She pushed the chair in, and before she crossed to the door, she nodded coolly at the man who had once filled her dreams. He stared back at her and shook his head. Something was bugging him but with the stuck-up attitude he had, she wasn't going to hang around and find out what it was.

"Theodore." She gave him a tight, cool smile as she reached for the door handle. Mr Theodore Brown dropped his eyes and his gaze raked her from her toes up, lingering on the expanse of bare thigh revealed by the short skirt. Rosie fought the urge to pull it lower. *Damn him.* Aunt Aggie had requested they wear colour to her funeral and the colour and length of her skirt were none of his business.

How the hell had she thought he was a nice guy for so many years?

Not only were those posters coming down, but they would also go straight into the trash.

Chapter 3

Rosie hurried out to the car park at the side of the building, her high heels clicking on the concrete path. She had driven herself to the chapel—over the past six years she'd virtually had a parking space reserved for her at the aged care facility. She'd always kept her appointments clear from two till four in the afternoon, so she could come and sit with Aunt Aggie. In the last few months, Aggie had stared at her vacantly and even though it had been hard, she had still visited every day.

She slammed the door of her old car and sent a quick wish up to the universe that the old girl would start for the second time today; her reliability had been hit-and-miss over the past weeks, and this was the first time she'd had the car out since Aggie had passed on last week. A new car was the last thing she could afford and if things panned out the way she was beginning to suspect, she wouldn't be able to afford much at all. Rosie wanted to escape before Theodore caught up to her and started asking questions.

The black sports car with a sleek surf logo parked beside her could belong to no one but Taj Brown. Not that it took an Einstein to figure out that the sleek surf logo with the letters T and B flowing through the wave referred to anyone else apart from the famous surfer. She resisted the temptation to take out her key and scratch a shiny panel. That would not achieve anything apart from a childish satisfaction at besting the idol who had now turned out to be not only a pain in the proverbial but someone who was going to impact her future.

Her heart had finally resumed its normal pace, and all of the excitement of finally being in the presence of her pinup boy had quickly calmed with his cool reaction. Okay, the shock of him being related to Aunt Aggie was something she was going to have to process, but she had a four o'clock appointment at the house and she'd have to hurry to get back in time. The old car's engine fired on the second turn of the key and Rosie sent up a swift thank you, ignoring the ominous rattles and clanks that came from beneath the bonnet. She'd give some thought to the dilemma ahead—and she had no doubt there was going to be one—when she looked after her client. It was Joey Carmichael this afternoon and he was a non-talker and that would suit her just fine.

As the car groaned up the hill, the wind off the ocean buffeted the car. The first splatters of rain hit the windscreen and she flipped the wipers on, groaning as they stuck in the middle of the glass. Was nothing going to go her way today?

The car came to a halt with a final gurgle when she reached the back gate of Aunt Aggie's property. Damn, she always thought of it as Aunt Aggie's and in her usual dreamy state, hadn't really considered the future. That was all about to change.

She opened the back door of the house and pulled her high heels off and threw them at the shoe rack at the side of the inside porch before hurtling through the kitchen.

"Well?" Sonia pushed her chair back and grabbed Rosie's hands and she came to a standstill. "What happened? What did Mr Pepper want?"

"Later. I've got Joey now." She tried to pull her hands away from Sonia's tight grasp. She wasn't ready to talk about the solicitor's news until she gave it some thought. Not even with her two best friends because it would affect them just as much as her.

"Uh uh." Sally shook her head from across the table. "He cancelled. Football training was brought forward because of the storm."

"I saw the lights on at the ground when I drove up the

hill. Storm's going to be a beauty." Rosie jumped as the window panes rattled and the whistling wind confirmed her words.

Sonia—or damn Lily whatever— burst into the room, pulled out a chair and pointed to the vacant chair at the end of the table. "Sit. We're all done with our appointments for the day and we have some very serious things to discuss."

Rosie shook her head as she saw the teacups lined up in the centre of the table. "I'm not in the mood, Sonia."

"I've changed my name legally this time. Sonia has gone. Out into the ether." Ocean Lily waved a vague hand toward the ceiling and Rosie couldn't help the giggle that rose to her lips. Sonia's crazies were just a normal part of their day

"So you can call me Lily."

"Okay. But I'm really not in the mood, Lily." Rosie sat and exchanged a smile with Sally across the table.

"You might as well settle in, it's not looking good." Sally's words conveyed the same level of worry that Lily's had.

Lily picked up the first cup and peered inside. "This is mine." Her forehead wrinkled in a frown as she poured tea from the pot into a white cup sitting on a deep saucer. She pushed it across the table to Rosie. "Not good at all. And Sally's was worse."

Rosie rolled her eyes at Sally when Lily looked away. She could tell them both what was wrong without going through a damn tea leaf reading, but if it kept Lily happy…

Rosie's alternative therapies were all in the health field, and although she respected Sonia's ways and saw the huge clientele she had, some days it was a bit hard to take.

"Clear your mind and sip it slowly." Sonia stared at her as Rosie took a sip of the Earl Grey tea she loved. She relaxed as she drained the cup and tipped it upside down into the saucer and pushed it back to Sonia…damn it…Lily.

Lily pushed it back. "You have to read your own. That's how we know it's right for you. It's what you see." She lowered her voice to a sonorous monotone—almost a chant—and Rosie stifled another giggle.

"Now clear your mind, start from the handle and go clockwise. What do you see?"

Rosie rolled her eyes again and stared into the cup. It didn't matter what she could see, she knew very well what was about to happen without any magic tricks or tea leaf readings. As she opened her mouth to speak a huge clap of thunder shook the house and the lights flickered. Even though it was only late afternoon, it was almost dark outside. The southerly buster had roared up the cost and the spring weather of the morning was now a distant memory.

Okay, maybe Lily's hocus-pocus had some worth.

"I can see a house with a cross through it. There's a snake slithering along the bottom and a set of unbalanced scales." Rosie was hard-pressed to keep a straight face, even though the worry of what was ahead slithered through her stomach. She felt mean when Lily drew in a gasp and Sally paled.

"Oh my God, a warning. End of comfort and home, and someone we can't trust." Lily's voice shook and she raised an unsteady hand to her forehead with a dramatic flourish.

"And justice will not prevail." Sally finished the definition of the symbols.

"I'm getting my tarot cards." Lily pushed her chair back and it fell to the old linoleum floor with a crash to rival the thunder that now boomed outside.

"I'm sorry." Rosie put her hand back and pulled the elastic from her hair and shook her hair free. She was getting a headache and maybe letting her hair hang loose would fix it.

And maybe not.

"Forget the cards. I was being smart." She stared across the table at her two very best friends in the world. "I'm sorry, gals. I think the time for the Divine Soul Sisters is destined to come to an end."

***

The windscreen wipers whipped backward and forward as Taj turned the car into Ramsgate Avenue. He'd taken a few wrong turns as he'd tried to get to the top of the hill but finally, he'd seen the sign for Ramsgate Avenue. The motor of his car purred softly as it cruised to the curve of the cul-de-sac at the top of the hill. He had to see it for himself. The thought of his aunt's graceful old house being turned into a brothel was unbelievable. Barely in her grave, and by all accounts, Rosie and her friends had been using the house for their own purposes for God knew how long.

Up until he'd put two and two together and realised that the house his mate had referred to was Aunt Aggie's, Taj couldn't have cared less who it was left to. But no way on God's earth was he going to see it go to a little upstart madam who had turned it into a brothel. Or an escort service—whatever it was called. But he didn't care. Aunt Aggie's graceful old mansion was being used to sell sex, and it was not on.

Aggie had been liberal, but she'd turn in her grave to know what the place was being used for. At his meeting with Mr Pepper and Miss Rosie Pemberton next week, he'd fight tooth and nail to take it from her clutches. He'd intended to look for another property to develop and the house on the hill would do very nicely. And it would keep it in the family. Now that surfing was out of the question, he had to diversify his interests. Developing a familiar property and maybe turning it into a block of units could be very lucrative and satisfying.

Colourful wisps of material mounted on two poles on

either side of the gate flipped back and forward in the strong wind. Taj pulled the car to the side of the curb and narrowed his eyes waiting for a lull in the wind so he could read what was on them. As he watched, a car drew up in front of the gate and three men in business suits climbed out and ran through the driving rain and stood on the front porch.

The wind dropped and he peered through the windshield that was now streaked with rain.

"Divine Soul Sisters." The large words confirmed his suspicions. This was the place. He squinted to read the smaller writing on the bottom. "Where your deepest wishes can come true."

Bloody hell. The hide of them.

As he watched, one of the women from the funeral, the one in the striped colourful dress, opened the door and ushered the men inside from the porch. There was no doubt; this was the place his mate had told him about.

The same front porch, where he'd played as a young child and propped his boogie board against the old cupboard. The same one that was still there.

He frowned as another car pulled up and a second group of men crossed to the porch. Should he rev the engine and drive away now? If it took millions, he'd fight tooth and nail to keep the house. The will hadn't been read and it still belonged to the Brown family. And Miss Rosie Pemberton would not get a cent.

Chapter 4

Rosie opened her diary and ran a finger down the day's appointments. Old Mr Hollis was booked in for a massage on his sore shoulder, Mrs Pitt had her weekly appointment for her lymphatic massage but after lunch, Rosie had five sports massages in a row. Since the local Rugby League Club footballers had started attending Sally's yoga classes, Rosie's appointments for a remedial massage had picked up. Corked thighs, strained hamstrings, and twisted knees. She'd got to the stage of watching the Sunday night sports news to see which players had been injured in the weekend game and it was a good indication of how busy her following week would be.

She'd been invited out so many times by the various football players, she'd lost count. Work and pleasure did not mix. And besides, she wasn't interested in a relationship. Not now, and maybe never. Growing up as a foster child without her own family made her very wary of getting involved with anyone.

Maybe in the future, but there were definitely never going to be any kids in the mix.

The complication with the house and what they would do in the future was taking up all her time and energy now. Maybe it was a good time for this to happen. The conservatory at the back of the house was big enough for Sally's yoga and Sonia's—damn—Lily's exercise classes. The only problem was if they couldn't use Aggie's house for their alternative therapies centre anymore, there was no way they would be able to afford big enough premises around Bondi for the three of them to have their treatment rooms.

All of their clientele was local and it had taken a couple of years to build it up. Rosie fought the sigh that threatened to escape. Okay, so I was naïve expecting that we could just stay here. No matter how many times she read the letter from the solicitor it still didn't clarify his words about a difficult situation ahead.

The bottom line was—just like the seating at the funeral—she wasn't family and she shouldn't have expected to inherit the house. There had been a constant stream of realtors knocking on the door since Aggie's stroke and she'd got used to sending them away.

It was time to think about the future. She was due at Mr Pepper's office at four o'clock. Rosie crossed to the window and looked out over the sea. Last night's storm had cleared and the ocean glistened in the morning sun. A line of surfers bobbed in the gentle swell out behind the break and she pressed her forehead to the cool glass wondering if one of them was Taj Brown.

##

There was no time for a shower before she left for the legal appointment. The uncertainty of the outcome of the reading of the will had filled her thoughts all day and it had been hard to focus on her technique. It was only when Joey Carmichael had let out a yelp as she pressed her elbows into the soft tissue above his butt, did she realize that she was putting her frustration into her remedial massage.

"Crikey, Rosie. I'm sure my butt bruises are going to read 'Rosie was here'."

"Sorry, but if you want to play football next weekend, it has to hurt." But she'd lightened up the pressure and Joey was happy with the treatment by the time he limped out.

A quick change of clothes, a spray of perfume to cover the smell of the Tiger Balm massage oil that seemed to permeate her hands these days and a quick brush of her hair had to make do. She called out to Sally who was just winding up her yoga class. There was no sign of Lily; she must be in an appointment. Of the three of them, her clairvoyant appointments and tarot card reading kept her busier than Rosie and Sally.

"Wish me luck." Rosie mouthed and waved as she slipped through the hall and out the door. She tried to lighten her mood. Lily had finally got the tarot cards out last night and a positive outcome had been promised. Hah…if you put your faith in such things.

Stay positive. Time will tell. She tried to ignore the little flutter of nerves at seeing Taj Brown again.

As luck would have it, it took five attempts to get the car started and of course, she caught every red light through Bondi Junction. Finally, she found a spot to park the car, only two streets away from Mr Pepper's office.

She rushed up the stairs; it was quicker than taking the lift to the first floor. "They're waiting for you in the office." The secretary stood and led her down the hall, disapproval stiffening her stance.

"Thank you." Rosie smoothed her hand over her hair, tucking in the loose fine strands that would never stay in place. She bit her lip and then stopped, pushing the nerves away. There was nothing she could do about the outcome of the meeting, so there was no point being nervous. Taj Brown nerves? No more.

She'd left the posters up and spent the last few mornings lying in bed trying to reconcile the sexy, carefree surfer with the uptight guy in the suit at the funeral. If it hadn't been for the tangle of blond curls tied back, she could have even pretended it wasn't him.

"Come in, my dear. "Mr Pepper took her hand and shook it, and she focused on his face, trying not to look around the room. Not that she had to look. She could feel the gaze burning into her back. Turning around slowly, she nodded coolly, fighting the urge to wipe her sweaty palms on her skirt.

God, it was so unfair that one man had the looks of a Greek god. Theodore Brown—she was not going to think of him as Taj—stood and held out his hand and a whiff of citrus aftershave floated over to her, covering up the musty smell of the room.

"Rosie. Good to see you finally got here." She ignored the jibe and squeezed his hand, hoping the lingering remnants of Tiger Balm on her fingers burned his palm. She hadn't counted on the nervous jolt that ran up her arm and settled into a fluttery feeling in her chest. She willed the flutters to stay there and not head south as they had at the funeral service.

"Would you like a cold drink? Or a cup of tea?" Mr Pepper had to be all of seventy-five yet he fussed around like a mother hen.

"No, thank you." She slid into the chair he had pulled out for her at the same time as Taj sat down across the table. "I have appointments booked tonight so I have to get back as soon as I can."

Taj's blond eyebrows rose above those baby blues, and he stared at her. "So your service is by appointment?"

"Of course it is. How else would you run a business?" She stared back at him, trying not to drown in his stare. Not that it was remotely sexy. It wasn't even friendly.

"How else." His voice was a low mutter and his face held a strange expression as his eyes locked on hers.

"Congratulations, Rosie. I read in the local paper that you girls have picked up a contract with the football club." Mr Pepper took his seat at the head of the table and steepled his fingers in front of his wrinkled face as he smiled at her.

She ignored the snort that came across the table.

What is his problem?

"Yes. So we are really hoping that once the legal stuff

from Aggie's estate is sorted out, we can stay there."

"The whole football team?" Taj's interruption was filled with disbelief and it gave Rosie great pleasure to nod back to him.

"Yes, the whole team. First grade and the reserves too."

He shook his head and turned to the solicitor. "Can we just get on with this please?"

"Certainly." Mr Pepper shuffled his papers. "You may be wondering why the rest of the family is not here, but Agatha made it quite clear to me when she made the changes to her will, that the split with her family was irrevocable." He turned to Taj. "Except for you, Theodore. She followed your career closely and was very proud of what you achieved. If your parents had been alive, I am sure she would have spoken to them eventually. I know she was very upset that there was a rift with them that hadn't been resolved before they passed away."

Rosie sat quietly, confused thoughts swirling through her mind as she waited for him to begin reading. There must have been a family fallout before Aggie took her in. She'd never mentioned family. She frowned, remembering that Taj had said yesterday that he'd met her when they were children, but as much as she concentrated, she had no memory of anyone ever visiting the old house. Apart from the few old girlfriends that Aggie had stayed in touch with over the years. Rosie smiled. That group of old dears had been the first to take on Sally's yoga when she had kicked the class off.

Mr Pepper began to read and she switched off as the usual legalese that said nothing filled the air. Being of sound mind...

"Now we come to the division. I bequeath all of my worldly goods to my ward, Rosie Pemberton—"

Rosie gasped and looked across at Taj who had placed

his hands on the table and shot to his feet.

"No way." His expression was grim. "Did she have any idea what you were doing in our family home? Or did you just start that up when she didn't know what was going on and couldn't object?"

"Theodore. Theodore. Sit down." Mr Pepper glared over the top of his spectacles. "Please let me finish. To my ward, Rosie Pemberton, and to my great nephew, Theodore Alfred James Brown. My house, my possessions and all of my assets—" He looked at each of them in turn and cleared his throat. "This is where we may strike some difficulties. They will be divided equally between the two beneficiaries on the condition that each of them resides in the house for a period of three months from the reading of the will."

Rosie closed her eyes and took a deep breath as the words sank in. Maybe all wasn't lost. The room was quiet; you could have heard a pin drop.

"I'll buy you out." Taj broke the silence. Rosie glared back at him. She'd just about had enough of Mr Attitude over there.

"What gives you that right? So where were you when Aggie was sick? How many times did you visit her in the home? I've been more family to her for the past fifteen years than anyone. Blood ties or not." She folded her arms and sat back, her glare fixed on him. She could look at him now without her heart fluttering and her nerves skittering all over the place. "I am family. Or rather I was her family. She was all I had, and for many years, I was all she had." Her voice broke and she dug into her handbag for a handkerchief.

I will not cry.

Theodore stared at her and she stared back. Damn, she should have sat on the family side at the service and made it clear, she was going to fight. *Good. Hold onto that temper.*

"Please. Both of you." Mr Pepper spoke over them as,

together, Rosie continued and Taj replied loudly.

"We had each other."

"I'll have you know—"

Mr Pepper's chair scraped back on the wooden floor at the same time the door opened and the secretary peered around the edge. "Is everything all right, sir? Would you like me to call security?"

He waved her away. "Thank you. We are fine here. Aren't we?" His voice was stern as he looked at them as though they were naughty children.

"I'm sorry." Rosie's voice was quiet.

Taj folded his arms and scowled at her.

Those posters would be shredded as soon as she got home.

Chapter 5

It had taken a lot of self-control and some sweet talking from him, but Taj had finally convinced Rosie Pemberton that they needed to calm down and consider the options open to them. That was after Mr Pepper made it quite clear that the conditions of the will were iron-clad. If they didn't live together in the house for three months, the property was to be sold and the money to be donated to foster children's care. The wily old bird had obviously thought she'd known them both well enough to know that they would follow the instructions. Taj couldn't have cared less about the house until he'd found out what it was being used for. Now his resolve was set in concrete.

After thanking Mr Pepper, they'd taken a silent lift ride down to the ground floor of the building to the coffee shop in the foyer. Taj wrinkled his nose as the fragrance of Rosie's perfume filled the lift. It was unusual but pleasant. Familiar, but he couldn't remember where he'd smelled it before. The doors slid open when they reached the ground floor and he stood back to let her exit first, biting his lip as his knee locked. Perspiration beaded his brow as the pain shot down his calf and he drew in a deep breath. Rosie waited for him, a quizzical expression on her face. He reached out with one hand as the doors began to close and forced himself to step out, ignoring the pain and trying to hide his limp.

"What's wrong with your leg?" Rosie's brow wrinkled in a frown and her voice was pleasant for the first time since Mr Pepper had dropped the news.

"Surfing injury." He forced a smile onto his face and followed her to the table, holding a chair out for her. A strange feeling unfurled in his stomach when he stopped, and Rosie looked up at him. She was so close he could see the gold flecks in her hazel eyes.

"Let's sit outside. It's a lovely afternoon." Her voice was light, but her expression was still serious.

And it was very pleasant out there; the late afternoon sun filtered into the small courtyard between two buildings and the empty tables were dotted with colourful umbrellas. The light breeze had dropped and the brick walls of the buildings had trapped the last warmth of the spring day. Silence reigned again as the waitress came over and took their order.

"Last order," she informed them. "We'll be closing up shortly."

Taj nodded and switched his gaze to Rosie. "What time is your...er...appointment?"

"Six."

"Okay." He spread his hands, palms up on the table and thought carefully before he spoke. They'd had their blow-up in the solicitor's office and there was nothing to be gained by arguing again. "So how are we going to play this?"

Those hazel eyes held his for a long moment and that nervous jolt moved up into his chest. How the hell did someone with so much to offer to get into the escort business?

"I guess you're going to have to move in."

"I guess I am." Taj nodded slowly. Mr Pepper had quite clearly laid out the terms of the will. Three months living together in the house on the hill and then they could come to a mutual agreement about what would happen after that. Taj had every intention of buying her out.

Now that he couldn't surf, at least he'd be near the ocean. He'd focus on developing the house into units and fill in his days with that.

"So..." He paused. This wasn't going to go down well. "You know I'm not happy about your business operating from the house. How about—"

"How about what?" Her teeth were gritted but her voice was quiet.

"How about you call a halt to it for the three months that I'm there."

"Really! You do realise some of us have to work for a living. And I have clients and commitments. And so do Sally and…Lily."

"Whoa. Stop right there." Now his temper was building again. "Don't go assuming that being on the surf circuit is all roses. It's bloody hard work. And I've worked at it since I was sixteen."

"And I work hard. Just because I—we—work from home—or where we live—doesn't mean it's easy. I can't just drop it and pick it up again. Besides I've just signed a twelve-month contract with the football club."

She pushed her chair back and began to stand but Taj reached out and caught her hand before she could get up. That damn nervous jolt ran up his arm. "Wait. Come on. We have to work this out."

"Your way? So I have to give up my practice? The girls have to take a three-month break. Live on fresh air and roses?" She tried to pull her hand back, but he held on tight. "You get a lovely old home on the beach to live in and we'll all be happy? I don't think so."

"Your practice? What practice?" Taj stared across the table at her and the first glimmer of uncertainty hit him.

"How can you call it a practice?" He screwed up his eyes and lowered his voice trying to figure out what she meant by practice.

"My practice is my job. My livelihood, my income."

"Tell me what you do?" Taj stared at her as his uncertainty grew. "What exactly is your work?"

Maybe she had better spell it out for him. He was beginning to think he had made one almighty mistake.

"I'm a therapist. I specialise in remedial massage, Reiki and lymphatic massage."

In a flash, he realised what the familiar fragrance was. It was the massage oil that his physiotherapist used. That was the smell he'd recognized in the lift.

Hell, he'd made a mistake. One almighty, bloody mistake.

"And you do that in the house?"

"Yes." Her voice was very patient. He was beginning to feel like the biggest dolt ever.

"And what about the others?"

"We all work from the house. The bottom floor has three consulting rooms and a large area where Sally holds her yoga classes. One used to be the conservatory, and the other two were the living areas. The formal one and the informal one. You probably don't remember much about the house because you haven't been there for such a long time."

He ignored the cheap shot.

"And of course...the football club." He had made assumptions and he'd been way off base. Would he own up to what he'd thought?

As he considered his next words, the waitress placed their coffee on the table. He dropped Rosie's hand and pulled out his wallet and paid for the hot drinks. But a smile twitched at his lips.

"Thank you." Rosie tucked her hair back behind her ears and he followed the movement of her hand. Her nails were unpainted and clipped short. "Now are you going to share what's so funny? I can't see the slightest thing to smile about. You don't want to live in the house and we don't want you to." She leaned back and folded her arms and watched him reach for the sugar as she lifted the cup of herbal tea she'd ordered. "Sugar's bad for you…and so's coffee. Now are you going to tell me what is amusing you?"

"I don't know if I should. Especially if I'm going to be living in the same house."

Rosie propped her chin in her hands and the first glimmer of a smile tilted her pretty lips. He loved her name. Her cheeks had a slight rose-tinge to them and her lips were a deep natural rose. She was well-named.

"Spill." At least her voice was a bit warmer now.

"I misunderstood when I saw your sign the other night. One of my surfing buddies told me about an escort service called Sister Something and I jumped to the wrong conclusion."

For a moment she stared at him and then her laugh pealed through the courtyard. The waitress looked over curiously.

"Sin Sisters? Sin Sisters that used to be across from the beach? You thought that was us?" Her shoulders shook with mirth and his coffee sloshed into the saucer as she bumped the table. "Oh my God. Wait till I tell the girls."

"Sin Sisters?" He watched her eyes as they came alight with laughter.

"Yes, they used to run an escort service from one of the apartments on the corner but they moved on a few months back."

He smiled at her thinking how pretty she was when the anger had left her face.

"Gosh, I don't know whether to laugh or be cross. You thought we were looking after the football club?" Tears filled her eyes as she almost howled and her shoulders shook with laughter, and Taj caught a glimpse of the little girl that he'd met all those years ago.

"No wonder you were so uptight. God, Aggie would roll in her grave." Her smile disappeared and she sobered up as she mentioned his aunt, the person who was responsible for this situation of having to live together. "So do you know what she was up to? Making us live in the house together?" Her eyes were wide as she held his gaze.

"Not sure. I didn't know her well enough. What do you think?"

Rosie dropped her gaze and her attention was focused on her cup.

"Probably just as bad as your assumption in a way." She lifted her chin and stared at him. "I don't think, I know." She squared her shoulders and looked away as her eyes filled with tears. "She was matchmaking."

Chapter 6

Rosie blinked away the tears that threatened as she thought of Aggie being up to her old tricks even from the grave. She'd known the 'thing' that Rosie had had for Taj and had never once let on that he was her great nephew. Maybe she was trying to make amends by this crazy condition.

"Matchmaking?" He tilted his head to the side and she lifted her eyes back to hold his, ignoring that stupid little flutter in her chest.

Taj Brown. Her hero was sitting across from her, his blue eyes fixed on hers, the little laughter lines making small white lines fan around his eyes in the deep tan of his face.

"Yep, but you don't need to run a mile. No fear of that."

"That's good to hear."

"So, when do you want to move in? I guess we need to do it and then see what happens after the three months are up." She held his gaze steadily, a gaze which was now full of warmth and humour, and the sun-bleached lock of hair that fell across his forehead sent a delicious shiver down her back. She needed to race home and pull down the posters of him that were all over the wall of her bedroom. Not because she was angry at him anymore, but because she didn't want to risk him seeing them. There was no need for him to know she'd followed his career for years. She'd have to make that very clear to the girls and make sure they didn't mention her teenage obsession with him.

"I've got a suite at the Intercontinental over in the city, so as soon as it suits you. The quicker I move in, the sooner we can sort out selling the house. Three months will go quickly."

His words were like a dash of cold water. The

Intercontinental? She'd forgotten how wealthy he was. And selling the house? No way.

The easy mood between them disappeared. Rosie drained her cup and stood. "Thanks for the tea. When will we expect you?"

"I'll come after lunch tomorrow if that suits you?"

"What about your...your job? Don't you have to be somewhere?" She waved her hand. "At some surf competition or something?"

A shadow crossed his face. "No. Not at the moment." He looked at her curiously. "Who's we?"

"The other two girls with me at the funeral." She frowned as his eyes narrowed. "As well as working out of the house, they live there too. The three of us live on the first floor. And don't worry, we all pay rent into Aggie's account."

##

Rosie parked her car in the garage and hurried to the kitchen. She checked the small whiteboard stuck to the fridge. Sally and Lily had filled in their schedules for the day and both had clients now. She'd be lucky to see them before her client arrived in a few minutes.

She scrawled a note and stuck it under a glass on the kitchen table. 'Don't go anywhere. We need to talk. I finish at seven.'

Her six o'clock was a regular client who liked to chat while she was having her back treated. Rosie hadn't shared with Taj that she was also a qualified physiotherapist; she'd sensed that he was a sceptic when it came to alternative therapies. Many people were. She'd seen the look on his face when she'd mentioned Reiki and lymphatic massage. Yes, they were new age treatments and had made a huge difference to the health and lives of her clients who were prepared to open their minds.

When Taj met Ocean Lily, his eyes were going to be

even wider. She stifled a grin and focused her thoughts on her client as Mrs March told her about the day she'd spent with her grandchildren.

An hour later, Rosie waited at the door until Mrs March was safely in her car across the road before she went back inside and washed the massage oil from her hands. Her back ached, and her wrists were sore. A delicious smell of herbs and tomato sauce met her as she opened the kitchen door.

Sally and Lily were sitting at the table, their iPads propped up in front of them as the pot of sauce bubbled away on the stove.

"Double, double, toil and trouble." Rosie put on a deep voice.

Sally lifted her head and grinned. "By the pricking of my thumbs, something wicked this way comes."

"You're not wrong there." Rosie pulled a face and flopped into the third chair.

"So the cards were right?" Lily had dyed her hair and Rosie reached over and lifted a purple plait.

"Cards? You mean the tea leaves?"

"I read the cards at lunchtime. They were the same. Change is in the wind." Ocean Lily dropped her voice. "So tell us how bad is it?"

Rosie sat back and folded her arms. "Well…it could be worse."

"Rosie!" Sally tapped her fingers on the table.

"We have a guest coming. Well, technically he's not a guest, he's a beneficiary. Like me."

"A guest? What? Coming to stay here? Why?" Sally was the worrier of her family. "And who?"

"Because Aunt Aggie put it in the will. Three months with Taj Brown as a house guest and then we can do what we want with the house. The problem is I think we may want different outcomes at the end." She turned to Lily, who looked like the cat that got the cream. "What are you smiling about?"

"I had a dream last night." Lily nodded sagely. Damn if she could get used to that name. Lily was the last name Sonia reminded you of—lilies were cool and calm, everything that Sonia was not.

"And?"

"All will be well."

Rosie laughed. "How so? You mean I can forget the pricking of my thumbs?" She lifted both hands and moved both her sore thumbs in a circle.

"Yep. I dreamed he came and stayed here. And he stayed."

"What do you mean he stayed?"

"I mean, Rosie, all your teenage fantasies came true. He's going to fall in love with you and it will all work out. You'll find your happy ever after, live in the house and fill it with little surfers."

Rosie stood and crossed to the stove and picked up the spoon, giving the sauce a thorough stir before she answered. "No, Sonia—and forget that Lily crap, I can't get used to it—you know how I feel about relationships and kids." She stared at her two friends. "After my childhood, you know I don't believe in love and happy ever after. There's no such thing. I don't know what Aggie was thinking about. It's not going to happen."

Sonia's smile got wider and she nodded again. "You'll see. Trust me. When have I ever been wrong before?"

Rosie picked up the tea towel and laughed as she threw it at Sonia. "This time you will be. And wipe that smug grin off your face.

"You'll see. You have to trust the cards." Sonia

removed the towel that had landed on her shoulder and folded it neatly on the table in front of her. "They never lie." She nodded sagely at Rosie. "Trust me, Ocean Lily knows best." She ducked as Rosie reached for another tea towel.

Chapter 7

Taj arrived with supplies and a peace offering. A huge bunch of flowers and a bottle of wine. He rang the doorbell of the house on the hill before he turned to watch the surfers making the most of the perfect waves. It was a beautiful spring afternoon. A light westerly wind was making the super long, clean groundswell stand up as it rolled in from the southeast. It was unusual for Bondi to have such great waves in the late afternoon; the northeast chop would usually be making conditions unpleasant by now. Taj let out a sigh; he would have given anything to be out there. One of the hardest things about living here was going to be watching the surfers out there every day. Almost as hard as ignoring the effect that Rosie had on his libido. The last thing he needed was to get involved with her.

His last appointment with the specialist had not been promising. The doctor was talking about surgery and only a fifty percent chance that Taj would surf again if he went down the surgery path. The doctor was surprised the injury hadn't responded to the physiotherapy regime and he was awaiting the results of the latest MRI before he decided if surgery was going to fix the problem.

Taj turned away from the hollow beach break as a lone surfer caught the wave and rode it to the shore. His career was most likely over and it was time to think about his future. Money wasn't a problem but one thing was sure; he wouldn't be going into the family stock broking firm. Aggie had been loyal to him by leaving him a share of her house and assets; it would be traitorous of him to join the family who had ostracised her as soon as her husband had died. Maybe he'd go into developing real estate on a full-time basis. He'd always had a knack for finding good deals.

He turned with a start as the door was flung open and the woman who'd worn the multi-coloured tent at the funeral stood there with a huge smile.

"You must be Taj? Come in, come in."

He handed her the flowers and held onto the wine. She chatted gaily as he followed her down a long hall leading to the back of the house.

"I'm Lily…or you can call me Sonia, whichever you prefer. Rosie hates Lily, so I guess I can answer to Sonia. Sally and Rosie have appointments so I've been keeping an eye out for you. Lovely afternoon, isn't it? So pleased you're coming to stay, there's a bit too much estrogen here at times. Although now the footballers are coming every second night, it's all jock straps and testosterone."

He opened his mouth to answer but she kept on.

"Rosie told us what you thought we were. What a hoot! Got us mixed up with the old ladies of the night. Not a bad idea. All the money worries would be gone then. But we'd have others, I guess. Other worries that is." His expression must have changed because she dug him in the ribs and let out a laugh that was almost a cackle. "Don't worry. Just joking. Now as soon as you're settled, I want to do a reading."

"A reading?" Taj knew his voice was faint. A door closed behind him and rescue came in the shape of another woman; not Rosie but obviously the third one who lived here. The other one he'd seen at the service. She held her hand out and took his between both of hers and looked him in the eye.

"Hi, I'm Sally. Welcome to the 'House on the Hill'. She exuded calm and the tension that prickled at his neck at the thought of a 'reading', whatever that was, dissipated.

Taj stood the bottle of wine on the table as she switched the kettle on. Nothing like an Aussie cup of tea to break the ice.

"It's our morning tea break. Rosie'll be out soon. She'll show you your room. Tea?"

"Coffee would be great, thanks."

"Sorry. We don't have coffee."

Taj made a note to buy some. He wouldn't last a day here without coffee. "Tea will be fine. Thanks."

"What sort? We have plain green, green with mint, apple and cinnamon, chamomile, berry—" The nonstop talkative one who'd answered the door counted them off on her ring-bedecked fingers.

"Just plain tea please." Taj smiled weakly. He wasn't sure what to call her. This was going to be a very long three months.

"Then we can talk about changing the roster." She didn't draw breath between words.

"The roster?"

"Yep, the cooking and stuff. Shopping, cleaning. Pleased you're here actually. It'll free us all up a bit. Although Rosie said you've got a gammy leg?"

"I'm fine. I can do whatever is needed." Silently, he was screaming inside… *get me out of here.*

"Be good to have a man around. You can take the garbage out."

Is she for real?

A little giggle escaped her lips and she put her hand over them. He joined in with a laugh as he realised she'd been teasing him.

"Are you trying to scare me off? Did Rosie put you up to it?"

"Hello, Taj. Welcome to Aggie's house on the hill." The cold voice came from behind him before Sonia could answer.

He spun around as pleasant anticipation disappeared.

"The house on the hill? Is that what you call it?"

##

Rosie had all morning to prepare herself for Taj's arrival. She woke up out of sorts after the little sleep she'd had was broken by dreams of surf and a blue-eyed blond surfer. But the water in her dream had been brown and murky, and she knew how Sonia would interpret that dream.

Trouble ahead. Now trouble with a capital T stood in front of her with a huge smile on his face. Her damned stomach jumped and twitched, and the discomfort travelled even lower as she stared at him, ignoring the strange ache that lodged between her thighs. She took refuge in a bad mood. Damn him, she didn't care what he thought of her.

"Yes, it's always been the house on the hill to us… and to the locals. And it will always be Aggie's house on the hill to me."

He nodded and kept his eyes fixed on hers and she fought the temptation to straighten her hair, or lick her lips, or move, or something. Anything to stop him from looking at me.

Eventually, she folded her arms and returned his steady gaze. "So have you brought your gear with you?"

"Not yet, my PA is driving over this afternoon with my luggage and a couple of my boards."

Pah. His PA. Of course.

He looked around at the room and smiled apologetically. "You'll have to bear with me, I've got nothing personal…like towels and stuff to contribute. I'm used to living out of hotels, not private houses."

"Of course you are." She waved a dismissive hand. "We can sort that out." She turned away, conscious of the other two girls following their conversation. She shot a frown in Sonia's direction before she turned her attention back to Taj.

"So where is home for you?"

As she watched, he ran a hand through his hair and that sexy, stray lock fell over his forehead again.

"No one place really. I've followed the circuit for more than a few years now."

"But you must have a home base?"

Finally, he shrugged casually. "Yeah, I've got a couple of properties."

"Where?" Rosie knew her voice was waspish. So if he had a couple of places, what did he want with Aggie's house on the hill? Why did he need to live here and get his hands on it? *On my home?*

As she watched, he squared his broad shoulders. Those gorgeous, tanned shoulders she was more used to seeing bare on the posters on her wall.

"I've got a villa up at Airlie Beach, and—" he hesitated.

"And?"

"And a house down at Bell's Beach...and a small place in California."

"Three?"

"Actually, I have small farm in North Queensland too." He lifted his chin as he stared back at her and his challenging expression pushed her buttons a bit more.

Every time he opened his mouth it was easier to harden her heart. *Keep it coming, surfer boy.*

"So what are you doing here now?" She folded her arms. Damn, she knew she was being unfriendly, but he didn't need this place. They did. It was their home and their livelihood and here was a relative who appeared out of the woodwork when Aggie was barely cold in her grave. Rosie ignored the gasps that came from Sonia and Sally at her rude tone.

So be it. He hadn't even brought his luggage in and she'd thrown down the gauntlet. "How about we have this conversation when you're in a better mood." Taj's smile had gone and his eyes were narrow.

It was like being on centre court at the Australian Open. Sonia and Sally's heads were moving from left to right as each verbal thrust whizzed from one to the other like the spinning tennis ball.

"How about we don't have it at all? How about you just go back to where you came from?"

Rosie didn't like the smile that spread over his face as he turned his palms upwards and gave a very French shrug. Trying to be sophisticated, is he?

"Okay. So you want me to leave? You're quite sure of that?"

She hesitated at the glint in his eye but then stood her ground. "I think it would be better for all concerned, don't you?"

"No skin off my nose, babe."

Babe!

Rosie opened her mouth and closed it as she held back the splutter that threatened. An overwhelming feeling of being out of control, the thing she feared most in her life was clawing at her throat. The only way she knew to overcome it, was to come out fighting.

"So you're happy to move out too?" He quirked an eyebrow as he continued. "You heard what old Dr Pepper said."

Sonia interrupted him with a giggle. "Dr Pepper?"

"Ah, I should say Mr Pepper. Very confusing. Dr Pepper Drinks sponsored me once."

"What?" Rosie planted her hands on her hips. She wasn't going to let a glimmer of a smile cross her face despite his Dr Pepper jokes. Bloody inappropriate time to be making jokes. Obviously at her expense. She really could get to dislike this Theodore Brown.

"If we don't share the house for three months, you know it goes to neither of us. So it's your choice, babe."

Sally stepped forward and put a hand on Rosie's arm. "Calm down, sweets. Take a deep breath." She turned to her sister. "Lily, will you please take Taj upstairs and show him the two spare rooms? Let him choose whichever he wants. They're both made up. Rosie, I'll make you a cup of tea and then we'll all sit down and have a nice chat.

Rosie swallowed and hid her misery. Taj sent her one last look as he followed Lily out of the kitchen.

"What is your problem?" Sally's usual calm had disappeared and her voice was the loudest Rosie had ever heard her speak. "Do you want to lose everything?"

Rosie shook her head as warmth flooded her cheeks. "He just makes me feel so…so…"

"So what?" Sally crossed to the sink and filled the kettle. "A cup of chamomile tea for you, my dear."

"So out of control, Sal, you know. I thought I was in love with that surfer dude for most of my teens. He was my hero. Now here he is in our house, threatening to take everything from us. And he's nothing like I thought he was."

Sally raised both her eyebrows and stared. "And you don't think you are overreacting a bit?"

"No." Rosie felt like stamping her foot as she had with Aggie as a confused little eight-year-old, fifteen years ago. "I know what it's like to be rootless and have nobody. I don't want to go there again." She flopped into the kitchen chair and cradled her head in her arms. A gentle touch on her arm a minute later had her lifting her head as Sally pushed a steaming cup of fragrant tea toward her.

"I knew that was upsetting you. "Sally put her hand on Rosie's shoulder and she closed her eyes as the calming warmth seeped through her thin shirt. "Sweets, you have to go with the flow. Don't fight it. You know the universe has a plan for you. This may be the first step to something else. Something better may come of this. Don't fight it."

She sat across from Rosie and a cheeky look crossed her face. "Lily read his aura while he was waiting on the front porch and *wowsa*." She lifted her hand and fanned herself. "Once you take down this barrier you've put up, you're in for the ride of your life."

Chapter 8

The sound of a door closing quietly woke Taj just after dawn. To his surprise, he'd slept well. The lull of the waves on the rocks below the house had sent him off to sleep almost as soon as his head hit the pillow. After Sally had calmed things down, he'd headed upstairs with Lily and chosen the front room, and then he'd left the three of them sitting in the kitchen. Doing whatever they did.

Hocus-pocus of some sort. The smell of incense through the house reminded him of the place in the Maldives he'd surfed for a few months. The resort had been a place of supposed soul renewal and inspiration too; not his scene at all. And neither was this house. Tarot cards, herbal teas, Reiki and yoga. He was way out of his comfort zone.

Everywhere he turned there were little gold Buddha statues and silky drapes with inspirational messages on them. Lily had offered to read his cards for him when she'd shown him to his room, and he'd high-tailed it out of the house as soon as he could. It was like he'd landed in some sort of crazy house.

His preference would be to stay in the hotel until he got his medical problem sorted but he had to put up with this for three months. He had to. This house had been in his family for almost one hundred years and although he wasn't overly sentimental, he didn't want to see it go. Even though there'd been a huge split in the family, it was still the house of his blood relations. He already had plans for a modern renovation. Hell, once the place was his—because he had every intention of buying Rosie's share out when the three months were up—he'd get the builders in. Once it was modernised, it would make a great base. Even better if he was back surfing. If not—well he'd wait and see what happened.

Taj called a taxi; his car was still in the car park under the hotel. He hadn't been sure if there was anywhere to park it here but when Sally had given him a spare front door key she'd shown him a four-car garage that was accessed by a laneway at the back of the house. As soon as the taxi arrived, he gave the three of them a quick wave from the hallway. Sally and Sonia waved back and Rosie ignored him.

He'd headed back to the city. Dinner with Rick, a surfer from California, had cleared his head a bit. After a few drinks, some laughs and lots of reminiscing about surfing trips and his good mood was restored.

Almost. By the time he returned, the house was in darkness, apart from a low light burning in the front hall. He'd let himself in quietly and made his way up to his room.

Rosie's attitude had pissed him off. Okay, so it added to his guilt about not having seen Aunt Aggie for so long, but he'd had no idea that she was going to involve him in an inheritance battle.

Now with the sun peeking through the gap in the drapes onto the wall behind him, he rolled over, pushed back the light cotton blanket and climbed out of the huge bed. Walking over to the window, he ignored the tug in his right knee. He had an appointment with the specialist this afternoon and he was anxious to get the news. If surgery was necessary, he wondered if the time out would count towards the three months. By his calculations, the three months were up on New Year's Eve; he'd give old Mr Pepper a call today.

He pulled back the heavy drapes, wrinkling his nose at the cloying smell of incense that wafted around him. It seeped through the whole house. A glorious morning greeted him. Shafts of gold light shot into the sky behind the low clouds that hovered above the horizon. Lines of white-edged breakers rolled into the shore and the sea was dotted with black figures paddling their boards out through the lines of the swell to catch the first waves of the day. It was a perfect morning and brilliant waves were curling out wide.

"Fuck." Taj slammed into fist onto the window sill. All he wanted to do was grab a board and hit the waves, losing himself in the green caverns of water as they formed around him and pushed him towards the shore.

If he couldn't get in the waves, he'd go and sit on the sand and immerse himself in the salt and the spray. His suitcases were lined up along the wall and he reached for the small one that held his board shorts and T-shirts.

As soon as he changed, he opened the door to the hall and looked out. The last thing he wanted was another confrontation with Rosie, although he knew it was inevitable. He paused and listened, but the house was quiet as though it, too, was sleeping. He slipped into the huge bathroom that Sonia had shown him last night, ignoring the underwear draped over the shower curtain.

Five minutes later, he let himself out the front door and stood on the porch trying to remember which way he'd gone to the beach as a youngster. Across the road, a small park fronted the rocks and he spotted a beach access sign. He looked around as he crossed the road. Blocks of units led from the old house on the hill down to the intersection; he hadn't noticed how much the street had been modernised as he drove up in the rain the other afternoon. His plan to renovate the house would go down very well. Once he reached the park, he turned to look at the house and a feeling of nostalgia flooded through him.

The building stood gracefully on the top of the hill, the weathered timber glowing warm and rich in the morning sunlight. He leaned back and looked up; he'd forgotten about the widow's walk, the small railed platform above the top storey. He caught his breath as his mother's voice filled his head as though she was there beside him.

"Your great, great grandfather married a girl from America and she insisted that he put the widow's walk up there. She loved watching the sea."

Hell, he'd been so immersed in his surfing and clawing his way to the top, he'd pushed family thoughts from his mind. It had helped with the grief of losing his parents in that awful accident on Highway One. Cutting ties with his family and his memories had been deliberate. It hurt less than remembering.

Maybe Aunt Aggie had a reason for leaving him a part of the house. It had reconnected him with family and, although it was still a huge part of him, the ache of loss was bearable now.

Taj turned thoughtfully away from the house and looked for the steps that led down to the rocks and along to the northern edge of Bondi Beach. The tide was low and the rock platform was dry as he carefully made his way along to the two ocean pools that were built into the rocks. Swimmers crawled their way through the water in that distinctive lazy Aussie swim style, and others who had finished their morning swim lay on the rocks letting the warm sun dry them.

"Gidday."

He breathed in deeply and smiled back at the jogger who'd spoken to him. *God, it's good to be home.* Even if he couldn't surf, he would enjoy being back in Australia. As much as he loved touring the world, he loved his home country. The friendliness, the irreverent and iconic humour, and the mateship were unique.

And the beaches. The best in the world. He put his hand to his eyes and absorbed the brilliant blue of the water. The only other place he'd seen that depth of colour was in Bora Bora in Tahiti. As he watched, a young boy caught a medium size wave that had formed off the point. Admiration for the surfer's skill filled him as the teenager sliced his way across the top of the wave before he turned and headed down the face, gaining speed as the spray flew around his board. The wave curled and he disappeared into the tube and Taj held his breath, finally letting it out with a whoop as the boy shot out of the left-hand side of the gas chamber.

His knee held up as he hurried down the last few steps leading to the sand and watched as the boy paddled back out to catch the next wave.

Another professional in the making.

Taj knew how hard it was to crack the circuit these days. He'd give the lad a word of encouragement when he came in. He walked over to the low line of rocks and found a good perch to sit and enjoy the sun and be entertained by the wave riders.

The boy sliced up the next wave and Taj found his whole attention focused on the graceful movement as he turned into the right section of the wave ready to ride it to shore. The third wave he caught brought him closer to the northern edge of the beach and Taj caught his breath as the point break brought the surfer closer to him and he realised the surfer wasn't a boy. It was a girl.

And not a teenager.

"Well, I'll be damned." He muttered under his breath as he stood and watched as Rosie paddled through the white water to the edge of the sand where he waited.

***

Rosie had noticed Taj walking along the edge of the ocean pools as soon as he'd stepped into the sunlight. Even with the slight limp, she knew that walk well; she'd watched him on enough surfing shows over the years. The only thing that was missing was the surfboard beneath his arm and she wondered how bad his injury was.

The distinctive swagger and the loose blond curls confirmed for her that Taj Brown was now sitting on the beach watching the surfers. If anyone else recognized him, he'd be mobbed.

Her mood was mellow and she wasn't going to let his presence on the beach upset her. If he was going to live in the house, and it looked like he was, she was just going to have to wear it.

She reached the shallows and stood, tucking her board beneath one arm as she waded to the sand. Her wet hair stuck to her cheek and she reached back with one hand and wound it into a ponytail at the back of her head. As she squeezed the salt water from her hair, cold trickles ran down her neck and she shivered.

It was the cold, not Taj watching her from the edge of the path that sent goose bumps running up her arms beneath her wet suit. Her nipples pebbled as the shiver continued down her back.

Thank goodness, I put the wet suit on. She'd briefly considered surfing in her bikini this morning. If Taj was going to make a habit of coming down to the beach of a morning, she'd wear a wet suit for the whole three months.

Focusing on her breathing and staying calm, she walked across the glistening sand. A small child ran ahead of her scattering the seagulls, which took to the air squawking raucously. Three joggers waved as they passed her and she waved back. Her mornings on the beach always followed the same pattern. Familiar faces, friendly greetings. She couldn't imagine beginning her day any other way…or anywhere else.

"Hello." Rosie stopped beside him and wedged the end of her small board into the sand.

"Morning." His blue eyes crinkled as he smiled at her. "You're a surprise packet."

"I am?"

"Surfing. Somehow, it's not what I expected." He reached up and pushed the hair back from his eyes. The wind was increasing and the golden curls whipped around his face. Rosie focused on that, even though her eyes wanted to stray down to the muscles outlined by the snug-fitting white T-shirt.

"What did you expect?"

His shoulders lifted in a casual shrug and she gave in, letting her gaze settle on the broad chest with a sprinkling of blond hair peeking out of the V at the base of his throat.

"I hadn't really thought about it."

"I suppose you're used to the tanned, blonde surf girls." She looked down at the strands of black hair that blended in with her wet suit. "Even in the summer, I don't tan. I keep the sun cream manufacturers in business with my fair skin."

"You're very good. A natural surfer."

She opened her eyes wide, surprised by the easy praise that came from his lips. "Thanks. Aggie bought me my first board ten years ago. On my thirteenth birthday."

His laugh was pleasant and sent those shivers running back down her spine, despite the warmth of the morning sun. Usually by now, she would have peeled the wet suit off for the walk up the hill, but today she'd wear it home.

"Me too. I was here on a holiday. I guess that's about the time I met you. That would make you twenty-three now?"

"Yes. Five years younger than you." Damn, she'd let slip she knew how old he was but hopefully, he'd assume she'd done the addition in her head. She rushed on with a light-hearted joke. "So you've got five years of surfing practice on me. Maybe there's hope for me yet to hit the circuit."

"You're good enough. Have you ever thought about it?"

Rosie laughed and shook her head. "No. And I couldn't leave Aggie."

The smile left his face and he stared over her head toward the horizon. "I'm sorry you had the burden alone. If I'd known, I would have helped out. I feel guilty that I didn't even know she was sick."

"It was a sad ending to her life."

Taj pushed himself off the rock he was leaning against as Rosie lifted her board. "I'll walk back up with you."

He fell into an easy step beside her as she headed for the path that led to the pools. "I lost touch with Aggie and everything I left in Sydney when my parents died."

"I'm sorry to hear that. And I'm sorry I don't remember you." Rosie meant it; things would have been easier now if Aggie had mentioned him, or if she'd known to contact him when Aggie first got sick.

Taj's voice was low as they walked along the edge of the pool that sat naturally in the rock platform. "My parents died in a road crash in California."

"I can't believe that Aggie never mentioned it."

He shot her a glance. "Things in this family have never been smooth. That's why I was so surprised that she included me in her will. Maybe she was trying to make amends."

"What for?"

"When my Dad's uncle married her, there was a split in the family. I don't know why. My parents never talked about it. Something else happened when I was about fourteen and we never came to visit again."

"She was always happy, so don't feel bad." Rosie hitched a breath as a sob threatened. "Even when dementia took hold, she was always happy. She used to call me Maureen when I'd visit."

Rosie turned as his breath hissed in.

"That was my Mum's name."

"So see, she must have been thinking about you." She tucked her board up higher as they reached the steps. "And you were in the will, so don't feel bad." Not about that anyway. Over the next three months, she was going to do her best to see if she could get the money together, somehow, to buy out his share. There was no way she would let the house be sold to a developer. Because that's what would happen. The house occupied a prime piece of real estate at the edge of the most famous Aussie beach, and they'd been after it for years.

Taj's deep voice interrupted her thoughts as they reached the top of the steps. "Can I carry your board?"

"No, it's fine. Thanks anyway."

They walked in silence until they reached the park across from the house.

"So tell me about Sonia—or is it Lily? —and Sally? Why weren't they in the will too?" Taj paused at the gate that opened into the park and she looked up at him.

"Why would she?"

"I assumed that they were foster children too? Like you were?"

Rosie pursed her lips as her temper threatened to take over. They'd managed to have a civil conversation for fifteen minutes and she'd even felt sad for him when he talked about his parents. But the way he said 'foster' children pushed her buttons. It was as though he was trying to remind her of where she stood in the scheme of things.

"No."

She strode off ahead of him not waiting for him to keep up, but by the time she reached the road, he'd caught her up. As she looked down the hill to make sure the road was clear, a strong hand gripped her arm.

"Stop."

"What?" She shook him off and began to step out, but he grabbed her arm again.

"For someone who lives in a house of sweetness and

light, you can get awfully pissy." His voice was cold as she glared at him. "What did I say to upset you this time?"

"Nothing." She pulled away and hitched the board up again. It was getting heavy.

"Yes, I did. Or I mean, yes you are. Moody, that is." He ran his hand through his hair again and a pang of regret hit Rosie.

Okay, time for honesty.

"It was the way you said 'foster' children."

"I don't get the way you think." Taj shook his head as she looked up at him. "I didn't mean anything by it. I was just wondering about the other two in the house."

"We were friends at high school. They weren't Aggie's children." Rosie kept her voice strong. "I was the last one that Aggie ever took on. And she lost touch with the earlier kids. I considered myself very lucky."

"You were." He held up his hands as she opened her mouth. "And I don't mean anything else when I say that. She was a fine woman and you were lucky to have her."

Rosie kept her voice low. "Sally and Sonia only moved in to help me with the costs. Because Aggie's property is valued so high—and I don't mean that in a greedy way—shoot, that's not the right word. I mean I'm not thinking of the place for me. Or what it's worth for me." Rosie struggled to find the right words to explain. "Do you know anything about how aged care works? For a place in a facility, you have to put up a bond and it's worked out on how much your property is worth. Because this place is so valuable, I had to find a bond of half a million to secure Aggie a spot."

Taj looked at her with disbelief written all over his face. "I had no idea. I thought people just went into aged care facilities."

"Yeah, it's not something that you really know anything about until you need to. If Aggie had gone straight into the dementia ward when she first went in, there would have been no cost. They call it high care."

"So, how did you find the money?"

"Aggie had organised power of attorney and enduring guardianship for me. She was pretty switched on before she had the stroke. I was able to borrow in her name against the house and pay the bond to get her a place there. It's an interest-only loan and the girls moved in to help me out. They pay rent for living here and also business rent for using the place for their classes and stuff." She lifted her chin. "And I pay rent too. It's only fair."

"Does Mr Pepper know this?"

Rosie shrugged. "Probably not. I did it all through the bank."

"You need to tell him. It might make a difference to everything."

"Everything?"

"Yes, maybe he can sort something out to get you out of the debt."

"Or maybe he can sort something out so you get the house quicker." Rosie jutted her chin out. The feeling of being in control of her life and future was slipping away with every word he said. Three months she could deal with if she had to; it would give her time to get used to the idea of losing everything. Unless they sold, or she let Taj buy her out, she had nothing.

"I didn't mean that." His voice held steely control.

Alright for Mr Surfer Boy here. He had everything to gain and nothing to lose.

"I'm going for a shower. I don't want to talk about it." Rosie was just holding herself together. She turned away from him and strode across the road leaving him staring after her.

Chapter 9

Taj let out a frustrated sigh as Rosie strode across the road to the house without a backward glance. Her shoulders were straight and her long black hair was plastered to her wetsuit, reaching down to her butt. And a sweet view it was too. The wet suit moulded her trim curves and even in her temper, her hips swayed gently as she walked away from him. The clang of the metal gate shutting behind her pulled his attention back.

He couldn't understand her. One minute they'd been getting along just fine. Shame her temperament wasn't as sweet as she looked. Although to be fair, it sounded as though she'd been doing it tough and had put herself out on a financial limb to help Aggie. He shook his head as he stepped onto the road and a slice of pain knifed through his knee and his leg locked. Anger filled him as he limped across to the gate and pushed it open. The front door was closed but not locked and it opened quietly when he turned the ornate knob.

Maybe he'd forget the whole inheritance thing and leave town. Go back to North Queensland. But he couldn't. The best orthopaedic specialist was here in Sydney. And Aggie had caught him too. Not only would the house be sold and leave the Brown family, but now that he knew what a financial load Rosie had taken on to look after Aggie, he couldn't move out and see it sold out from under her either.

Equally, at the end of the three months, he could see no possible solution. She wouldn't want to be bought out.

Or maybe she would. Her loan would be cleared once the bond was returned. And if he bought her out, she could set up business elsewhere.

Hell, he could afford to buy the place ten times over.

The house was quiet as he crossed the foyer. He groaned as he looked up at the two flights of stairs with the landing in the middle. He'd run a hot shower and get some heat onto his blasted knee and then he was going to go and see the solicitor.

Climbing the staircase was slow, and he was drenched in sweat by the time he reached the first floor. As he lifted his foot onto the last step, his knee clicked back and the pain disappeared as quickly as it had come.

Bloody unpredictable injury. It had the specialist mystified but all Taj wanted was to get back to normal and into the surf.

He wondered which bathroom Rosie was using as he crossed the wide hall. The floor up here was checkerboard black and white tiles, and a large window at the end turned it into a wide and airy space. Even though a bit tired and old, it really was still a beautiful home. It would be a bit of a shame to have the renovators in; maybe they could keep the 1930s look and work around some of the existing features. There were at least three bathrooms on this floor that he'd seen so far. Even though he'd used the one closest to his room, there'd still been lacy underwear draped around and he suspected it was the bathroom Rosie used. He tapped on the door and waited but all was quiet. Pushing open the door, he grinned as he stepped into the foyer and closed it behind him. How many modern bathrooms had a foyer? He reached down and pulled his T-shirt over his head and threw it onto the chintz-covered sofa against the wall. Slipping his hands into the waistband of his board shorts, he took a step through the arch that led to the shower and barrelled straight into a wet, soft chest.

"What the—?" He lifted his head and looked into a pair of gold-flecked hazel eyes but not before he'd got a brief flash of a small black bikini bottom.

"What the heck do you think you're doing?" Rosie gasped and crossed her arms in front of her bare breasts.

"I knocked but you didn't answer."

"I had the water running. Surely you heard it?"

"No. I didn't hear anything. I was going to take a shower." He couldn't stop the appreciative grin from spreading across his face. "But now I'm appreciating the view."

Rosie took a step back and the view got even better. He dropped his gaze and skimmed his glance from the red-painted toenails up long, toned legs. Her fair skin was accentuated by the flush on her cheeks as red as the rosy lips that were now pursed in disapproval.

"Well, you can just stop—"

Taj couldn't help himself. The last thing he wanted was another spray of words from this little firebrand. He leaned forward and pressed his lips to hers and the gasp that followed warmed his lips.

"If you haven't got anything nice to say, just don't say anything. Okay?" he murmured against her mouth.

***

Oh.My.God. Had she died and gone to heaven? Was she asleep and dreaming or was she almost naked in her bathroom with Taj Brown's lips locked on hers?

Rosie closed her eyes and revelled in the warmth of his lips against hers and the roughness of his bare chest against the backs of her hands. Years of imagination, and dreaming about this moment made it impossible to pull back. Why not just give into the dream for a few seconds and worry about what happened after that? His lips moved into a smile she could feel against hers when she snaked her arms around his neck and held on tight. She opened her lips to welcome him, ignoring the quick flutter of panic that rushed through her when he pulled back. The dim light falling through the skylight highlighted whorls of blond chest hair and broad, muscled shoulders. The glorious muscles were well-defined and continued down his abs. Rosie lowered her hand and traced a gentle finger around his nipple and smiled as he sucked in a breath as his lips met hers again.

Awareness of time and rational thought fled as his mouth plundered hers. His teeth scraped over her lips and a jolt of pleasure hit every nerve ending in her body. An exquisite quiver tingled between her thighs, a pleasure that she'd not indulged in for over a year. Too busy with Aggie to think about sex. But sex had never been like this with anybody. This was her wildest dream coming true. The sensation of his hands gripping her butt was soon replaced by the hard erection against her bare stomach. Only his thin board shirts were between her and heaven.

Another shaft of excitement whipped through her as his fingers slipped beneath the edge of her bikini bottoms. Beneath his hungry mouth, she was aware of her breath catching and her pulse pounding, but she didn't want him to stop. He walked her back towards the wall and she moaned as he slipped her bikini down a little.

"Rosie? Are you in there?" Reality hit like a bucket of cold water as Sally's voice came through the door. Rosie gasped and pushed him away, grabbing for her bikini bottoms and then trying to cover her naked breasts at the same time.

Thank God, Taj was quick thinking.

She gathered her thoughts, and a towel, as he crossed to the door and called out. "No, I'm in here, Sally. But I won't be long if you want to use the bathroom."

"No, it's okay, Taj. I was just looking for Rosie. Take your time. There are plenty of other bathrooms in this house."

A pair of twinkling eyes met hers as Sally's footsteps faded. Taj took a step back towards her and that damned sexy smile almost broke her resolve.

"Did you hear that? We can take our time." His eyes were heavy with need and for a moment she was tempted but she put one hand up, as she clutched at the towel with the other.

"Uh uh. Not going to happen, surfer boy. I don't know what happens in your world but I need to know someone longer than twenty-four hours before I sleep with them."

Again the sexy grin crossed his face. "But we've known each other for fifteen years."

"Good try. But not on." She hitched the towel higher as he stared at her. One more minute and she was going to melt into a puddle in his arms. "I'll go and wait in my room while you take a shower."

Without looking at him, she scurried over to the door and listened. When she was sure there was no one outside, she opened the door and hurried across the hall and almost fell into her room. She closed the door and leaned on it with her eyes closed.

Finally, when her heart had stopped pounding erratically, she opened them and let out a huge sigh as posters of Taj Brown looked down at her.

They were coming down now.

Chapter 10

Dr Brennan shook his head as he looked up from the report in his hands. "You're a mystery man, Taj. There's no sign of anything in the reports and I'm really at a loss to understand what's causing your knee pain."

Taj leaned forward dangling his hands between his knees as he stared back at the specialist. "So what does that mean? Is it good or bad news? Can I get back in the surf?"

"The only thing I can suggest is that you've twisted too far, either on your board or even just walking. The ligaments around your knee can stretch but only a certain distance. If you try to put the joint through too much motion…who knows what it's done." The doctor shrugged. "But there's no sign of any tear or damage on the MRI scan. We could open you up and have a look but quite frankly I don't think there's any need."

"Well, that's one good thing, I suppose." Relief shot through Taj, but it was tempered with uncertainty. "Should I get out in the surf and see if it holds up?"

"Entirely up to you. The source of the pain and the way it just happens is something I can't understand. If it was there all of the time, I would say there was an injury, but"— Dr. Brennan's shoulders raised in another shrug— "it appears that there is nothing. Maybe it's psychosomatic? You need to think if anything sets it off. Stress? Come back and see me if it's still like it in three months."

Taj muttered to himself as he walked back to the car. "Bloody three months." His whole life seemed to be on hold for three months. He picked up his pace daring his knee to give way, but he strode along the footpath without a problem. His mood deepened into frustration which wasn't helped by the lingering memory of Rosie's body pressed up against his in the bathroom this morning. It had taken fifteen full minutes in a cold shower to get rid of the hard-on.

He focused his thoughts on the present, trying to sort out what he'd do. There was a surfing competition coming up at Narrabeen in two weeks. If he got out in the surf, and his knee held up, he could stay at the house, and get back onto the circuit at the end of the three months. The problem was if he was out for much longer than that his world ranking would plummet.

He turned into the lane at the back of the house just as the sun was setting. As directed by Sally—who seemed to be the only sane person in the household—he opened the door manually from the outside, drove in and then locked the garage from the inside.

Great. There were three other cars in there which meant the Witches of Eastwick were all home. He grinned at his joke and his mood improved. No point being shitty, there was little he could do about either situation. And the anticipation that filled him at seeing Rosie again gave him a pleasant buzz. Hell, the way she'd responded to him morning—if Sally hadn't interrupted them when she did, things would have gone past the point of no return. And he wouldn't have minded that one bit.

Taj liked to be organized and he formulated a list in his head. One—live in the house for the three months and get to see the solicitor about Rosie's debt as soon as he could. Two—get back into the surf and test his bloody knee. Three—get into Rosie's bed. As soon as he could.

He pushed open the door of the kitchen. Sonia was standing at the stove stirring a huge pot and the witch image flicked through his head.

"That smells good." He walked over and peered into the pot. Meatballs floated in a rich red sauce. "You must tell me about this roster. I don't mind helping out with the cooking, too."

Sonia stepped back and smiled. A strange smile as though she could read his thoughts.

"Hmmm. Feeling a bit needy, are you, Taj?"

"What? You mean hungry?"

"Uh-uh." She shook her head and shot him a cheeky grin. "Your aura is fair pulsing red. You'd better hurry up and do something about it."

"My aura?" He barely managed to choke the words out.

"Yep. Looking good. Shame Rosie's got her sights on you because I'd take you on without hesitation."

"Rosie?" This time he did choke. *Did they share everything in this house?*

Sonia ignored his question and tapped the wooden spoon on the side of the pot. "But I could be wrong…the red could just mean you are a high achiever or an adventurer. You'll have to let me read your cards and we'll sort it out."

"Sort it out?" His voice was weak now.

"But it can also mean heat too. Do you have any injuries? It could be that crook knee of yours that's causing it too. But Rosie could fix that." He almost waited for her to cackle as she stirred the pot.

"Whatever it is, Rosie can fix it. That's where your future lies." With those enigmatic words and without a backward glance, she put the spoon down and left him in the kitchen alone.

Taj shook his head and dropped into the chair, shaking his head. What did she mean Rosie's got her sights set on me? What games were being played? He'd been quite surprised when she'd almost jumped him this morning and then quickly changed her mind.

The women in this house were doing his head in. The

door opened again and his head flew up but this time it was Sally. She walked gracefully into the room and her calm settled his mood.

"Hi, Taj. Are you going to have dinner with us tonight? It'll give us a chance to get to know you better."

"Yeah, that'd be great. What time?" Like she said, it would be a chance to get to know them and more about Aggie's final years. Maybe he could piece together what had happened to rip the family apart.

"We eat early because I've got classes and I know Lily's got a couple of appointments, but I'm sure Rosie will keep you company."

"Okay, I'll just shoot upstairs and get changed. Anything I can do to help?" He wondered how Rosie would feel about that. He could disappear to his room if needs be but getting to know her much better was high on his agenda.

"Not yet. Maybe you can help clear up."

Taj nodded and headed upstairs. He wanted to see Rosie before dinner. Coming face to face with her for the first time after the bathroom interlude might be embarrassing for her, and he didn't want to complicate matters between them any more than they were already.

***

Rosie rolled up the posters she'd taken down from the wall and slipped an elastic band over each one and placed them in a row that covered her entire bed.

Time to get over all that juvenile stuff. She should have taken them down years ago. She squashed the Blu-tack into one big blob and stuck it on the side of her desk and glanced at the clock on her bedside table just as a knock sounded at the door. Must be Sally.

"Come in." Sally wanted to sort out a roster now that Taj was part of the household and they'd just have time to talk before dinner. As far as Rosie was concerned, she just wanted to pretend he wasn't here in the house, but it was only fair that he helped out. Even if he is a world-famous surfer.

She shook her head; she still couldn't believe that Taj Brown was here in the house, in this very house and that she'd been up close and personal with him in the bathroom. No more of that. The door opened slowly and she threw the last poster onto the bed. They could go down to the garbage bin later. "Well, I did it. My walls are bare."

"They sure are. Are you redecorating?"

Rosie jumped and put a hand to her chest as Taj walked in and pulled the door shut behind him. Her heart pounded in her chest and trembling in her legs began again. "Oh, I thought it was Sally."

He looked down with a grin. "Nah, last time I looked I was me."

"Very funny." She folded her arms over her chest and stared at him. "What do you want?"

"That's not very friendly." He strolled across the room and plonked his butt on her desk. "I wanted to talk to you about this morning. In private. Before we have dinner."

She drew in a deep breath, willing the trembles to stop and the heat creeping into her neck to disappear. Taking a step to the side of her bed to hide the rolled-up posters, she tried to appear as nonchalant and casual as he was. "Nothing to talk about. Just forget it."

"That's the problem. I can't. You've been in my head all day."

A warm shiver ran down Rosie's spine as he stared at her with those blue eyes. His gaze was intense, and she fought to keep her face expressionless as she shrugged. Not only had he filled her thoughts all day, but she also couldn't get rid of the feel of him against her skin. Lusting for him from afar for such a long time had deepened her reaction to his touch this morning. He was imprinted on her senses and she didn't think she would ever forget the feel of his chest against her bare breasts. *And his lips against mine. And his erection against my skin.*

Her lips parted as she stared at him and he must have read the need in her eyes because he pushed himself away from the desk and took a step towards her.

"Oh, no you don't." Forgetting the bed was close up behind her, she backed away and fell on top of the rolled-up posters. "Damn."

The posters crackled and rolled beneath her as she tried to get up and as he held his hand out to help her the elastic band on one of the rolls broke with a twang and the poster unfurled onto the bed.

More heat rushed up Rosie's neck as he stared down at an almost life-size photo of himself surfing at Bells Beach. It was the biggest poster and obviously needed a stronger elastic band.

"Where did you get that?"

Before she could answer, his gaze scanned the pile of posters on the bed and his lips pulled up into a broad smile. "And there's more? Can I see the others?"

"No."

"So these were on your walls?" If it was possible, his smile got even wider, and mortification settled in Rosie's chest. She could actually feel it, like a solid object.

"And now they're bare?"

"No. I mean, yes they were." She dug deep for an excuse. "But it was Aggie who followed your career."

"Really?"

Somehow, he'd got close enough to her that she could feel his warm breath on her skin. Either that or she was about to spontaneously combust with embarrassment. She dropped her gaze as her face burned red. All was quiet until two gentle hands cupped her chin.

"Rosie, look at me." She lifted her head and blinked away the tears of embarrassment. How much worse can this get? Why hadn't she taken the damned things down before he'd arrived? Never in her wildest dreams would she have imagined that Taj would end up in her bedroom. However innocently.

"I'm flattered. In fact, I'm more than flattered. I'm really stoked that you had surf posters of me on your bedroom wall."

She kept her voice low, conscious of his thumb slowly stroking her cheek. "I've always admired your surfing." That was as much as she would admit to. His thumb moved over to her lips and she lifted her head slowly. The look in his eyes mirrored what she was feeling and the movement of his lips towards her was as natural as the next breath she took. Slowly and gently his lips covered hers and Rosie closed her eyes as a different sort of warmth rushed through her.

Everything she'd imagined in her dreams was in that kiss. It was nothing like the sexual moments they'd shared that morning. A gentle passion, a kindness, and a friendship sealed as their lips met and clung for a few seconds.

Slowly he pulled his head back and a quizzical smile crossed his face. "We still have some things to talk about, though."

"I guess we do." Rosie stepped back and folded her arms across her chest. She still wasn't ready to open up to him.

Chapter 11

By six o clock, they were all sitting around the kitchen table, eating Sonia's meatballs. Rosie grinned; no matter how many times Sonia tried it on, no one would call her Ocean Lily. She'd managed to calm down as Taj followed her downstairs. For some reason, her awkwardness in his company had fled and she was getting used to him being around. If you could take the inheritance and the house out of the mix, everything would be pretty good.

"Tell me about your days." Taj put his fork down and rubbed his stomach. "I'm interested in how you all work. "I'm not used to this alternative health stuff. It sounds fascinating."

Rosie tipped her head to the side, wondering if he was genuinely interested or just being polite. Sonia had done the usual aura reading when they'd all sat down, but skipped by Taj, saying, "I did his before," by way of explanation.

"Mine was good. Yoga classes back to back all day." Sally smiled serenely. "What better job could there be?"

"I had three readings and then I read a really interesting article on past lives. Rosie, did you know you can take someone back when you do massage?"

Rosie shook her head as scepticism crossed Taj's expression. "No, you know me. Straight old sporting injuries." No way would she admit to being interested in it with Taj in the room. He just didn't seem the sort of guy who appreciated alternative anything.

Sonia frowned at her and then swung around to Taj. "What about you? How did you fill in your day?"

Rosie put her head down and thought about how the day had started and the familiar quiver settled between her legs. His sexy voice across the table made it even worse. She could still feel the vibration of his lips on hers.

"Not good. I went back to the specialist and he didn't have good news for me."

Rosie's interest was piqued. "What's wrong with your knee?"

"Nothing according to the quack."

"So you can surf again?"

"If I want to risk it locking out there. But I don't particularly fancy drowning if it happens two hundred metres offshore."

"Why don't you let Rosie take a look?" Sonia's smile was as innocent as that of the cat that got the cream.

Taj shrugged and his eyes met Rosie's across the table. "Guess I'm prepared to give anything a go."

"Anything?" Her voice was cold. "No point having a treatment with me if you're not prepared to open your mind."

"Is that a challenge?" His smile was innocent. Just as innocent as when he kissed her this morning. Her heartbeat skittered up a notch, hoping, praying he'd decline.

"I'm prepared to have a look if you're prepared to open up your mind."

"It's my knee that needs treatment." The smile slipped a little from his face. "Okay. I'm game. When?"

"Why don't you do it tonight? We've both got appointments. Might as well all get to work." Sally looked as innocent as Sonia. Honestly, she'd kill the pair of them when she got a chance.

"Sounds good to me," Taj agreed.

Rosie held his deep blue stare. "Eight o'clock then. My therapy room is third from the left on the ground floor.

"See you then. Thanks for dinner. I'll clean up, seeing you girls all have to get to work."

***

Taj pottered around the kitchen and loaded the dishwasher after the others left him in the kitchen. As he wiped down the benches the front door opened and closed a few times, and cheery voices carried down the hall. He could get used to this; sure beat the hell out of a soulless hotel room. Flicking off the kitchen light, he headed upstairs to take a quick shower before his 'appointment' with Rosie.

"Shit." He grabbed for the handrail as his blasted knee locked and pain shot down his leg. Gripping the rail tightly, he took a deep breath and waited for the searing pain to ease.

"Bullshit, there's no injury," he muttered as he pulled himself up the last stairs. Another specialist and another opinion were needed. He'd phone his doctor tomorrow for another referral. Brennan was supposed to be the top sports doctor in the country, but he'd been a waste of time.

"Nothing wrong, my arse."

By the time he showered and limped back down the stairs, the house was quiet. He tapped on the door of the room Rosie had directed him to and waited for her to open the door. He didn't want to seem too eager.

"Come in." Her voice was brisk as she stepped back to let him enter the dimly lit room. A strong smell of massage oil wafted over to him as she pointed to the privacy screen at the back of the small room.

"Strip down to your jocks and lie face down on the table. Give me a call when you're all settled."

She stepped outside as he walked over to the screen and stripped down, hanging his jeans and shirt on the hook provided. He was looking forward to this. He always enjoyed a remedial massage and Rosie's hands on him would make it even more enjoyable.

"I'm done," he called out as he settled face down on the table and put his face into the soft vinyl ring and looked down at the floor. A click was followed by soft music; the same sort of music they'd played in that alternative soul place in the Maldives. He closed his eyes as two warm hands gripped his calves and straightened his legs.

"Hmm." Her voice was soft but with a tinge of concern.

"What's wrong?" Taj tried to lift his head and look around but his position face down on the massage table made it too difficult. Rosie stretched his leg back and then the other.

"Which knee is the bad one?"

"The right one."

"Hmm."

"Hmm…what?"

"Your left leg is a fraction longer than your right. Do you have back problems?"

"No. Just the bloody knee. I'm as fit as a Mallee bull apart from the knee."

"Hmm."

Taj closed his eyes and let Rosie work her magic. He tried to focus on the remedial aspect of the massage but her firm hands sliding up and down the backs of his calves and thighs, and the smooth sensation of the massage oil on his skin sent tingles up to his groin. He swallowed and focused on the patterned carpet on the floor beneath the table. He counted the roses and then counted the leaves on the winding stems. The tightness that had been building in his groin began to lessen until her warm hands reached his lower back.

God, he didn't want to have a hard-on when she rolled him over. But then all thoughts of pleasure flew out the window as her firm fingers hit a nerve at the base of his back and she pressed. Hard. Bloody hard.

"Holy shit." He almost jumped off the table. "What the fuck's that?"

"Breathe it out."

"Breathe it out! I can't bloody breathe. What the hell

are you doing?"

"You want your knee fixed?"

"That's not my knee."

"Trust me, Taj. It's all about trigger points. Now breathe it out."

"Sorry, but that hurt!" He regretted the stream of swear words he'd let fly and bit down on his bottom lip as she continued.

By the time, Rosie's fingers had worked her way over the bloody trigger points from the base of his back to his shoulders Taj was in a lather of sweat. How could such a slim-built woman have such strength in her hands?

"Brace yourself."

Bloody hell! She was using her elbows on his back. He'd never had a massage like this in his life. But strangely the more pressure she applied and the greater the pain, the better he began to feel.

"Okay." She lifted the towel that was covering his legs and a sensation of cool air swept over his thighs as she held it up. "Roll over for me."

Taj obliged and settled his head on the low pillow she eased beneath his neck, grateful that there was no hard-on tenting his boxers. Hell, his whole body was as weak as a kitten's.

He closed his eyes again as she started on his feet and worked her way up his legs, kneading muscles and stretching his legs.

"I'm not hurting your knee?"

"Uh-uh. All good."

Her hands left him for a moment, and he let his mind drift. He was back surfing the Pipeline at Oahu. The air rushed past him and he could feel the spray on his face as he curved down the face of the perfect wave. The flawless water tube held him as his legs stretched and the board flipped and weaved as the power of the wave took him down the face. He flopped onto the board and let the white water take him into the shallows as the sun warmed his back. Gradually his doze lifted as the warmth spread to the front of his legs. His right knee was burning hot and he opened his eyes with a start, expecting to see a heat pad on his leg. He pushed himself up to his elbows and stared.

Rosie had her hands in a horizontal plane hovering about six inches above his right knee.

"What the—"

"Sssh. Lie back down."

He lowered himself and watched quietly as she focused on his knee. Although he was now wide awake, a deep calm rushed through him and he relaxed his body as the warmth lessened on his knee. Rosie lifted her hands and with one finger she lightly rested it on his knee, his lower stomach, his chest and his throat before lightly touching the top of his head.

"Stay there as long as you like. When you're dressed we'll talk out on the front porch."

He watched as she walked to the door and turned with the sweetest smile before she slipped outside.

***

Rosie sat on the front porch watching the moonlight dance on the waves. She'd filled two glasses with iced water from the dispenser in the foyer that there was there for their clients. She was exhausted. As her fingers had travelled over Taj's body, all sorts of fantasies had filled her mind. She'd had to fight to focus on being professional. The temptation to lower her head and let her lips follow her fingers had been overwhelming. Once he'd rolled over and she'd sensed the toxic energy, she'd called on everything she had to balance his physical state. The heat that had come from her hands had surprised her. It was the strongest healing she'd ever done and she had no doubt that his knee would be okay now.

She jumped as the door opened and Taj pulled up the chair beside her. She passed him the glass of water and watched his throat muscles work as he drained it. The moonlight played on his golden hair and her breath caught. No matter what happened in her life, she would never be able to put aside her feelings for him. Now that she'd met the flesh and blood Taj Brown, everything she'd known was true.

"Thank you. I needed that." He put the glass down on the table between them." I don't know what you did in there but I feel bloody amazing. So calm, and yet energized. I even dozed off while you worked."

"I didn't hurt you too much?"

He grinned at her and his perfect teeth flashed in the dim moonlight.

"A little, but I'm tough. Sorry I let fly with the f-bomb." He tilted his head to the side and observed her. "What was that thing you did at the end?"

"With your knee?"

"No, with your fingers."

"The long explanation or the quick one?"

"The quick one will do for tonight."

"I balanced your chakras. I listened to your body as I worked and I found what was needed."

"Oh."

She'd expected a sceptical reply, but Taj looked at her thoughtfully. "Whatever it was, I feel great. I could grab my board and go for a surf right now."

She pulled a face at him. "Ah, it's a bit dark for that."

"Seriously, do you think my knee would hold up for a surf in the morning after…whatever it is you've done."

Rosie tried not to smile too smugly but she had no doubt the Reiki treatment had fixed the imbalance in Taj's body. "Trust me; your knee will be fine now."

A nervous jolt ran up her arm as he reached over and took her hand. "Thank you."

The words were simple but his tone was heartfelt.

They sat there quietly watching the lights across at Bondi Beach. Even though it was dark, crowds of people walked the esplanade, joggers were still out on force and the sound of music from the units next door added to the mood of the night. The silence was companionable. Taj kept hold of her hand and Rosie revelled in the feel of his skin against hers. It was hard to believe she'd only known him a few days; it just felt right.

His deep voice interrupted her thoughts. "This is nice. I'm usually in a hotel room by myself."

"You don't get home"—she shot him a grin—"wherever that is, very often?"

He shook his head. "So what are we going to do about Aggie's place, Rosie?"

She shrugged. "Let's not talk about it tonight. The night is too nice and I don't want to worry."

"No need to worry. I have an idea." He hurried on. "How about I take you out for dinner tomorrow night and we'll discuss it rationally—without getting angry?"

She nodded slowly. "Okay."

"And do you want to come for a surf with me in the morning?" His smile was wide and her stomach curled. "I'd love the company."

Chapter 12

Rosie barely slept. Taj had let her hand go and bid her good night, and her dreams of him kissing her on the porch evaporated like the salt spray beneath the streetlights on the esplanade. She woke at dawn and jumped out of bed, grabbing her wetsuit and taking it to the bathroom. There was no sign of him; he'd said sunrise and she'd be out there at sunrise.

She made her way down to the rocks and looked out, catching her breath as her gaze settled on him. He was already out there carving up the waves like there was no tomorrow. Closer to the beach, she passed a group of people watching him from the rocks.

It was one of the most spectacular displays of surfing she had ever seen and for a moment she hesitated, putting her board down. There was no way she could go out there with him. He was the king of the surf. Pride rushed through her that he had put his trust—and his knee—literally in her hands.

She grinned. Stuff it; she would go out there. So what if she looked like an amateur? It would be fun.

And it was. Ninety minutes later they paddled into the shore side by side after sharing wave after wave.

Every time Taj had passed her as she'd paddled back out, he'd let out a whoop and given her the thumbs up as he'd shot down the face, or out of the tube. Each time, she'd watched the flexing of his muscles, his chest, his back and his legs. He was beautiful to look at as he carved up the face of a wave, glorious in his element.

Rosie slid off her board and waited in the foamy, ankle-deep water at the edge of the beach until he caught her up.

"You are one amazing woman. My knee is as good as

new." He threw his board down and grabbed her, planting his lips on hers before she could draw a breath. Heat sizzled down her legs as need rushed through her. No one had ever kissed her with such intensity. Her stomach clenched as his tongue slipped between her lips and his hands cupped her butt.

"Woo hoo. Way to go, man." A few other voices joined in with a cheer.

Rosie looked around, disoriented, as Taj lifted his head and a grin crossed his face.

"Whoops, we have an audience."

The sound of clapping surrounded them. The crowd that had been watching Taj surf when she'd first come down had swelled, and now there seemed to be dozens of people standing there grinning at them.

As heat rushed up her neck and into her face, a teenage boy with a boogie board ran across to them. "It is Taj Brown. Oh wow. How cool."

Taj shrugged but the sexy grin stayed in place. "Sorry. Welcome to my world."

Rosie stepped away and left him chatting, and posing for pictures as people pulled out their phones.

"I'll see you up the hill," she called over her shoulder. He nodded and waved but she could feel his eyes on her as she walked up the sand.

"Good surf, sweets?" Sally was waiting on the front porch, her iPad on her lap.

"The best."

"And you're trending on Twitter too." Sally's smile was wide. "Sonia was right about the auras and it looks like you've fixed his knee too. All you have to do now is sort the inheritance out."

"What? Twitter? What are you talking about?"

Sally held up the iPad. "The power of social media.

Hashtag is #sexysurferTaj."

"Show me." Rosie groaned as a brilliantly clear picture of Taj kissing her with his hands firmly planted on her butt filled the screen. "Oh my God. How embarrassing."

"Really? I thought it was all your dreams come true."

She grinned. Sally was right. It was just like out of her dream but this time, it was the real deal. No need to look at posters anymore.

***

Part of being on the circuit was supporting young surfers and every damned one of them seemed to stop to talk to him as he walked up the beach, over the rock platform and past the pools. He'd finally shaken off the last fan just before he'd reached the park. He jogged lightly across the road and put his board on the porch, before peeling off his wet suit and leaving it over the low brick wall near the front door.

"Rosie?" he called as he opened the door. She couldn't have started work already. They had unfinished business to sort out. Sally stood in the kitchen doorway.

"She's up taking a shower."

"Thanks." Taj shot her a grin and vaulted up the stairs, his knee not giving him one ounce of trouble. He tapped lightly on the bathroom door before he opened it and poked his head around. You in there, Rosie?"

"Ye…es."

"Can I come in?"

"Give me a minute."

He closed the door and waited. It was only seconds before it opened and Rosie stood there, a towel hitched around her and tied at her breasts.

"I wanted to say thank you."

Her eyes lowered, and colour tinged her cheeks as a small smile played about her lips. "Well, you'd better come in here then."

As his lips took hers, she wondered whether he could feel the thumping of her heart. This time his lips were slow and soft, and he murmured against them.

"How long till you have to start work?"

Rosie pulled back and held his intent gaze. "I don't have anything on this morning."

"That's good." His cheeky smile filled her vision until his lips took hers again, and they moved gently back and forward across her open lips like a whisper. He was hard against the flat of her stomach and she reached between them and undid the knot of her towel and it slipped to the floor. Taj glanced over at the small sofa in the foyer of the bathroom. "Sofa or bedroom?"

"Sofa will be just right." Her voice was throaty and sexy, and she felt a need rush through her. She laughed as Taj scooped her up into his arms, walked across the checked tiles and placed her gently on the old-fashioned sofa.

"I wonder what Aggie would say," he said softly. He stepped out of his board shorts and she drew in a deep breath. He was magnificent. All over.

After that rational thought fled as he lowered himself beside her on the soft couch. She shivered under the heat of his stare as he lightly trailed his fingers across her bare breasts. Her nipples had been tight since she'd left the cold surf, but now they budded even more tightly in response to his questing fingers. He lowered his head and caught one between his lips, rolling his tongue over it until Rosie gasped with pleasure. Exquisite tendrils of pleasure were wrapping around her nerve endings and building between her thighs as his fingers went lower and hovered at the edge of her sex.

"You are so beautiful, Rosie." His voice was husky and she smiled up at him as he lifted himself above her. He nudged against her sex, and his lips lingered on her neck. Goose bumps ran down her arms and a delicious shiver ran through her. Her body was a mass of rampant nerve endings sending messages of need to her brain.

"Have you got a condom?" she managed to breathe out.

"Shit." He laughed but it was rueful and he pulled back. "You have me so bewitched I didn't give it a thought, and no, not here, I don't."

"In the cupboard above the basin."

Her skin, but not her ardour, cooled in the few seconds he was gone, but he was sheathed and ready for her as he lay back down beside her. He took her face in his hands and kissed her, his tongue dancing with hers. Rosie couldn't help herself. She pushed against him, rubbing against his solid thigh. "I can't take this much longer."

As his eyes held hers, a strange feeling ran through her. A feeling of balance and rightness as though all of her chakras aligned in perfect harmony. She had never experienced such bliss before. He held her gaze and shifted over her, his eyes holding hers, unblinking. She opened her legs and grasped his shoulders before running her hands down the well-defined muscles of his back. With one thrust, he filled her and stars filled her vision as she let go of the waves of pleasure filling her.

***

Taj was very pleased that Rosie had no appointments until after lunch. She filled his mind, his senses, and his emotions, and no matter how many times he kissed her, a need like he'd never experienced before consumed him. It wasn't just the sex; that was awesome too— he just couldn't get close enough to her. After the first round, they showered together, and when they couldn't hold back, he'd had to dash from the shower back to the cupboard. Amazing what desire a cake of soap and bare skin could create.

They'd walked innocently across the hall to his

bedroom, each draped in a towel, but there'd been no sign of the others. When Rosie opened the bathroom cupboard to take the box of condoms, she giggled as he'd shaken his head.

"Plenty in my room. I just don't carry them when I surf."

It was a beautiful morning, and he'd indulged in the pleasure of having her in his bed. Her black hair was fanned across the pillow and her lips were rosy red. An unfamiliar feeling settled in his chest, and it was crazy, but he couldn't imagine leaving her. She had come into his life suddenly and it was right. Now that she was here, he didn't want her to leave it—or leave him. The realization hit him like a thunderbolt.

"What's wrong?" Her hazel eyes locked with his, and he reached over and cupped his hand beneath her chin as she stared at him, uncertainty filling her eyes.

"Nothing. Just looking and admiring." He didn't want to put words to his feelings. Not yet. "It's time we were up. I've got some places to go after lunch."

Rosie let out a gasp. "Lunch? What time is it? I've got a noon massage."

Taj rolled over and picked up his watch. "You have twelve minutes."

He enjoyed the view of the lush bare butt as she scurried across to the door, grabbing the towel on the way.

Chapter 13

Mr Pepper shook Taj's hand as he stood before walking him to the door.

"An excellent outcome. Excellent." The elderly man cleared his throat. "When I draw the papers up, I'll call. After you and Miss Pemberton come in and sign them, it will all be ready to settle early in January. Excellent." He rubbed his hands together.

Taj glanced down at his watch. The appointment had gone later than he'd expected and he still had to book a table for dinner. He couldn't wait to tell Rosie what he'd come up with. A tiny niggle of doubt tugged at him, but he dismissed it. It was a great solution, and it would mean they could stay in touch so much easier when he was in town. He wanted to spend as much time with her as he could when he wasn't on the circuit.

Now that his knee was better—thanks to her unbelievable skill—he could get straight back into the competition field. As soon as the three months were up. And living in the house on the hill was perfect. He could surf and practise every day. Watch out world, he would make world champion one more time before he retired.

With a smile planted firmly on his face, and satisfaction settled in his chest, he jogged lightly to his car. *Life is good.*

Rosie finished at six and Taj had booked the restaurant at the Intercontinental in the city for seven-thirty. He'd seen her briefly before her last appointment and stolen a quick kiss in her massage room.

"Glam up, we're going to town."

His heart had skittered up a beat when she'd run her

fingers down the front of his shirt and tucked her fingers in the waistband of his jeans.

"Later, babe. Dinner and my news first. Then you can finish that at home." Regret tinged his voice. She had magic fingers and not only for healing. Shame they were out of time.

As soon as he was dressed in his suit, he wandered down to the kitchen following yet another mouth-watering aroma. A bottle of champagne sat in the middle of the table where Sonia and Sally were sitting each holding a long-stemmed crystal flute.

"Private celebration or can anyone join?"

"Aren't you driving?" Sally looked at him over the rim of her glass.

"No. I've booked a taxi. What's the occasion?"

The girls shared a grin.

"I won a bet." Sonia didn't elaborate. Her dress was a mishmash of brilliant colours and fell to the ground in loose swirls as she stood to get another glass from the cupboard above the sink. Her dress reminded him of that Jackson Pollack painting.

The door opened and he drew in a breath. Rosie stood there; her long legs left almost bare by the short classic black dress. Her hair was scooped up exposing her long, graceful neck, and she'd done something to her eyes. Sexy, smouldering shadows stared back at him, above scarlet-painted lips. The blood surged to his groin and he gripped the back of the chair. As he stared at Rosie, Sonia turned to Sally and high-fived her.

"That's enough, you pair. It's a business meeting we are going to." Rosie shot him a smile and his blood heated more. Maybe they should order in and discuss business privately upstairs.

Rosie turned to him. "The taxi pulled up outside as I came downstairs. Are you ready?"

The drive into the city was quiet and Taj smiled as Rosie slipped her hand into his as they sat together in the back seat. As they walked into the restaurant, heads turned and he knew it wasn't him that was drawing the attention. She was a knockout. The maître d' showed them to their table and Rosie smiled at the vase of red rosebuds at her setting.
"From you?"
He nodded. "That's what you remind me of."
"Thank you." A delicate tinge of colour flushed her cheeks and he waited for her to sit down. He reached over and took her hand as the waiter poured water into their glasses and placed the drinks menu in front of Taj.
"So, champagne to celebrate my brilliant solution?" He rubbed his thumb on the back of her hand.
"You'd better tell me what this great solution is first." Rosie snatched her hand away and for a moment he thought she was upset, but she grabbed for a tissue and sneezed.
"Bless you."
"Damn, I've had a scratchy throat all day. Mrs March had a cold when she was in yesterday. I guess she shared it." She smiled at him apologetically. "I hope you don't catch it from me."
The food waiter arrived with the menus and Taj ordered a bottle of the best champagne on the menu.

***

"So tell me what you've come up with. I've been trying to think of a way out of this, and I can't see a solution." Rosie reached for her water glass and waited for him to answer. She could think of a solution but it was one out of fairy-tale land. There was no way Taj Brown, a world-famous surfer, would want to have her in his life permanently. Her teenage dreams of weddings and brides with her hero waiting at the front of the church were just that.
Dreams. She knew where she stood. They were having a fun

time together but it was only a temporary thing. Aunt Aggie should have known her matchmaking would lead to a simple fling and should not have complicated matters with that condition in the will. Her heart beat a little faster as he looked at her.

Dreams can come true sometimes.

But his next words were like a dash of cold water on her skin.

"I went to see Mr Pepper today." He reached for her hand again and she let him take it.

"What for? Why did you go without me?"

"You were busy. I wanted to talk to him about the bond and everything you did for Aggie."

The cold settled as a feeling of doom crept over her. Maybe it was the head cold, or more likely maybe it was because she knew she wasn't going to like his solution. "You don't think that was my business?"

"Yes. But you know, Aggie was my aunt and I really should have been there to help out financially. It was not your responsibility. It was a huge burden you took on by yourself."

"But I did and I was happy to." Rosie tightened her lips. "So what's this solution of yours?" She pulled her hand away on the pretext of pulling a tissue from her small purse. She didn't want to be holding his hand when he spoke the words she knew would follow. Her dream had come true for a couple of days…maybe she should just be happy with that.

"He's drawing up the papers and if we sign now, it will all go through smoothly in the New Year."

"What will go through smoothly?" As much as she hated to put a dampener on things, she couldn't help noticing his excitement.

His eyes lit up as the words rushed from his mouth. "I'm going to pay you out for half of the value of the house. It should be at least a million. That will be plenty for you to set up a clinic somewhere local. At first, I was going to sell the place, but now I've decided to get the house renovated. Turn it into a block of apartments." His face lit up as a huge grin showed his teeth white, against his tanned face. That recalcitrant lock of hair fell over his forehead and Rosie closed her eyes for a second.

When she opened them he was staring at her, still smiling.

"And you think that's what Aggie would have wanted?"

He obviously didn't notice her mood. It was as though her world was shutting down.

"I think so. And the best part is to come."

She opened her eyes again; he was like a child at Christmas and he obviously had no idea that every word he uttered was destroying her dream. No matter how much fun they'd had, his motivation had been driven by something very different to hers.

"I'll sign over one of the units to you, I'll keep one and if Sonia and Sally want to rent one, I'll do them a good deal. That way we all win."

"We do?"

"Yes." His face fell as she reached for her bag. "What's wrong?"

"Can you call me a taxi, please? I'm not feeling very well."

He fussed around her and called the waiter over and explained they were leaving.

"There's no need for you to come with me. You might as well stay and eat. I just want to go home to bed."

His mouth tightened and she saw the second that comprehension dawned for him. He looked just like he had the first time in Mr Pepper's office. Everything had to be Taj Brown's way or the highway. She'd been a fool to fall into

his arms.
> *Chasing that silly dream.*
> No more.

Chapter 14

Taj had been concerned about her when he had escorted her to her room after the taxi dropped them back to the house on the hill. Rosie had sneezed most of the way home and she'd insisted that he sit in the front of the taxi. She needed to be alone; she couldn't think straight with him around. All she could think about was being in his bed and the crushing disappointment in the restaurant when she'd realised that it had only been to suck her in. To entice her, so that she fell in with his plan.

His plan to destroy the beautiful old house and turn it into a sleek apartment block.

He probably had a girlfriend in every surfside town, and stupid Rosie with her childish posters had been an easy target. She turned her face into the pillow trying to ease her burning cheeks.

Stupid, stupid, stupid.

But really, if she thought about it, she had no right to the house. It had been in the Brown family for generations, and it was rightfully his. Torn between not wanting to accept his solution, because she didn't want to take his money, and knowing that at the end of the three months, she would be entitled to half anyway, she tossed and turned in and out of a fitful sleep.

Even then they would have to agree on what they would do with the house. Apartments? Aggie would turn in her grave. She'd loved this place and Rosie did too.

Tears dampened her cheeks as she fell into a deep sleep.

She woke suddenly to a pitch-dark room. Her throat was dry and her head was throbbing.

"There's a glass of water on your bedside table."

She rolled over and stared. Aggie was sitting on the side of the bed. How could she see her in the dark? Her grey hair was wound up into its usual beehive hairstyle and the lavender perfume she loved filled the room. Her soft fingers reached out and smoothed Rosie's brow.

"Oh, darling. You're burning up. You always did get a temperature with a head cold when you were little."

Rosie stared back at her. It had been five years since Aggie had been able to have a conversation with her. She closed her eyes as the cool fingers rested on her cheek.

"Aggie?" She tried to sit up but Aggie's gentle hands pushed her back to the pillows.

It must be the fever. *I'm delirious.*

Aggie's voice surrounded her. "He's falling in love with you, you know. I knew he would."

"No. He's just sleeping with me to get me out of the house." *Am I really talking about sex with Aggie?* "He wants to pull it to pieces. Your beautiful house." Rosie shook her head.

"He'll realise what is right for you both. You have to learn to trust."

"I don't know what to do, Aggie."

"Follow your heart. You've always loved him. I can still remember you following him around when you were a little girl."

"I don't remember."

"Trust, sweetheart."

The wind whooshed through the open window bringing the sound of crashing waves into the room. The old lace curtains fluttered, and the smell of lavender surrounded her. She turned back to Aggie but the room was empty.

##

Rosie rolled over and groaned as a bright shaft of sunlight hit her in the face. She put her hand up over her eyes and dragged herself up to a sitting position. Her headache was gone but her nose was streaming. She reached over for the box of tissues she kept by the bed and wiped her nose. There was a glass of water beside the bed; she didn't remember getting that.

A wisp of a dream tugged at her and she sat bolt upright as she remembered Aggie sitting beside her through the night.

Trust. The strangest dream.

After she'd showered, Rosie headed for the kitchen, picking up the water glass on the way. Sally came in the back door, carrying her walking shoes.

"How was dinner?" She looked closely at Rosie. "You look dreadful."

"Head cold." She held up the glass. "Did you bring me a glass of water through the night?"

Sally shot her a cheeky grin. "I wouldn't have been game to come anywhere near your room through the night. I didn't want to interrupt anything."

Rosie flopped onto a chair as Sally filled the kettle. "You wouldn't have. I blew it."

The door flung open, and Sonia burst into the room. "So what's the deal? What happened?"

"What do you mean?"

"Taj packed up and left early this morning. He drove out as I was coming back from my walk." Sonia stared at Rosie. "You look dreadful. Have you been crying? Did you have a fight?"

"No, I have a cold and no, we didn't fight." Rosie grabbed for her tissue as she sneezed. "Sonia, did you bring me a glass of water through the night?"

"No. I didn't know you were sick. So where's he gone?"

Rosie shook her head. "I don't know."

"What about the house?" Sally's voice was calm.

"I guess we're all going to have to find somewhere else to live."

Chapter 15

Rosie called Mr Pepper to see what was going to happen now that Taj had decided not to stay for the three months.

"We don't have to worry until the time is up. But if you want to, you can still come in and sign the contract I drew up. I thought that was quite a workable solution, Miss Pemberton."

"I'll give it some thought, thank you."

Not likely. She was being polite.

Rosie disconnected the call and tried to push away that gloom that had hung over her since Taj had offered to buy her out. She knew she had been unfair to him and she'd blown it. It had been an overly generous offer that he hadn't needed to make, and he had not forgotten Sally and Sonia either. Losing her parents and not being wanted by anyone until Aggie had come along, had left her wary of trust. To be fair, she knew that Taj had come up with a workable solution, and she'd overreacted. What she hadn't believed was that he'd said he wanted to see her more.

She let out a sigh as she stared at the surf. He had come into her life for a week. Could she really have fallen in love with the flesh and blood Taj Brown in a week?

Trust. That strange dream of Aggie sitting beside her wouldn't leave her. Rosie wasn't so sure it had been a dream. It was time to take control and trust her feelings. It was time to take a risk with trust.

He's falling in love with you, you know.
***
Taj took the lift down from Mr Pepper's office and glanced into the coffee shop on the ground floor. Everywhere

he looked there was a memory of Rosie. Hell, he couldn't even take a shower without thinking of her. Now that he didn't need to stay in Sydney, he was going to head to California and leave it all behind him.

The legalities of the house on the hill were underway and he could forget all about it. Forget all about his dysfunctional family, Aunt Agatha, and more to the point, a black-haired, rosy-lipped woman who had stolen his heart.

Time to move on.

The traffic from Bondi Junction into town was heavy as the afternoon peak hour approached. Lost in his thoughts, he missed the entrance to the Cross City Tunnel and ended up in the back streets of Rushcutters Bay before he got back to the main road and tried again. His mood worsened as he sat in the line of traffic. Maybe he'd forget the States; maybe he should go to the Maldives where life was slower.

He pounded his fist on the steering wheel. Damn, he didn't want to go anywhere apart from that house on the hill at the top of Bondi Beach. But the problem was, he knew he wasn't welcome.

He left his car with the parking valet at the Intercontinental and slowly climbed the marble stairs to the foyer. He'd call the airport and change his flight. Surfing in the Maldives appealed more than anything. *Almost.*

If he couldn't have what he wanted, he'd go and find the best waves he could.

"Taj."

He stopped and turned as the soft voice reached him. A tiny sliver of hope unfurled in his chest, but he pushed it away, not daring to hope.

"Rosie. What are you doing here?"

"I...I wanted to talk to you." Her cheeks were flushed and her nose was red. But she was beautiful.

"Do you want to come up to my room, or sit in the

lounge down here?"

"Your room would be fine."

He led her across to the bank of lifts that led to his suite. They stood silently as the lift whizzed them up to the fourteenth floor. He held his security card above the lock until the light turned green and reached past her to open the door, standing back as she stepped inside.

His suite had a magnificent view over the Harbour Bridge and the Opera House. Two red leather sofas flanked the window that looked out over the vista.

"Sydney's a beautiful city, isn't it?" Her voice was scratchy, and she lifted a tissue to wipe her nose as she sat on one of the sofas. Taj sat opposite her on the other one. Even with her red nose and puffy eyes, she was beautiful and he couldn't trust himself not to touch her.

"It is. What are you doing here, Rosie? Has Mr Pepper called you already?"

"Mr Pepper? No, I called him the other day to see what we had to do now that we weren't living together for the three months. Why would he call me?"

"Before I tell you why, you tell me why you're here to see me."

She raised her eyes and held his gaze and he leaned forward. His fingers ached with the need to touch her. But he waited.

She cleared her throat nervously. "Can I ask you something first?"

He nodded but her question was unexpected. "The other night before you left, did you bring me a glass of water?"

"No." He stared at her as a slow smile sweetened her face. Every nerve ending in his body stirred.

"Aggie came to see me. She told me I had to trust." Her hands moved jerkily as she reached up and gripped them in front of her chest. "I'm sorry I was so quick to judge you the other night." He watched as she flexed her fingers, curling them and uncurling them. When he lifted his gaze to meet her eyes, he was surprised to see a sheen of tears.

She rushed on and her words fell over each other. "I'm sorry. I know I've only known you a short time, but I think Aggie was right in putting us together. I just wanted you to know that before you go anywhere. And I don't care about the house on the hill. It's only a house and we'll manage. Whatever you decide to do."

Taj stood up and held her gaze as he sat beside her. He reached out and took her clasped hands with his. Her fingers were icy cold.

"The house is yours."

"What?" Her eyes widened and she shook her head. "It can't be. If we didn't make the three months, it had to be sold."

"It has been sold. I bought it and the money has gone to the foster children like Aggie wanted. But I have given the house over to you. Mr Pepper will have the documents ready for you next week. I thought that's why you were here."

"No, that's not fair. It's your family house."

Taj took her face between his hands and ignored the rush of feeling that shot through him. "No, Rosie. It belongs to you. You were Aggie's family. You were the one who loved her and looked after her, while the rest of her family abandoned her. Mr Pepper told me why they cut her off and it was all to do with greed and money. I'm not proud of the Brown family."

"Oh, Taj. Aggie was right. She told me to trust and—"

"What else did she say?"

"You really believe that she visited me?"

"Rosie, I trust you. If you say Aggie came to visit, then she did. What else were you going to say?"

Her fair skin deepened with a blush and the look in her eyes as she gazed up at him was enough for Taj.

"She told me you would fall in love with me," she said shyly. "So it was obviously a dream."

"A dream you wanted to come true?"

Rosie nodded. For a long minute, he held her gaze and he saw everything there that he wanted to see.

He pulled her to him gently and smiled as he lowered his lips to meet hers, but she pulled back.

"You'll catch my cold."

"I don't care. I'll take anything you want to share with me."

Epilogue
Five years later

"Hurry up, Theo. The surf's waiting."

Rosie looked up and grinned at Taj as he hitched the boogie board under his arm and held out his hand to the four-year-old boy who was sliding down the grassy hill. His little board shorts were covered with grass stains, and his long golden curls were full of grass and twigs.

"Mummy, Theo's pants are dirty." His twin sister carried her boogie board and looked impatiently at her brother. "Hurry up, Theo. The waves are waiting for us."

Taj waited for them to catch up and smiled at his wife. "Surf does look good." He lowered his voice to a whisper. "Makes up for this pair of grommets getting us out of bed so early."

"We can always hope they have a sleep this afternoon." Rosie grinned back at him. She looked up at the house; the renovations were almost finished, and the house had been restored to the former glory of a 1930s mansion.

"Look, the builders have painted the widow's walk. She frowned and blinked as the sun glinted on the railing. For a moment, she could have sworn that she caught a glimpse of a tall, graceful lady in a long purple dress, standing on the narrow balcony at the top of the house on the hill.

Taj lifted a hand and waved.

Rosie's mouth dropped open. "Who are you waving to?"

"Aunt Agatha." He leaned in and kissed her as the children ran ahead. "She was right, you know."

Rosie's lips opened beneath those of the man she loved with all of her heart. The man who'd just won the world surfing championship for the fourth consecutive year. As they'd travelled the world, they'd supervised the house renovations from afar. She lifted her head and stared over Taj's shoulder as the wisp of purple faded into the pale blue autumn sky.

"Thanks, Aggie," she whispered.

Sally's story

Beach Music

Annie Seaton

Dedication

*This book is dedicated to my dear friend, Sharyn.
She had a real Otis.*

Chapter 1

Sally leaned her head against the cold glass window of the bus and stared out at the depressing scene of a rain-swept street. After the dismal view became too much, she closed her eyes and imagined a tropical beach, but the only picture she could summon up was Rosie and Sonia waving to her from Waikiki.

She was still stuck on a bus in the peak hour of a miserable Sydney winter.

Thanks, girls. Catch some sun for me.

Sally hated winter. Water droplets ran down the outside of the dirty window and she put her hand on the back of the seat in front of her as the bus lurched to a stop at yet another set of traffic lights. The man beside her pulled out a handkerchief and she tried not to breathe in as he coughed.

That's all I need. A dose of the flu would cap this winter off perfectly.

But she could only take the blame herself. She could have gone with Sonia, but as usual, her work ethic kicked in. The weather had been bleak, and business had been slow in the house at the beach. The engine roared as the bus took off again and Sally turned her attention back to the grey world outside. A flash of lightning relieved the dim vista and the thunder rumbled soon after. The gutter at the edge of the footpath was running, and spouts of water were streaming over the rubbish that was being swept along in the torrent. A young woman stood waiting to cross the road and as Sally watched her red umbrella turned inside out when the chill wind gusted in from the sea. The girl's eyes were wide, and she looked as disgusted as Sally felt at the moment.

She closed her eyes as the bus stopped to let passengers off and a blast of cold air roared up the passageway of the bus. The southerly busters had arrived one after the other this winter and last Friday night on the news, the weatherman had said it was the coldest Sydney winter for fifty years.

'No shit, Sherlock,' Sonia had commented as she lounged on the sofa beside her. She'd picked up the postcard that had arrived from Hawaii and read it aloud for the third time.

'Gals, we are renting a huge condo right above the beach. Come and visit, I'd love to see you both it's been too long. All it will cost is an airfare and there are deals at the moment. Ring me when you are going to arrive, Love Rosie.'

When Sonia arrived home the next afternoon and waved a ticket at her, envy had almost eaten up Sally.

'Come on, Sal. Book a ticket too. Get away from this cold weather,' she'd pleaded. 'I'm leaving Monday. Free accommodation in Hawaii. Sun, surf and sand. Come with me. Pleeeeease?'

'Monday!'

'Yep, no point hanging around. Business is slow, and I'm off to have a good time. They've been few and far between lately.'

'What few customers?'

'No, good times. I need a fun roll in the hay.' Sonia giggled. 'Or maybe the sand.'

Sally shook her head. Honestly, even though they were twins—fraternal—she and Sonia couldn't be more different. Sometimes she thought life might be more fun if she did have a free and easy attitude like Sonia. But Sally had inherited their mother's cautious and considered manner. Anything she did had to be thought through and planned.

Not like Sonia taking off for Hawaii on a whim.

'Come on, Sally. We could have a great time.' Sonia tipped her head to the side. 'You need to do something to get out of the rut you've been hiding in since—'

'I can't.' Sally had folded her arms and cut Sonia off. 'I've got commitments now. I can't close my appointments book off now that I'm working over at the Wellness Centre.'

'I don't know why you ever started work there. We've got our own centre.' Sonia glanced across at her twin sister as she filled the kettle. 'Or we did have. You want a coffee?'

'Yes, please.' Sally pulled out a chair and looked down with a smile as her kitten wound his way around her ankles. 'I did it because my appointments here dropped off after the footy team folded. And you know it's not been the same since Rosie moved away. Besides who'd look after Muggins here.' She reached down and smiled as the rag doll kitten snuggled into her chest.

'You can't call her Muggins. That's an awful name for such a pretty little girl.'

'It's only temporary until I think of the right one.'

Sonia rolled her eyes. 'And you make up your mind so fast, she's likely to be Muggins when she's old and grey.'

'Don't be sarcastic. I like to think things through, not like you. Mrs Rush-Tear-and-Bust. Sally pursed her lips. 'I still can't believe you've bought a ticket to go to Hawaii.'

Sonia frowned and pulled out the chair beside her twin. 'Sal, don't be so boring. I worry about you. It's bad enough that I'm still living here in the same house that Aggie let us move into with Rosie when we were starting out. But at least I do things and go places. When was the last time you took a holiday?'

Sally bit her lip and looked down at the kitten in her lap. 'I don't need a holiday.' She gestured to the window. 'Look, we live in the most vibrant city in the world and Bondi Beach is at our doorstep. I don't need to go anywhere.'

'You're never going to get over him, are you? He really did a number on you.'

'Sonia.' Sally kept her voice low and she injected a warning note into it. 'Don't go there.'

'I'm going to. You're turning into a boring recluse. God, Sal. It's been three years since Blake dumped you for that…that bimbo. When was the last time you spoke to a man who wasn't a client?'

Sally had stood, held the kitten tight and glared at her sister. 'I'm happy in my life. Okay? Forget the coffee. I've got work to do.'

'You really need to be pushed out of that boring comfort zone you've settled into.'

If she'd seen the calculating look on her twin sister's face as she strode out of the kitchen, maybe she would have bought a ticket to Hawaii.

Sonia had been gone five days and when Sally stepped off the bus on Friday afternoon into rain and wind, she muttered beneath her breath. 'Not only the coldest winter for fifty years, but the damn wettest too.'

Muggins was waiting at the door as she pushed it open, and Sally dropped her umbrella onto the tiles before she shouldered her coat off. It was so damp it would need to go in front of the fire.

If she could be bothered lighting one. It would mean a trip out to the back shed to get some firewood, and she was pretty sure that she'd used the last of the split kindling the other night. Taj had offered to put reverse cycle air conditioning through the house on their last trip home, but Sally had shaken her head.

'Waste of money, guys. It doesn't get cold enough here to need it.'

And what she didn't say was that it would hike up the power bill, and she and Sonia had to watch their finances lately.

Especially now that her work had dropped off so

much. At least tomorrow was Saturday, and she could stay home. She would get the fire going late. It would warm some of the house for what was looking like a bleak weekend.

And a bleak life. The words flitted through her mind. She straightened her shoulders and reached down to pick up the kitten; her purr was at full throttle and she was warm in her hands. It was time to stop feeling sorry for herself and listen to Sonia. This weekend she would do something out of her comfort zone.

Sally fed Muggins before she pushed her wet hair back from her face with a sigh and headed for the bathroom. A hot bath, her winter PJs and dressing gown and some hot soup would warm her up. As she headed back to the kitchen to pour a wine to take into the bath, the front doorbell pealed.

For a minute she considered ignoring it, but then realised it could be a potential client. Every one counted.

Juggling the wine glass in one hand and the door key in the other, she headed for the door.

Chapter 2

Solomon Brown looked curiously at the two men who pushed past him at the gate. He held the gate open and approached the front door of the house with something akin to reverence. He folded down the black umbrella and leaned it against the low wooden wall of the porch of the grand old mansion. As he'd walked up the hill in the gusting wind, he'd passed a constant stream of people walking to their parked cars and down to the bus stop. But he forgot about that and opened his eyes wide as the graceful old house on the top of the hill overlooking Bondi Beach filled his vision. It stood tall and proud, the stormy sky providing an atmospheric backdrop.

This was meant to be. When he'd read the advertisement yesterday, the address had snagged his attention; so much so that a cup of coffee in his hand had gone flying when he realised the ad was to do with this house.

The same house that had called to him for years. The house he'd always loved.

If he believed in things like that, he'd almost say he'd been led here this afternoon. But he didn't believe in the paranormal.

Not completely anyway.

Despite not having the medical mind to suit his family, Solomon still had a scientific bent. This beautiful house had always struck a chord in him. He'd admired the graceful old building since he was a kid walking up the hill with his boogie board slung over his back, fascinated by the architecture of it. The steep roof with the widow's walk around the top had caught his attention when he was still at primary school. He'd imagined sea captains, and ghosts, and elegant parties held there in years gone by. The house was the same as he remembered it from twenty years ago and the same thrill tingled down to his toes. It was an anachronism set amongst the bland and boring apartment blocks that overlooked the beach. The square boxy minimalist apartments that people forked out millions of dollars for these days only added to its appeal. For a while there the old house had spurred on his career dreams, and he'd decided he wanted to be an architect.

Then after he'd rescued the cat and the litter of kittens from the drain behind their house at Rose Bay, he changed his mind and decided to study veterinary science. Of course, all of this was enough to send his mother into one of her 'nervy episodes', because the expectation was that Sol would join their exclusive medical practice at Double Bay. With his grandfather and his father, he was destined to become the next young Dr Brown and pander to the whims of the matrons of Rose and Double Bay. He'd soon learned to shut his mouth about what his future would be. He'd almost finished his vet science degree when he'd become fascinated with psychology.

Although Sol was almost a doctor—when he finished his doctorate his mother could put doctor in front of his name— it was lucky that his older brother Tobias had graduated with the required medical degree at Sydney University because, as his maternal grandfather was wont to tell him, 'you just don't cut the mustard, boy.'

Or what he meant was that a study of psychology and an almost completed doctorate were not good enough for the esteemed Brown family of Vaucluse.

The vet dream was on the back burner since Sol discovered psychology. Now he was at the final stage of his thesis and there would be another Dr Brown in the family.

If I get my research completed in time.

But it was the wrong sort of doctor to make his family

happy.

He should have known back in the days when he walked from Vaucluse to Bondi Beach so he could hang out with the friends he'd made at the local public school, that he was a misfit in his family. The boys he'd attended St Joey's with— the private high school that he'd been forced to attend— were now all part of the 'network', and making their mark in the city or in high-flying international careers. Sol was a tutor at Macquarie University and ignored his mother's comments that even if he had to follow "that career" surely, he could be a professor. Her mouth always twisted in a funny grimace as she articulated the words. *That career.*

He could almost have written a thesis on the psychology of his mother's disapproval and what each expression conveyed. To put it in the old-fashioned words of his grandfather, psychology just didn't cut the mustard. Sometimes Sol would smile as he wondered what his mother would think of the topic of his thesis.

But there was no fear of that ever happening. Anything studied away from his father and grandfather's Alma Mater, Sydney University, was not worthy of family interest.

Sol was sure he'd been abandoned on his parent's doorstep as a baby—like that litter of kittens he'd found when he was in Year Six—and that his parents had taken him in to avoid any scandal. Maybe he'd been born in the old house on top of the hill above the beach.

But the one time he'd asked his mother if he was adopted, her professionally plucked eyebrows had arched and her mouth had formed a perfect O. Merely another question that had sent Mother—not being allowed to call her Mum like his mates called their mothers had only reinforced Sol's idea that he was adopted—scurrying to the sideboard to the sherry decanter.

Heaven forbid that anything would taint the esteemed

Brown name.

So even though he'd had to drive over sixty kilometres to answer the ad this afternoon—it had stated clearly to apply after five o'clock on Friday afternoon—he was buzzing with anticipation. The answer to his immediate problem, and the house he'd admired from afar for so many years.

He jumped as the door opened in front of him, only half aware that he'd pressed the old-fashioned doorbell as he'd mused about his family woes.

'Oh um, hello,' he said. Despite the chill wind and the water droplets running down from his hair, his face heated as he stared at the woman who opened the door. Although she was really pretty, she looked tired and a scowl pulled her pretty face into an unwelcoming expression.

'Before you say a word,' she said as he stared at her lush lips wondering how such terse words could come from such pretty lips, 'I did not place an ad in the Bondi View.'

***

Sally's temper flared as she pushed the door shut. Or as she tried to push it shut. Her eyes widened when a brown suede desert boot wedged between the door and the frame.

Desert boots? She hadn't seen shoes like that since she was in high school. She stared at them.

And brown corduroy jeans. Was this guy super trendy and dressing retro, or was he a charity case? Who knew from the different types she'd had knocking at her door for the past hour?

'Do you mind?' Her words came from between gritted teeth as she tried to shove the door shut with both hands.

'Actually, yes.' The cultured voice was more confident now and the desert boot stayed wedged firmly between the old wooden door and the porch. And every second it stayed there her hot bath was getting colder. 'I've come a long way to answer your ad.'

Honestly, this was turning into the night from hell, to follow the day from hell. She'd taken the bus to the other side of the city to run a class, and not one person had turned up. And then she'd missed the early bus home and had sat in a cold and draughty coffee shop—with shit coffee—for an hour and a half until the next Bondi bus came through. She didn't give a thought to being scared of the guy at the door. The constant stream of callers to her door had let her know that someone had used her address by mistake for some advertisement. If the truth be known, this guy would be wise to be scared of her because his foot in the door was really pissing her off.

'It's not my ad.' Sally reiterated but the boot didn't move. And when being pissed off was combined with cold and hunger—and the thought of her hot bath getting colder by the minute— it wasn't going to be a good night.

I should have gone to Hawaii.

Since Sally had turned the bath taps on an hour ago, she'd met a procession of men, and two women, at the door, all claiming to be here about the "ad". She was still damp and cold and now she was cranky and out of sorts. The taps had been on and off for an hour.

And she was hungry too.

Every time she'd come downstairs to answer the door her bath was getting colder. And the hot water system wasn't terribly reliable either. There was a good chance it would have run out and the once steaming hot water in the bathtub was sure to be cold by now.

'Look I have no idea about what ad you, or the other people who have interrupted my night, are talking about.' Her voice was as cold as the water in the bath upstairs.

A strong gust of wind roared in from Antarctica, and the windows rattled. Sally hung onto the door so it wouldn't slam shut. She didn't want to injure his foot.

Not very much.

'I really need to talk to you about the ad. It's perfect for me.'

For probably the fifteenth time since Sally had arrived home, wet, cold and thoroughly out of sorts, she repeated. 'There is no ad. It is not my ad. You have the wrong house. I am not selling anything.'

Fourteen times, she'd answered the door to an 'I've come about the ad.'

Fourteen times in the past hour and a half, she'd replied, 'You have the wrong house,' and the person had apologised, looked slightly embarrassed and left. None of the other callers had been as persistent as this one.

'Does someone else live here? Someone called Sally?'

She peered around the door and lifted her eyes from the boots to the face.

'What?' Shaggy brown hair stuck to his cheeks like wet rat's tails. It was one of the worst haircuts she'd ever seen. He actually had a fringe. 'How do you know my name?'

'That's the name in the ad.' His voice was patient now as though he was talking to a child. 'There is an ad. With this address. And the name of the person to see is Sally. After five o'clock today.' He dug into his pocket and pulled out a folded piece of newspaper. 'I've driven from Peats Ridge.'

Sally huffed a sigh and let the door open a little bit more. 'That's the ad?'

He nodded but held onto it.

'So can I see it? And then I can tell you for sure you've wasted your time.'

He handed over the small square of paper and she squinted. It was too dark to read the words, and she'd left her specs up in the bathroom, next to the book she'd been waiting to read.

She reached up and flicked on the light switch and the

front porch was bathed in bright light. Her visitor put his hand over his eyes and took a deep shaky breath. She stared at him as she held the piece of paper, wondering what he was going to do. He shoved his hand into his coat pocket and for the first time, nerves shimmied up her spine and she backed away.

A knife? A gun? She'd been watching too many movies at night since Sonia had gone away.

But the only thing that came out was a polka-dotted handkerchief that he quickly put over his face to catch a sneeze that almost rattled the roof tiles.

'Bless you,' she said with not an ounce of sympathy. 'I hope you're not getting a cold. Good night.'

He'd pulled his foot back when he'd passed her the piece of paper and she took the opportunity to push the door.

'Wait.' The voice was deep but uncertain and she hesitated for a moment.

'You can't just take the ad and shut the door in my face.'

For the first time, a smile tugged at her lips. 'This is my house'—well technically it wasn't but he didn't have to know that— 'so I can do what I want.'

Determined to have some peace and quiet, Sally leaned on the door but Mother Nature had different plans for her. A huge gust of wind rocketed in from the sea and the door slammed back against the wall taking her with it. The ad fluttered from her fingers and landed on the garishly patterned rug that Aunty Aggie had bought back in the 1950s. Sally stumbled and gasped as a torrent of water poured in through the open door.

'Quick, come inside.' Common courtesy won out. 'You can't stay out in that.'

The man stepped beside her and as he pushed the door shut a huge crack of thunder shook the house, and the lights went out.

'Bloody heck, 'Sally muttered. 'Can it get any worse?'

Chapter 3

Sol reached into his pocket and pulled out the small LED flashlight that was attached to his key ring. He flicked it on, and a dim light lit the small foyer with ghostly shadows in the corners. He lifted the beam slightly and his lips twitched as the feisty—or was she simply cranky? —woman stared back at him. Large brown eyes were framed by a delicate face with high cheekbones. She was slightly built although the navy-blue work shirt and trousers did hug some curves.

From the way the ad had been worded, he'd imagined an alternate—and definitely approachable—woman. Not the one who was now tapping her foot and glaring at him.

'Should I be worried?' she said.

'Worried?' He frowned and lowered the flashlight.

'You were checking me out? Am I about to be accosted?'

Sol's lips twitched again, and he fought back the chuckle that was threatening to rumble out of his chest. 'I think you're safe. And I wasn't checking you out. I was checking you were okay. You hit that wall pretty hard. For a minute there I thought there's been a lightning strike. I've never seen the wind gust like that.'

'No,' she said thoughtfully. 'Neither have I. The porch is protected by the high wall. And I thought the storm had passed.'

As she spoke there was a loud bang upstairs, and Sally frowned.

Aggie.

'Look, let's start again.' He took a step towards her.

'Whoa. Stop right there. I still haven't decided if I can trust you.'

'You can,' he said quietly.

'I'll be the judge of that. And Aunt Aggie will too.'

'Aunt Aggie?' He peered around her into the living room. 'Do you want to get some lights going?'

'Aunty Aggie doesn't need lights.' She folded her arms. 'She's a ghost, but you try any funny business and you'll be sorry. She looks after us.'

Sol tipped his head to the side and wondered what he'd encountered here. Excitement curled in his stomach. Her stories were exactly what he'd imagined finding in this house. He didn't usually read the community paper, but the fish and chips he'd sat on the beach and eaten at lunchtime yesterday—before the weather had closed in— had been wrapped in this week's local newspaper. The ad had jumped out at him; if it hadn't said call after five, he would have run up the hill and pounded on the door straight away.

Okay, despite her appearance, a little alternate, and the face had a fairy-like quality with those huge eyes and the pretty red lips, maybe she was what he'd imagined from the ad. 'Us?'

She waved a hand. 'Don't worry.'

He bent over and shone the light on the scrap of newspaper that was on the patterned rug. Reaching down he picked it up and handed it to her.

'In the ad, it says to call in here at this address, after five pm today and ask for Sally. I'm just pleased that I found it today. It was meant to be.'

'I wonder why none of the others asked for me by name.' She shook her head slowly. 'You'd better let me read it. I'm getting a bad feeling about this.' Reaching up, she pulled the tie from her hair and massaged her scalp. Long, silky, dark hair tumbled to her waist and it was tempting to reach out and run the long tresses through his fingers.

He held out his hand instead and tried to inject professionalism into his voice. 'I'm Sol Brown. I'm probably here for a different reason than your other callers.'

She took it and it was as though an electric current ran up his arm. 'Sally Smith.'

'Perhaps we could have a chat, Sally? Or make an appointment.' Not that he wanted to wait. The ad was exactly what he needed, and he wanted to talk to her now.

'Look, it's storming too much to send you back out there'—her voice was brisk—'come into the kitchen and I'll make a cup of tea while we sort this out.'

'Thanks. That'd be great. I really didn't want to wait too long. I'm on a pretty tight deadline.'

'Follow me. I can turn the gas on and put the kettle on. That'll warm us up, and the stove will dry you out a bit.' She looked at him curiously as she held her hand out. 'Pass me your light please.'

Sally—she'd said that was her name—turned and walked into a large room off the entrance foyer. It was too dark to see much, but the dark shadows and bulky shapes hinted at old furniture filling the space. He followed her through another three smaller rooms and then into a long hall that led to what appeared to be a separate wing at the back of the house. As they walked along the corridor, there was a series of bangs from the floor above.

He raised one eyebrow at her at the last particularly loud one as she pushed open a door.

'Don't worry, it's only Aggie or Muggins.'

'Muggins? You have two ghosts?' He looked up but it was so dark he couldn't even see the ceiling.

'No. Muggins is a cat.' She shone the light onto an ancient stove. 'Taj was going to replace this, but we insisted on keeping it.'

Sol looked around as his eyes became accustomed to the dim light.

'Sit down. I'll get the stove going.' She crouched in

front of it and there were a couple of clicks before the smell of gas surrounded them as he sat at the large wooden table.

'Bugger,' she cursed. 'That would just top off the day. Blowing off my eyebrows is not what I want. Aunt Aggie did it so often, in the end, they didn't grow back.'

Sol swallowed. A ghost with no eyebrows, no less.

Finally, with a whoosh, blue flames danced in the ring on the top of the stove. Sally handed the torch back and he slipped it into his pocket.

'Yay.' After she filled the kettle and put it on the hob, she crouched down and lit the oven. Sol held his breath waiting for a bang, but her eyebrows remained intact.

'So...' He searched around for something to fill the awkward silence after she sat across from him. 'Divine Soul Sisters? There's more than one of you?'

Sally frowned and he couldn't help thinking how pretty she was. Her posture was straight, and her movements were graceful. Maybe it was the soft light from the flame and his small flashlight, but her face looked ethereal. He wandered off into a daydream, thinking about some of the fairy-tale heroines he'd studied as part of his first Master's degree. His supervisor had wrinkled her brow, unable to see what he was trying to convey in his thesis when he'd first presented the idea but he—

'There were three but now we are two.'

His head flew up and he frowned. As usual, he'd lost the thread of the conversation; it drove his family crazy, but they were used to him by now. He saw it as being blessed with an intellect that was prompted by free-thinking; his family called it being off with the pixies.

'Sorry. What was that?'

'I said there were three to start with.' She was staring at him.

'Three what?'

'Three divine soul sisters.' She leaned forward and folded her hands on the table. 'Now it's just my twin sister and I. Rosie's on the circuit.'

'The circuit?' The last thing he'd imagined was a circuit for his research topic.

'And does your sister do the same thing as you?' he asked.

'No.' From the tone of his voice, he sensed that she wasn't happy with that.

'And um, how do you run your business?' Sol leaned forward and put his hands on the table too. 'I need to know if I'm going to be able to use you.'

'Use me? You just make an appointment.' She shook her head and confusion crossed her face. 'The paper must have run an old ad. I haven't advertised my business for years. But maybe it's not such a bad idea if that's the sort of response I get on a stormy afternoon.' She bit her lip. 'Since the football club folded, my clients have dropped right off.'

'The football club?' He knew his eyes were wide. 'The whole football club?'

'Yes, they used to keep me busy. They'd fill a whole class, so I'd run an extra one on a Friday night. The coach used to say he could guarantee a win on the Saturday after the class.'

Sol swallowed. This was not what he'd imagined at all. 'Um, you run classes?'

'Yes. It's not very effective one-on-one. And I'd never make a living if I took clients individually.'

'Maybe I could come to a class and watch?'

'I'm not sure that watching would be beneficial. But if you want to see what a class entails, sure. But you'd still have to pay the class fee.' Sally looked at him as though he had two heads. 'But isn't that why you came knocking on my door?'

'No.' He shook his head slowly. 'I thought that I could get more information from an individual interview. But maybe watching a class…' Heat ran up his neck. Reading research articles and interviewing practitioners in the field, he was comfortable, but he didn't know how he'd feel like being an observer in the room. He'd felt uncomfortable sitting by himself watching some of the DVDs that he'd sourced from the German Association.

The kettle whistled and Sally stood. 'People usually just turn up.'

'But how do you know that they're right for what you do?'

'You can generally tell by first look whether they will be able to cope in one of my classes. I even have some clients in their eighties.' She held up something and he squinted.

'In their eighties?' Sol knew his eyes were wide.

She nodded at the tea bag in her hand. 'Tea or coffee.'

'Ah yes, tea would be good, thank you.' He was fascinated by her responses. 'White, no sugar.' He nodded his thanks and waited while she poured water into a mug. As she passed it to him, he tried to get his head around what she was saying. 'You're giving me a whole new perspective for my area of study. But it's too late to change now. In their eighties, you say? Wow.'

'When Aunt Aggie was alive'—she glanced at him as she passed over the mug—'she was in the nursing home across from the beach and I'd run a couple of classes there most weeks.'

Sol spluttered as he sipped his tea and the hot liquid sprayed from his mouth. He reached into his pocket and pulled out his handkerchief to dab at his shirt. Sally stared at him as he wiped his mouth and Sol felt more gauche than he usually did. The newspaper in his pocket crackled as he pushed his damp handkerchief back in. He pulled the ad out and put it on the table as Sally tipped her head to the side.

'And what do you mean by area of study? I thought you wanted to enrol in a class,' she said reaching for the newspaper clipping. 'From memory, my ads just advertised class times. And the times have changed since I ran the last ad.'

She held the ad up to her face and shook her head. 'It's too small to read in this light. Can I have your torch again please?'

Sol passed over the small LED light and flicked it on for her.

Chapter 4

The lights came back on and the kitchen was bathed in bright light from the old-fashioned fluorescent circle above the table. Sally's mouth dropped open and she carefully put her mug down. She placed the advertisement beside it on top of the old, scarred table.

Oh. My. God.

She leaned back and closed her eyes and put her hand over her mouth to stop the tirade of curses that were threatening to explode.

'Um, are you okay, Sally?' The concerned voice broke through the red mist of rage that was burning her eyes. It's a wonder they weren't bleeding.

Her fingers caressed some of the marks on the timber table and she focused on them to try and calm down. The burn beside her mug was where Aunty Aggie had put a hot saucepan one night when she was trying to tell them something exciting that had happened to her that day. Of course, she'd needed her hands to talk with the expansive gestures she'd always used, and she'd put the pot straight onto the timber tabletop. The knife mark was where Rosie had pushed the top of the paring knife into the table one night when they were playing cards, and she'd got excited and missed the cheese platter.

Rosie had never won at cards, and that night had been a standout one when she'd won every hand.

Memories. The table held beautiful moments. Her eyes filled with moisture, but they weren't bleeding. Those times had gone now.

Aunt Agatha had passed on—although at times they all wondered how far she'd actually gone.

Rosie and Taj were married and had gorgeous four-year-old twins.

And Sonia—cut to the re-entry of the red mist—her sister, Sonia, was in deep trouble.

Deep shit was a better term.

'I will fu— freaking kill her.'

I wonder if I can disown a twin sister. Sonia had done some stupid things in their lifetime, but this was going too far.

Sally opened her eyes and stared at Sol. As her temper took hold she'd forgotten he was there. He was leaning forward and his expression was full of concern as his brow wrinkled. Sally stared at him and his eyes locked with hers. Now that the light had come back on, she took a good look at him. His eyes were the deepest blue, she'd ever seen. They were surrounded by sooty black lashes and full of sympathy. And he didn't even know why she was so upset.

She pointed to his cup of tea. 'Drink your tea. I need to make a call.'

'Do you want me to leave?' His voice was as warm as his eyes and she wondered why the warm flutters started low in her tummy.

It had been a long time since she'd been so aware of a man. And despite his strange clothes and dorky short haircut, he was a very good-looking man. His shoulders were broad and a sprinkling of dark hair peeped out of the V of his polo-neck shirt.

Not now. No time for that now.

And not later either, the little voice whispered in her head. She was over men for life since Blake the bastard had left. She'd become a spinster like Aunt Aggie. She'd had fun; her life hadn't been boring or dull.

'No, no.' She shook her head. 'Just wait there and then I'll explain.' She pulled her phone from her pocket and hit speed dial for Sonia doing the quick time calculation in her head, hoping it was the middle of the night. Her sister deserved to be woken up.

She shook her head.

Damn. It would be just after ten at night in Waikiki.

Sonia picked up almost immediately and she chuckled before Sally could speak. 'Hi Sal, you should have come with me. I'm sitting by the pool in the sun drinking a Pina Colada.'

'You are not. It's night-time.'

Another giggle. 'So how's your day been, Sal? Still sitting miserably in the Sydney winter or has life in the beach house livened up a bit?'

'I'll give you livened up! I hope you have no plans to come back to Australia, Sonia Smith because I'll kill you if you do.'

'Oh, sweets, come on that's a bit harsh.'

'Tantric massage, Sonia! Tantric massage? Honestly whatever possessed you to put that ad in the paper?' Sally's voice rose to a screech. 'And don't deny it, I know you did.'

'Have you had lots of interesting enquiries already?'

Sally huffed an impatient sigh. 'What do you reckon?'

'I did it for you. You needed something to get you out of that boring life you're stuck in. I worry about you. You're going to end up like Aunty Aggie. If you're not careful.'

'Dead?'

'No, silly. A single spinster.'

'There's nothing wrong with that. She was happy.'

'I only did it because I care about you, Sal. I'll put Rosie on. She wants to say hello.' Loud music filtered through the phone as she waited.

'Coward,' Sally muttered.

'Hi, Sal. Are you okay? Sonia told me what she did. She was a bit naughty.'

'Naughty's not the word! Where are you and what is that awful thumping music?'

'We're in a nightclub. Taj offered to mind the twins,

and Sonia is determined to get laid while she's here.'

'Get laid? I'll give her "get laid" when she comes home. You have no idea of the procession of men and women I've turned away from the door tonight.' Sally glanced up and caught a twitch on Sol's lips before he schooled his face back into a serious expression. 'Anyway, I've got to go. I have company.'

'Ooh, Sonia will be so pleased to hear that. Tell all. What's he like?'

'Why do you assume it's a he?'

'Because Sonia read the tarot cards for you. Now tell me what he's like.'

Sally knew that Sonia would be listening in, so she put her hand over the phone for a minute and whispered to Sol. 'Please ignore what I'm about to say.'

'Okay,' she lifted her hand and dropped her voice to a sexy whisper. 'Even though it's only seven o'clock here, he's asleep beside me.' She let her eyes linger on Sol's face. 'He's got short-cropped blond hair and the most beautiful blue eyes, surrounded by long black eyelashes. High cheekbones and lovely, lush lips.' She slowly dropped her eyes to his shoulders and down to his chest. 'Broad shoulders, well-muscled arms, and a gorgeous tan.' She held the giggle back as her eyes stopped at the tabletop— it was all up to her imagination from here on in—but damn if those warm flutters didn't set up a beating in her tummy and heading south. 'An all-over tan, Rosie. His thighs are powerful, and he has the most gorgeous feet. As for the rest of him, I'll leave that to your imagination but trust me....'

Sally wasn't surprised when Sonia's indignant voice came back on the phone. 'You're laying it on too thick. The ad only went in a couple of days ago.'

'Thanks for the vote of confidence, sis.' Sally was starting to enjoy herself. 'Sol came to the door this afternoon to see about a Tantric massage. We hit it off straight away, and he booked in, and well—one thing led to another—'

'One word. Bull. Shit.'

'That's two.'

'Well, I'm pleased you're not cross anymore, anyway. I'll see you next week and we'll read the cards again.'

'Oh, I'm still cross with you. For thinking you knew what was best for me. Oh, hang on. Sol's just waking up. I'll put him on.' She spoke quickly. 'Sonia is my sister. I hope you don't mind agreeing with what I told her?'

Sol's eyes were dancing, and he nodded as Sally passed the phone over. 'My pleasure.'

***

'Hi, Sonia.' Sol held Sally's eye as he waited for a reply, but there was silence. Gradually a wary voice spoke.

'Sol? Sol who? And what are you doing in my sister's bed?'

He made sure his voice was deep and sexy. He was supposed to have just woken up, presumably after a bout of energetic sex. 'Solomon Brown and Sally invited me to her bed.' He grinned at Sally as a choking noise came over the phone. 'I'll pass you back to her now, but I'll look forward to meeting you. I'll be around for a while.'

He winked at Sally as he handed the phone back. He hadn't had this much fun for a long time.

'Bye, Sonia. Someone needs my attention more than you do.'

Her voice was a throaty purr and Sol blinked as a rush of desire coursed through his veins. But it receded as she dropped the phone and stared at him, all playfulness gone.

'Thank you. I'm sorry I dragged you into that, but I really needed to teach my sister a lesson.' Finally, a sexy little giggle erupted from those pretty lips. 'I wouldn't be surprised if she jumped on the first plane to come home and check you out.'

'Where is she?'

'Hawaii.'

'And I'm guessing she put the ad in the paper, and you don't really practise Tantric massage?'

Sally nodded. 'Right on both counts.'

Sol dropped his shoulders as disappointment chased away any lingering thoughts of desire. Finding a local practitioner almost on his doorstep had solved the dilemma of his deadline. But turned out it was only a joke.

'Damn.'

'I'm sorry. It was a silly joke she played. I apologise for dragging you into it. I owe you for playing along.'

Sol waved his hand. 'That's okay. I'm just disappointed that this avenue closed.'

'What do you mean? You wanted a Tantric massage?'

'Oh, no. That's not why I came.'

Sally stood and picked up the mugs. 'Would you like another cup of tea?' She shook her head as she looked at him. 'I am turning into Aunt Aggie,' she muttered before she walked to the fridge and pulled out a bottle of wine. 'Sol, would you like a glass of wine before you leave, and you can tell me what you mean?'

'Are you sure?'

She nodded. 'My bath water will be stone cold by now. It's still blowing a gale outside. We need something more than a cup of tea to warm us up. That oven's not going to do much.'

She shivered as he watched her. 'Do you have any other heating in the house?'

'Yes, there's a gorgeous open fireplace in the living room, but I don't have any kindling split, and I didn't fancy going outside. Then by the time I answered the door about ten times, it was dark.

Sol stood. 'Where is it? Show me the way.'

'Oh, no. I can't impose on you for wood chopping. It's bad enough that I roped you into a disagreement with my sister.'

He walked over to the back door. 'Hey, I'll have you know that was my job until I left home. You might have wondered where these "well-muscled arms" come from. I was the kindling splitter champion in our household.'

'If you're sure, I would appreciate that. There's a lot of winter ahead yet.' She followed him to the back door, as a smile tilted her lips. 'And I guess that contributed to the broad shoulders too.'

'Spot on.' A warm feeling settled in his chest as they laughed together. 'Look, no need for you to come out in the cold. Just point me in the right direction.'

After she told him where to find the door at the side of the small woodshed, and where the light switch was, she tilted her head to the side. 'While you're doing that, I'll cook something for us.'

Sol wasn't going to argue. As usual, he was starving.

Sally stood beside the door as he put his head down and headed for the small shed. He pushed open the door and stepped back as a swathe of cobwebs brushed across his face. Reaching out he found the light switch that Sally had told him was there. The shed was full of logs and the axe was hanging on the hook where she said he'd find it, so he rolled up his sleeves and within ten minutes had a good pile of kindling chopped—enough for tonight plus some. He put the remainder of the pine chip slivers into the box that was sitting on the bench. Balancing the kindling on his forearm, he reached out for a newspaper off the pile that was beside the kindling box before putting his head down and making a quick dash back to the kitchen.

The smell of garlic and tomatoes made him twitch his

nose and his stomach grumbled in response. Sally was waiting at the door and she held it open as he ducked through it.

'No, I think the rain has let up a little bit but it's still freezing cold out there.

She led him through the kitchen, down a long hallway and into a large living room. She flicked the light switch on, and a myriad of magical lights danced immediately across the walls. He looked up to a magnificent chandelier full of crystals hanging from a beautiful ceiling rose.

'This house is everything I ever imagined,' he whispered almost reverently.

'You know the house?' Sally followed him over to the fireplace on the wall that backed onto the hallway.

'Yes. I've lived close by my whole life. I've loved this house since I was a kid.'

'It is beautiful. Just a shame it takes so much to keep it the way it should be looked after.' She looked at him curiously. 'I thought you said you drove from Peats Ridge?'

'I did, but I'm house—I mean farm—sitting.' He crouched in front of the fireplace and scrunched up some pages of the newspaper into a tight ball. 'Does the house belong to your family?'

'Oh no. I just rent, but Sonia and I have lived here for a long time. Our best friend and her husband own it, but Taj surfs on the world circuit so they don't spend much time here.'

'Not Taj Brown?' He looked back up at her as he scrunched the newspaper and rearranged the kindling.

'Yes. The surfer. Have you heard of him?' She shook her head. 'That was a silly question. Everyone's heard of Taj.'

'I have and he's a third cousin or something. From a different branch of the family, but I've never met him. I didn't know he owned this place.' He let out a low whistle and looked up from laying the kindling in a horizontal pattern on top of the newspaper.

Sally looked at him strangely and he wondered if she thought he was making up the connection to gain brownie points.

'Do you have any matches handy here?'

'Yeah, they're in the kitchen. I'll go and get them for you.'

By the time she came back, he had the makings of a fire ready with the newspapers and the kindling. As Sally handed him the matches her fingers brushed his and that warm feeling settled back in his chest again. He was looking forward to sitting down and having a wine and a meal with her; he hadn't encountered someone so interesting for a long time.

If the truth be known, he spent most of his days at the university in the small cubbyhole that was called an office or back at the flat where the space was not much bigger than his office. The current favour he was doing for Dave, his mate up at Peats Ridge, gave him lots of space, but the problems that came with it were making his life a bit difficult this week.

Her sister had called Sally boring, and Sol knew he fitted the boring mould way more than she ever would.

Maybe their conversation would spark him up a bit. He'd do his best to sound interesting.

'I'm pleased I came to your house, even though it isn't going to help me with my research.' Sol frowned. For the first time since he'd been at the university, disquiet replaced his usual complacency. His supervisor had warned him on Monday that he was cutting it fine. Three years of study would be wasted if you didn't get his thesis written. He had all the research finished but until he'd completed interviews with a practitioner, he couldn't write up his conclusions, even though Sol was sure of what he would discover out in the field.

The fire took hold as a gust of wind roared down the chimney and the windows rattled. He crossed back to the table and sat beside Sally again.

'I guess I'd better tell you what I need from you.' He sat back and folded his arms. 'Or what I hope you can do for me.'

Chapter 5

Sally waited while Sol Brown gathered his thoughts. He fascinated her; for such a good-looking man, he was dressed strangely. Old fashioned, like his manner and the precise way he spoke.

Aunt Aggie would have loved him.

Sally frowned as a thought struck her. 'You said you were related to Taj. So that means you're probably related to Aunt Aggie. Or were, before she died?'

Sol shook his head. 'I don't know. I grew up not far from here, but I don't remember ever visiting here when I was a child.' He tipped his head to the side. 'So is there really a ghost in the house or were you just trying to scare off an unwelcome visitor?' His grin was wide, and a rush of warmth settled in Sally's chest.

It was the first time she'd felt warm all day. Before she could answer there was a clatter from upstairs, and a wry smile crossed her lips. 'We like to kid ourselves, but it's probably the pipes in this old house. Who knows?' She lifted her shoulders in a gentle shrug. 'Okay, Mr Brown. Come back into the kitchen with me while I serve up, you can tell me why you thought I could help you. Then we can eat back here in front of the fire.' Sally had decided she could trust this stranger. He seemed genuine, and she owed him for chopping the kindling and getting the fire going.

Sol followed her back into the kitchen and then put the wine glass down, before he picked it up again, his fingers playing nervously on the tabletop. Finally, a chuckle broke the silence as he shook his head.

'I hope you find it amusing. When you said that you ran classes and that you also had a group of eighty-year-olds, I was under the impression that you were actually practising

Tantric massage.'

'No, sorry, I'm a plain old yoga teacher.' Sally stood and opened the fridge and took out some cheese to go on the sauce bubbling on the stove. 'And you wanted to come to a class to see Tantric massage?'

'On no.' This time the head shake was vehement. 'I simply wanted to interview you. To get the practitioner's point of view.'

Sally lifted a saucepan from the hanging rack about the stove and spooned in enough soup for two. 'And why would you need to interview me about that?'

'Because I'm doing a thesis, and my final report is due at the end of the month.'

'This month?'

He nodded.

'But today's the twenty-first.'

This time the nod was glum. 'I know. Nine days.'

Sally moved the saucepan onto the flame and stirred the sauce. 'So tell me about your thesis.' She closed her eyes as he began speaking. She could have listened to his voice all night. Deep, warm and soothing.

'My second degree is in psychology. I decided that vet science wasn't for me but this week, I wonder if I should have stayed with it.'

'Because you're running out of time for your thesis?' She put the spoon on the plate at the edge of the stove and sat at the table.

'No, because of the animals.'

Sally picked up her wine, and took a sip, letting the full-bodied red burst on her tongue. She was getting used to the way his conversation moved all over the place; she hadn't enjoyed herself this much for a long time.

A very long time. Pre Blake the bastard days, if she was honest.

'Okay, so what do animals have to do with your thesis on massage?'

'Oh, it's not on massage. My thesis is on "Ayurvedic Therapy and the Psychological Dimension of Illness."'

'Um, what does that mean?' Sally wrinkled up her nose. 'And what does that sort of science have to do with animals?'

'What I needed for the final research was some actual enlightening on Tantric Massage, the non-sexual, yoga application. And the animals have nothing to do with that, of course. They're at the farm I'm minding this week.'

'At Peats Ridge.' She was learning to follow his conversation as it darted about.

He nodded. 'Yes. I was mad to take it on, with it being so far from the university. I've not had time to be in the library much this week, so when I saw your ad—well, I thought I could get a hands-on—oops, poor choice of words— a first-hand—'

Sally couldn't help herself. She actually snorted before it turned into a laugh. 'So you're sure you weren't after a good old bout of Tantric massage.'

It surprised her to see the colour in his cheeks. His very nice cheeks. He had a cute cleft in his chin, and she was tempted to reach out and touch the dimple.

'No. Of course not. I told you'—the voice was very precise now—'interview only.'

'I might be able to help,' she said slowly. 'I've got a lot of notes upstairs in my study. When I trained at the college, I actually did Ayurvedic massage as one of my subjects. And I've implemented a lot of what I've learned in my classes—particularly with older people at the home.'

'Really?' As Sol sat forward, his whole face lit up. 'That would be lifesaving for me.'

'I'm happy to help, but it might take me a while to dig

it all out. I've got some references to a lot of academic research that might save you some time.' The sauce began to bubble on the stove, and she hurried across and lifted the pot. 'Leave it with me and I'll give you a call in a couple of days.'

She spooned the sauce into two bowls, sprinkled them with cheese and picked up the last two bread rolls that were in the breadbasket beside the stove. Sol stood and took the bowls from her and she led the way back to the fire.

'I'll pay you of course, for your trouble.'

Sally waved a dismissive hand. 'No, you won't.'

'Well, I'll owe you.'

The glimmer of an idea began to take shape and she smiled as she sat on the sofa. 'I might just take you up on that. But not until you meet your deadline.'

Chapter 6

Sally waited for Sol to reply to her text. She'd deliberately left it an extra day because she didn't want him to think that she was going to drop everything and find the notes for him. She was busy too, or she wished she was—the frequency of appointments had deteriorated along with the weather. Plus she'd spent two days telling herself that he was a man, and she had no interest in him, that way.

Blake Curtis had done such a huge number on her self-confidence, Sonia was probably right; she would end up old and lonely like Aunt Aggie. Maybe she'd still be in the house and take over the haunting when Aunt Aggie moved on to wherever ghosts went.

Despite what she'd told Sol about creaking and banging pipes, she did not doubt that Aggie still had a presence in the house. Nothing to be scared of, just a comforting sense of Aunt Aggie looking out for them.

That was another reason she should have known Blake wasn't for her before he flaunted bimbo girl in her face, the night she'd caught them together. He'd laughed the one time she'd foolishly mentioned Aunt Aggie still being in the house. Rolled up the sleeve of his very expensive business shirt, looked at his Rolex and made a hasty exit.

She should have known then, or maybe one of the other dozen times when Blake had ridiculed her, disparaged her profession and turned his nose up at the house. He'd never been meant for her, but she was too scared of being lonely to admit it to herself.

Pride comes before a fall. The words hung in the air around Sally, and she looked up with a smile.

'Yes, Aunt Aggie, they sure do.' And that was exactly why she wasn't going to fall for the charms of a bumbling research student who wore strange clothes.

No matter how good-looking he was. As she walked slowly upstairs, her phone rang.

Sonia. She ignored it for the first few rings, still cross at her sister for what she'd done. Finally, she gave in and pressed answer.

'Sally?'

'Yes.'

'Whoops, she's still shitty with me.' Sonia's voice was muffled but Sally heard what she said. 'Are you there, Sal? What's the weather like? Has it improved?'

'If I say no, will you stay away for longer?' Sally knew she was being a cow, but Sonia shouldn't have placed that ad.

'Probably.'

Sally paused at the top of the stairs and looked out the window in the little alcove where Aunt Aggie had loved to sit and read. The moon was full and the stars were strewn around the sky like glittering diamonds. It was a beautiful, crisp and clear winter night. 'Well, yes then, it's teeming down rain. Broken every rainfall record ever made. The sea is huge, and the storms haven't stopped since you left.' She stamped on the wooden floor. 'Hear the thunder?'

'Oh, come on Sal. You must be missing me. Aren't you lonely?'

'Nope.'

'So how did you get that guy with the sexy voice to pretend he was in bed with you the other night?'

Sally almost disconnected, but she kept her voice firm and calm. 'Pretending? There was no pretending about it.'

Sonia's giggle was the last straw.

'In fact, I need to know when you're coming back because Sol's moving in. I guess I need to check that's okay with Rosie and Taj.'

She nodded and satisfaction filled her. That had shut her sister up.

'Sal?' Rosie's voice replaced Sonia's. 'What's happening there? Sonia just held the phone out to me, she's lost for words. What did you tell her?'

Sally crossed the fingers of her spare hand. 'I'm pleased you're there, Rosie. I wanted to check with you that it's okay for Sol to move in.'

'Sol, who's Sol?'

'My friend from the other night.'

'Sure, you can sub-let any of the rooms, that's not a problem. As long as you don't mind having someone else in the house.'

Anger tugged at Sally's calm.

Why was it that everyone thought she was incapable of getting a man and holding him?

Any guilt at telling Rosie a porky disappeared like a puff of smoke up the chimney. She'd kept the fire going since Sol had lit it for her. 'No, Sol's moving in with me.'

Stunned silence. 'But didn't you just . . . um . . . meet him?'

'Yes. Love at first sight. And how long did you know Taj before you got together.'

'That was different.' The voice was indignant. Great, now she had Sonia and Rosie offside.

'Okay, as long as it's okay for him to move in. Thanks, Rosie.' She kept her voice bright and breezy and cut Rosie off before she could speak. 'Tell Sonia to text me when she's coming home. I have to go. Sol's at the door. Byeee."

She hit the disconnect button.

It was time to call Sol and put her plan in place.

She took a deep breath and went looking for the business card he'd given her the other night.

***

It had been three days since Sally had said she would be in touch. Time was running out and Sol was about to hit the panic button. Maybe he'd forget about this thesis before he went back to Sydney uni to finish off his vet studies. But one thing he hated was leaving anything unfinished. That was another reason he had to go back and finish his vet science work.

One quick text to say she'd found the notes and would be in touch for him to pick up the notes from the house was all he hoped for; he'd trusted her and he had not expected her to let him down but it would still be a relief to receive her call, even though he was cross at her.

Well, not really at her; it was a combination of things that had put him into a bad mood, but Sally was bearing the brunt of it because he couldn't get her out of his thoughts.

He didn't have time to find a woman attractive.

He didn't have time to spend any time with a woman he found attractive.

But she was so damn attractive, and such a sweet person—once she'd gotten over the grumps on Friday night, he hadn't been able to stop thinking about her. And he didn't have time to think about that.

The pressure was on him to get his thesis done, even though he knew that once it was done, he wouldn't be doing any more study in that field.

Although a little voice nagged, it would be a reason to stay in touch with Sally. He pushed away the voice of doubt that always plagued him. He wasn't good with women and this whole dating business. He'd been too busy studying for most of his twenties.

'If I want to spend more time with her, I'll ask her out,' he told the voice of doubt emphatically. 'What do you think I am? A nerd or something?' He straightened his shoulders as he trudged through the muddy paddock. This last week had opened up a clear path for Sol but he hadn't told anyone yet. Not the supervisor at the university, or his family.

Especially not his family. He could just see the eye rolls and hear the "tut-tuts" when he told them he was going to follow a different path for his career. The one he should always have followed. He was a grown man, and it was time that everyone around him realised it.

'Hah, and you're too nervous to ask out a beautiful woman,' niggled the voice of doubt. 'So how are you going to stand up to your biggest critics?'

'I'm not nervous,' Sol muttered as he picked up the bag of goat pellets and ripped open the top of the sack with more vigour than he'd intended.

'Oh fuck,' he said as the pellets scattered around in the mud and about a dozen goats came running at him.

As soon as he got this lot sorted and locked up, he'd call Sally back and organise a time to visit. And when he'd caught up on everything, he'd ask her out.

On a date. A real date. Nothing to do with the thesis.

His phone beeped as the first goat hit him in the back and his legs went out from beneath him. He lay in the squelchy mud and dug into his jeans pocket for his phone as the cold seeped through to his legs. He squinted and smiled when he saw who it was from; scrolling down, his grin got wider as he read the text.

Are you free to catch up tomorrow? I have no clients, so come as early as you like. I have a favour to ask you.

Sol nodded. Not even the cold mud or the goats nudging at him to get to the pellets in the mud could dampen his mood. He was going to see Sally again, and not only that she had a favour to ask.

Then all he had to do was finish the thesis, hand it in, enrol in his new course, go and visit his parents—maybe—and then he would be asking Sally out.

Life was looking good.

##

Sol tried to retrieve that good feeling later that night as he sat in the driver's seat of his old Land Rover ready to put it in the shed for the night. There was no way it would start the next morning if the day was cold.

'Come on, old girl. You can do it,' he almost crooned. On the tenth turn of the key, when the motor refused to turn over at all, he slammed his hands onto the steering wheel in disgust.

Okay, so the universe was telling him that this was a bad idea.

Another point of contention with his parents. The Audi they'd given him for his twenty-first birthday seven years ago was sitting unused in the spare garage at their house on the harbour.

Gertie, the old Land Rover had been for when he was going to be a vet.

Forget Sally. Forget the thesis. Why finish it anyway? Just to prove to his family that he could see something through to the end.

He climbed out of the car and grabbed his phone off the seat.

Sorry, Sally. Car troubles. Before he could think, his fingers flew over the keys of their own free will. **'Don't suppose you fancy a trip up to Peats Ridge tomorrow to deliver the notes. I'll entice you with a nice lunch, and reimburse your petrol.**

Chapter 7

Sally hadn't been up this way for years. Familiar signs flashed past: Avoca, Terrigal, Wamberal. Great memories—in their teens she and Sonia had spent a lot of time at the Central Coast, hanging out with their friends on weekends. Having fun, being silly, enjoying life.

When had it all stopped?

Two years and two months ago when Blake the bastard had broken her heart.

As she drove along the expressway after the built-up areas north of Hornsby, Sally let herself think about Blake. For a long time, she'd refused to think about the relationship or talk about it. When they'd been together, Blake hadn't liked spending time with her friends—or Sonia—and they'd gravitated towards his finance crowd. She'd made some acquaintances but hadn't had a lot in common with the wives and girlfriends who liked to "do" lunch and spend most of their time in beauty spas and dress shops. So no new lasting friendships had formed. She and Blake had been together for just over a year when he'd decided he wanted a change, but he hadn't had the courage to tell her.

No, she'd come across him and the bimbo in a bathroom at one of his work functions. The only satisfaction Sally had got that night—and by the look of things, Blake had been getting plenty until she'd walked in on them—had been tipping the whole jar of Dolce and Gabbana hand wash over his head.

By the time, she'd surfaced after the breakup, many of her friends had left town or were married and had moved west of the city to more affordable housing estates. Rosie and Taj and the kids spent most of their time overseas, and Sonia—well Sonia was just Sonia. She was the party animal and fitted in with all crowds. After the third time she'd dragged Sally out to a club, Sally had had enough and opted to stay home.

Where she was happy in her own company. Or so she tried to convince herself.

And thus Sonia's comment, "You're turning into Aunt Aggie" had been born.

But Sonia was right. Sally knew she'd been used and she'd let it affect her for way too long. And if she wanted to be catty, the sex hadn't been that good anyway. Blake had been more interested in how he looked than how he performed. A giggle escaped her lips and happiness lifted her heart as she looked forward to seeing Sol again.

Sonia's ad, and meeting Sol, had been the catalyst for her rethink.

From today, life was about having fun!

She turned the radio on and smiled as her favourite surfing song came over the airwaves. It made her think of Rosie and Sonia over in Hawaii; even though she'd forgiven Sonia for the ad she'd placed, it would still be fun to wind her up.

Sonia had always said Sally had lost her sense of humour since Blake was on the scene; she was about to find out it wasn't lost; it had just been buried in an avalanche of low self-confidence.

As long as Sol was willing to play along.

And if it meant that she had to spend a little more time in his company on the way, well, so be it. That would be a bonus.

Seeing the way he'd looked at her the other night had done wonders for Sally's self-confidence. Today she'd taken a little bit more care with her appearance. She'd blown dry her hair and put a tiny bit of makeup on, and taken care to choose a nice T-shirt to go with her slim-fitting jeans. She'd lost a lot of weight over the past year.

As Sally got closer to the Peats Ridge turn-off, she pulled over in a parking bay and opened Sol's text and typed the address he'd given her into Google Maps, and then let the robotic voice guide her to the place that Sol had said he was farm-sitting. She passed the Australian Reptile Park, and then Somersby Falls, but there was still some distance to go. The small township of Peats Ridge flashed by, and then the tarred road turned to gravel. When she turned onto Bloodtree Road, she recognised the address and knew she was going in the right direction.

Only a few more kilometres according to the digital map.

But it seemed to take forever as she wound down narrow dirt roads, over hills and through creek crossings.

No wonder Sol had been disappointed when she'd tried to fob him off on Friday night, after driving all this way into the city.

To answer her—Sonia's—ad. This place was hours away from Bondi Beach. Trees formed an avenue above the last narrow road and the lacy shadows danced on the windscreen. The closer she got as the small blue dot on her phone headed for the farm, the more the little niggles of excitement fluttered in Sally's stomach. It was like being sixteen again, and she had no idea what had caused the feeling. Maybe it was the decision she'd made to start having fun again.

Maybe Sonia's ruse had worked?

##

When Sally had agreed to drive up to the farm with her notes, Sol had fist pumped the air. He hadn't expected her to agree to come so far, and he'd become resigned to the fact that he would have to get his Land Rover fixed before he could drive to the beach house at Bondi and collect the notes. The deadline was looming and there was very little time to spare.

But she'd agreed to come…and she'd sounded enthusiastic too.

Sally had said she'd be there late morning, so once he'd fed the dogs and goats, searched out the cats and locked them inside and swept out the aviary, he let himself relax.

He boiled the kettle and was sitting out on the back verandah when two things struck him at the same time. He needed to get out of his pyjama pants and ratty jumper before she arrived, and at the same time, he realised he hadn't seen Otis around since he'd let him out when he'd got up this morning.

With a groan, he hurried out the back door and pushed open the gate that led out to the back twenty acres.

There was no sign of the silver Weimaraner.

Damn, he'd been put in Sol's care, and now he'd taken off.

Dave's words rang in his ears. 'Whatever you do, don't let Otis in the back paddock, or especially down by the creek. He humps wombats.'

Great, just great! A wombat-humping dog. Just what he needed today.

Sol thought back, trying to remember when he'd last seen Otis, but with no luck. He'd first ventured out at sunrise and the silver dog had followed him outside.

He walked down to the back boundary past the old wooden dunny covered in honeysuckle vines and called and whistled the damn dog. He tipped his head to the side; that had sounded like a bark from down near the creek on the top side of the farm.

As he walked back up the hill, another sound drifted across and he looked up.

A small red sedan was crossing the cattle grid at the front of the property. It was between him and the house, and he put his hands over his eyes.

No, it couldn't be Sally.

Not yet please God. He lifted his hands, and when he was sure it was indeed her, he estimated the distance between the back paddock and the driveway—and the house in between. He knew there was a pair of clean jeans sitting on the washing machine at the back of the house.

Anything would be better than getting sprung in a pair of blue-striped flannelette PJs.

He skirted along the back fence keeping an eye on the car as it drove up the hill before he dashed behind a stand of gum trees. He stood waiting for Sally to pull up at the front of the house. The car drove slowly along the drive and then she turned towards the shed where his dead Land Rover was parked.

With a groan, Sol stepped out from behind the tree and crossed to the shed. He had no chance of scarpering back to the house for his jeans.

He'd just have to greet her, apologise and then get dressed.

'Morning, Sally. You must have left bright and early.' He plastered a grin onto his face as she wound down the window and peered out at him.

Her eyes dropped to his legs and her smile was wide as she looked back up at him. 'Am I too early?'

'No, no, not at all.' He opened the door for her. If there was one thing that his mother had taught him it was how to be a gentleman. 'I've been looking for a missing dog.'

Sally climbed out and stretched her arms above her head. 'That was a long drive.'

'Thanks so much for coming. I really appreciate it.' he gestured to his Land Rover parked in front of her car. 'Since Gertie gave up the ghost, I'm stuck here until the mechanic arrives.'

As Sally walked around to the other side of the car and opened the back door, a cacophony of barks and bleats filled the air.

'Bloody dog. Wait here, Sally.' Sol left her at the car and took off at a run, puffing by the time he reached the top of the hill, but a groan took away his next breath.

The Weimaraner was in the goat pen and was having a wonderful time chasing the goats.

'Blast you, Otis.' He'd had nothing but trouble with the damn dog since he'd arrived to look after the farm. Now he knew why Dave had trouble getting the neighbours to look after the place when he went away.

'How can I help?'

He turned around to see Sally beside him.

Sol shook his head with another groan as the goats ran around in a mad panic. He could barely make himself heard over the bleating and the barking. 'If you hold the gate, I'll go in and get him. When I get back over here with him, open the gate and shut it behind us after I drag him through.'

Sally nodded and he vaulted the fence. His PJs caught on the barbed wire at the top and he grabbed for his butt as a blast of cold air hit his skin. But he didn't have time to worry about that. He grabbed the top of his pants and held them secure as he took off across the pen after the dog. After three circuits of the pen avoiding goat hooves, with a huge lunge, he crash-tackled the damn mutt and landed in the mud with the dog beneath him.

'Gottcha, Otis!'

***

Sally hadn't laughed so much for years. Okay, maybe she had a tiny bit of sympathy for Sol, but the sight of a grown man with a huge rip in his PJ pants, chasing a silver flash of a dog around a goat pen was one of the funniest things she'd ever seen. By the time, Sol was back on his feet and dragging the dog over to the gate where she stood guard Sally had managed to school her face into a sympathetic expression.

'Step back when we come through, you don't want to get flicked with mud.' Sol now had both hands through the dog's collar, and the dog was heading reluctantly towards the gate. 'Okay. Open it now.'

Sally pushed the gate open, and the dog charged through. She squealed as it headed straight for her and two muddy, smelly paws landed on her shoulders and a pink, very wet tongue licked her chin.

'Oh, God, I'm so sorry.' Sol tugged at the dog's collar. 'Otis, bloody get down!'

Sally snorted as the laughter took over again. She lifted her hand to her face and it came away wet with a combination of dog slobber and mud. Her best white T-shirt and designer jeans were flicked with mud. As Sol pulled on the dog's collar, the dog resisted, still licking Sally's face, obviously enamoured with a new human. Sally reached out and put her arms around him. She was already filthy, and he was the most beautiful pup, naughty behaviour withstanding.

'What a beautiful boy,' she murmured. The dog moaned as she rubbed his ears, and after a minute, he slid his paws down the front of her T-shirt and jeans on his way to the ground.

Sol stood there and looked at her, a stupefied expression on his face. 'I am so sorry. What a welcome.'

'It's fine. My clothes will wash. The goats seem to be alright, and the only damage I can see—' the laughter spluttered out again— 'is the huge rip in your pretty blue PJs.'

The grin stayed on her face as Sol went brick red and looked down at the dog.

'Now take me to a laundry, and I'll have a wash.' She

wrinkled her nose. What's that strange smell?'

'Probably wombat.' Sol rolled his eyes as he looked at her. His mouth twitched and then lifted in a grin. 'Trust me, you don't want to know.'

Sally stared up at him. 'Thank you. '

'Thank you?' Sol quirked an eyebrow. 'What for?'

'For taking me right out of my comfort zone.'

Sally looked down as the dog slipped out of his grasp and headed for the house. Sol held his hand out to her, and it seemed to be the most natural thing in the world to slip her hand in his.

Her heart filled as they followed Otis over to the old farmhouse.

Chapter 8

Sol showed Sally to the bathroom and went in search of some clothes. He stripped off his PJs in the laundry and had a quick wash under the outside shower when he was sure that Sally was inside. He pulled on the jeans and a T-shirt that he'd left in the laundry and went looking for some clothes for her. Surely Dave has something here that she could put on while he washed and dried her muddy clothes.

The farm had belonged to Dave's parents before they'd retired to the coast, and in the back room, he found some bags of clothes that seemed to be bundled up for the op shop. Digging in he found a pair of yellow track pants, a hi-vis work shirt and a purple hoodie. He knocked on the bathroom door and yelled through the door. There are some clothes on the floor outside for you, Sally.'

'Thanks,' came the reply. He heard the shower switch off and he hurried down to the kitchen where he'd fed Otis and locked him in. The dog looked up at him innocently. He and Sally had got most of the mud off his coat before they'd let him inside. Sally had been such a good sport.

'Stay there.' Sol shook his head as he pointed to the rug in front of the blazing fire, and the mutt settled in comfortably. He checked the back door was closed firmly and opened a window to let some fresh air in. The aroma of wet dog wasn't a pleasant one for a kitchen, but Sol didn't have the heart to move him away from the fire.

With a shrug, he crossed to the fridge and took out the pie he'd cooked last night when Sally had agreed to drive up. The oven in the combustion stove was warm and he slipped it in.

I owe her big time.

It was satisfying to be pottering around the kitchen

preparing a meal to share with another person. For too long, Sol had lived alone, choosing to house-sit for his friends. In between house sits, he endured being back in the apartment at the family home, and if he was lucky his parents would be travelling to some medical conference overseas when he had to stay there. It was about time he bought his own place, although, with his new career plans, he could end up anywhere. He stood at the window thinking about where he might end up and jumped when something brushed against his arm.

He turned around and looked into a mass of colour.

Sally stood beside him and smiled. 'At least they fit, even though I might be a bit bright.' She gestured down to the clothes he'd found for her.'

'You look . . .um . . . lovely.' His lips twitched again.

'Um, lovely?' She nudged him and a warm feeling shot down into his stomach and—

Don't go there.

'Yes lovely. And bright. Lunch is almost ready.'

Sally sniffed. 'Smells good.'

'It's killed the dog aroma anyway.' Sol pulled out a chair for her, but she shook her head.

'I'll go and get my bag and your notes first.'

As she opened the door, Otis was up instantly and out the door like a shot. Sol followed him out and crossed to the gate with Sally. ''He can't get out of the house yard, so I'll wait here and make sure the gate's locked when you come back in.

A short time later, he locked the gate behind Sally and Otis stayed outside as Sol followed her back into the warm kitchen. His lips twitched again as he looked at the outfit she was wearing.

'I've put your clothes in the washing machine. As soon as it finishes, I'll put them in the dryer.

'Thank you.' She sat down and put the notes on the table. 'I'll take you through this because there's so much there. I'm not sure exactly what your focus is.'

'Fabulous. Thank you. How about after we eat?'

'Sounds good to me.'

The bacon and egg pie was cooked to perfection, and the pastry was light and flaky.

Sol made two coffees with the coffee maker that went everywhere with him when he moved between house-sits. Sally leaned back in her chair and inhaled as it brewed. 'Yum. What is that?'

'Ginger and cardamom.'

'You're an interesting man, Sol Brown.'

He poured the coffees and carried them across to the table. 'Not really.'

She nodded and a whiff of fresh Sunlight soap wafted across.

Sexy. Sol shook his head. Stop it.

'You are. You have a mean hand with pastry. You make amazing coffee and you're writing a fascinating thesis.'

He grinned ruefully. 'You need to talk to my family. They would disagree.'

'Speaking of family. I have a huge favour to ask you.'

He tipped his hand to the side as he sipped his coffee. Sally's eyes were bright, and her cheeks were pink from the warmth of the fire crackling beside them.

'How can I help?'

'The day my sister comes home from Hawaii, I want to give her a shock. It's payback time. She thinks I'm too boring and staid to play a trick on her, and I know she'll fall for it hook, line and sinker.'

'What do you want me to do?'

'I want to pretend that you've moved in with me.'

The anticipation glinting in her eyes mirrored the

anticipation that shot through him.

'But only if it suits you. I'm not sure when Sonia's due home and you have the goats to look after and the dog. And I know you've got to get your thesis in too.'

Sol looked at her and grinned. 'Sounds like fun. But am I right in guessing payback is out of character for you?'

'You're very perceptive,' she said as she held his gaze. 'I'm the quiet twin. The one who always does the right thing, the one who fulfils everyone's expectations. I've been a bit introverted over the past couple of years. I had a relationship go wrong, and I've been licking my wounds ever since. For way too long. That's why Sonia decided to jolt me out of my comfort zone.'

'And you're happy she has?'

Her eyes sparked with mischief. 'I am. But she's not going to get away with it.'

Sol reached over and picked up his phone. 'I leave here on Friday and I was going to head back to Vaucluse for a couple of weeks, so I can come any time.'

'Thank you. I'll find out when she's coming back.'

'And I'll have to make sure Gertie's fixed by then. I don't want to be stuck out here with the goats and Otis when Dave comes home.' He smiled apologetically. 'Can you just excuse me for a minute? With all the fuss this morning, I haven't had a chance to ring the mechanic yet.'

Chapter 9

Sally picked up her coffee and walked across to the fire while Sol made his call. She stared into the flames as she sipped the wonderful brew. It surprised her how comfortable she was here with him. Maybe it was the incident with the dog and the goats that had broken the ice a bit more, but if she was honest, she'd felt just as easy with him at the house the other night.

As Sol disconnected, Sally crossed to the sink and rinsed her cup. Her mouth dropped open as she looked over at the shed. Around her car were piles of grey—she wasn't sure what—grey stuff. As she watched, Otis jumped from her car window with a mouthful of grey—

'Oh my God.' She yelled and took off for the kitchen door, pushing past Sol as she put his phone on the countertop. 'He's eating my car!'

The door slammed behind them as Sol followed her out. Sally pushed the gate open and ran across to her car, the sharp stones of the driveway sharp beneath her bare feet. She stood there with her mouth open, disbelief coursing through her. Sol stood beside her, his mouth open and his eyes filled with horror.

'Fucking hell, Sally. I'm so sorry.'

The interior of her car—the seat covers, the carpet and parts of the dashboard— were scattered around the driveway.

'I've never seen a dog eat a car before.' Her voice was hushed. As she spoke Otis squeezed his head through the open driver's window, a goofy smile—if dogs did smile—on his face and lumps of foam rubber stuck in the slobber around his mouth.

Sol opened the door and Otis jumped out. The dog came over to Sally and she crouched down when he flopped at her feet. She couldn't help but run her fingers over that silky silver coat as she chastised him.

'You are a naughty boy, you know that, don't you, gorgeous.' She looked up at Sol as he peered into the interior of her car. 'How bad is it?'

'Um, you don't want to know.' Sol shook his head. 'Don't worry, Sally. I'll pay to have it fixed.'

'Insurance should cover it.' She couldn't help but giggle. 'Puts a whole new spin on the dog ate my homework, doesn't it?'

'Maybe I could try the dog ate my thesis?' Sol's deep voice was full of laughter and Sally's girly bits quivered. They hadn't done that for a long time.

'Maybe.' She knew her smile was shy, and she stood and worked over to the car, and stood close to him as she peered inside. 'Um, is it drivable?'

Sol shook his head. 'He's chewed up the pedals too. Dave told me his previous owner calls Otis, the naughtiest dog in the universe, and that's why he got rid of him. Dave took him on as a rescue dog, but he didn't warn me about half of what he's done this week.' He put his hand on Sally's arm, and the butterflies in her tummy started dancing again. 'I'm so sorry. I'll pay for a cab to take you home later.'

'Oh. She bit her lip. 'I forgot your car was out of action.'

'Mac's coming out at five o'clock to take a look at it when he shuts the local garage back at Peats Ridge. If he gets it going today, I can drive you home tonight. We'll have to get your car towed to a panel beater for a quote.'

'Don't worry too much. It's a really old car. Sonia and I have shared it since we were in our teens. It's about time we got a new one. I just hope insurance covers interiors.'

'But I do feel bad. I'll sort out something.' Sol frowned at her. 'When's your next appointment or class?'

'Not till tomorrow night, so there's no rush to get

home.' The thought of staying with Sol for a few more hours filled her with happiness. He took everything in his stride and she loved the way he was. She shook her head as she thought of Blake coping with a situation like this. He would have lost it entirely, and he would have been rude about the outfit she was wearing. Sonia had been right all along.

'He wasn't a very nice person,' Sally muttered.

'Sorry? Who?'

Sally shook her head and smiled up at him. 'Nothing. I was just thinking out loud.' She tugged Sol away from the car. 'Come on, there's nothing we can do about that. And we need to go through my notes so you can get your work done.'

Three hours later, Sally stretched and looked over at Sol. He'd made pages and pages of notes, and his face had lit up constantly. She'd already told him to stop thanking her over and over.

'This is exactly what I needed. It fills the hole in my argument. And being clinical notes is perfect. I won't use the names of course, and I'll have to get you to sign a permission release for me—'

Sally waved her hand. 'All good. I'm pleased I could help. I guess Sonia's ad was worthwhile after all.'

'It sure was. He held her gaze and something shifted inside of her as he smiled. 'And not only because of your work, Sally. I've enjoyed spending the day with you.'

Sally felt like a teenager as warmth ran up her neck and filled her cheeks. 'Me too.' But a warning tugged at her. Hadn't she felt the same excitement when she first met Blake?

Why was this—if it went anywhere—going to be different?

She sat up straight and her voice firmed as the heat subsided. 'So tell me what you're going to do once your thesis is accepted. Will you start clinical practice yourself?'

Sol dropped his gaze and shook his head. 'No. I'm going back to my original career choice. Once this is finished, I've decided to finish my veterinary science degree.'

'Wow. That's a big change in direction.' She could have sworn that he looked uncomfortable for a moment before he answered.

'Yes, but it's what I want to do. Now can I offer you another coffee before Mac arrives?'

Sally reached down and fondled Otis' ears. 'Thank you.'

She sensed the subject of his work was closed.

***

Sol was cross with himself for feeling uncomfortable when he told Sally of his decision to change his career path. He'd half expected a response like he knew he'd get from his family, but then he realised Sally didn't know about his erratic career path.

How many courses he'd done—and how many times he'd changed direction. He should have stuck with vet science; he could have had a career well underway, and a practice set up by now. Instead of being at a loose end, still half living at home at the ripe old age of twenty-eight. As he picked up the coffee pod and put it into the machine, Mac's work truck trundled through the front gate. Mac was Dave's uncle and Sol had known him since he was a kid running wild in the orange orchards at the bottom of the hill when he'd come to stay at Dave's house. They'd met at boarding school, and it had been a long friendship. Dave was one of the few who understood Sol's need to study and search until he found his niche in life. Dave had followed his dream and he had a successful fashion label; he'd spent more time overseas in the past year than here at the farm.

Dave had asked Sol a couple of times if he wanted to

move in permanently but it was too far from the university for Sol to consider it.

'Is that the mechanic?' Sally had crossed the kitchen and was standing beside him as he daydreamed.

'Yeah, that's Mac.'

'Do you want me to finish making the coffee?'

He nodded. 'Thanks. If you don't mind, bring one out to Mac too. I'll go out and see what he's got to say.' He ran his hand through his hair and grimaced when he lifted his arm. 'Blasted dog. I think I pulled a muscle in my back when I tackled him this morning. I've stiffened right up.'

As she looked up at him, his face heated. Her fresh soapy smell stayed with him as he walked to the shed.

Mac climbed out of the old work truck and grinned at Sol as he crossed the lawn. 'Gertie's playing up again, is she?'

'Yeah. Flat battery, I think.'

'Blast it, I haven't got a spare in the workshop at the moment. The delivery's due tomorrow.' Mac scratched his head. 'If you need to go back to town tonight, I can jump-start you, if it is the battery.'

Sol went to accept and then hesitated. Sally said she didn't have any appointments till her class tomorrow night. And if she was happy to stay here tonight, he could almost knock over his thesis if he worked late, and then he could take it with him ready to print out and get bound at the university print shop tomorrow.

'Take a look at it and see what you think.' He walked around and looked at the motor as Mac fiddled and put a tool into the deep recesses of the engine that remained a mystery to Sol.

'Yep, she's as dead as a doornail. Do you want me to drop the new one out in the morning?'

As Sol nodded, the old mechanic stared at Sally's car

and the mess of foam that had stuck to the grass. 'Otis got out, did he?'

Sol nodded glumly. 'Yes. Got into the goats and then my friend's car.'

'He's a bugger. Always has been. At least he wasn't out chasing wombats.'

'He spent the morning doing that.'

Mac laughed and Sol couldn't help but smile too.

***

Sally found a tray under the toaster and loaded the three coffee cups onto that. As she balanced the tray and walked towards the shed, Sol and the mechanic were laughing.

'Sally, this is Mac.' Sol reached out and took the tray from her. 'Thank you.'

The older man wiped his hand on the side of his overalls and held it out to her. 'Nice to meet you, love. What are you doing spending time with this lazy fella?'

Sally swallowed, unsure of how to answer.

'Don't worry. I'm just having a lend of him. Goodness knows the little larrikin caused me enough trouble when he was a kid. Used to spend a lot of time out here on the farm.' He nodded at her car. 'Got a bit of car trouble too, I see.'

'Yes.' she nodded, with a wry smile. 'About time I got a new one. Otis just helped me along.'

'Nice girl.' Mac said to Sol as he took a mug from the tray. 'Good coffee, too, love. You hang on to this one, Sol.'

'Oh but—' She stopped. There was no need to go into what she was doing out here.

Mac drained his coffee and jumped up into the truck. 'See you in the morning.' He stuck his head out the window as he started the truck. 'Nice outfit, love. That hoodie used to be Pearl's favourite.'

'In the morning?' Sally frowned as he backed down

the driveway. 'And who's Pearl?'

'Aunty Pearl was Dave's mother. Mac didn't have a battery in stock. You said there was no rush to get home.' He stood beside her and wrinkled his brow. 'Are you okay about staying here with me tonight? In the spare room, of course,' he added quickly. 'I can always get you a taxi if you'd rather go back to the city.'

'That's fine.' She thought for a moment. 'As long as it's early. I left enough dry cat food and water out so Muggins will be fine. And I can take you through some more of my notes if you need more info.' Sally stared up at him. 'And besides a taxi would cost hundreds from here!'

'Okay, more work together would be great. I still have a couple of questions.' Sol winced as he took a step forward.

'Your back?' she asked.

'Yes.' He balanced the tray in one hand and leaned to the side. 'Damn dog. I honestly don't know why Dave keeps him.'

'Probably because he's a part of his family.'

'There's only Dave.' Sol shook his head. 'He's overseas lately more than he's home and I've become Otis's surrogate owner.'

'So what's wrong with that?' Sally asked as they walked back to the house.

Sol laughed. 'Are you serious? The woman who now needs a new car has to ask that. And before you argue, I'm going to reimburse you.'

'What, for a new car?' She laughed too until he nodded.

'It's the least I can do.'

She stopped walking and put her hands on her hips. 'Whoa. Stop right there. That is entirely unnecessary. I've got insurance and I'll sort it. Okay?'

Blake had tried to take over every aspect of her life,

and Sol's insistence about the car—and about paying for a taxi if she wanted one—riled her. It was a timely warning to put a stop to those little frissons of attraction that had been firing her nerve endings all day. But it was easier to decide that than to tell her body to stop it. As she looked up at him, the butterflies were almost stamping their feet on their way south.

'Okay.' He nodded. 'I'm sorry. I didn't mean to upset you.'

Sally lifted her hand. 'Okay, truce. You stop telling me what to do, and I'll stop being cranky.'

'Sounds good to me.

Chapter 10

Despite his sore back, Sol cooked an incredible pasta dish for dinner. Sally leaned back when her bowl was empty and put her hands on her stomach.

'That was close to the best meal I have ever eaten.'

'Only close?' He beamed so much he almost lit up the dim kitchen; they'd eaten by the light of the fire and one candle on the table. 'I did a few cooking courses between my degrees. I've got a Cert three in Commercial Cookery. When I worked in an Italian restaurant in Newcastle, Giuseppe taught me some fabulous dishes.'

'Between degrees?' Sally shook her head. 'You sure are one interesting guy.' She stretched and Otis stirred on the rag rug in front of the fire.

Sol drained his wine glass and pushed his chair back. 'I'll go and feed him.'

'I'll do the dishes while you do.' Sally pushed her chair back. 'It's the least I can do.'

She put her hand up as Sol opened his mouth. 'Don't say it. Don't thank me one more time.' As the delectable Italian sauce had simmered on the stove, they'd shared a bottle of red wine, and Sol had asked more questions about her notes, and he must have thanked her about ten times. She'd been relaxed, and the questions he'd asked about the more intimate aspects of tantric massage hadn't fazed her as much as they would have in the cold light of day.

'Some practitioners say it creates an altered state of consciousness, sometimes called an erotic trance state which is a taste of bliss beyond time.'

'But you?' A warm flush ran up her back as he held her gaze over the ruby-red wine in his glass. 'What do you call it? Do you ever use it?'

'There is a place for it in psychotherapy, but as a

simple yoga instructor, it's played an occasional part in my repertoire of skills.' She giggled at the look on his face.

'Oh?' he said.

Very restrained.

'Tantric yoga is a powerful combination of energies that you can use to build strength, clarity, and bliss in everyday life. For my interested clients, there's an excellent YouTube clip that I refer them to. But that's it. It's a bit too personal and hands-on for my comfort zone.'

Sol reached over for the plates and Sally shook her head. 'Uh uh. My job. You look after Otis, and then go and rest that back.'

For a second or two, she thought of suggesting a massage to ease his pain, but after the discussion on Tantric massage, she worried that he'd think she was coming onto him. And that she didn't want.

It was bad enough that she'd been buzzing before the wine, and since she'd drunk two glasses of red with the pasta she had to focus harder on staying distant and restrained.

Right out of my comfort zone now, Sonia!

Very. Sally giggled as a hiccup escaped her lips.

Sol glanced at her as he poured the dog kibble into a bowl. 'All okay?'

She nodded slowly. 'All good.'

Her clothes had dried before dinner, and she felt much more comfortable back in her own clothes again. Poor old Pearl's purple hoodie might have been warm but she hadn't felt quite herself in borrowed clothes. It was as though she stepped into a different world. Or maybe out of her comfort zone. Sally smoothed her hand down the side of her jeans as Sol came back to the table.

'Dessert?'

She looked up at his face highlighted by the flickering candlelight as he stood by the table. His eyes were hidden, but his smile was in evidence.

Oh, yes please, she thought, as she looked up at him and then cleared her throat. Those butterflies started flying around in her tummy again and she tried to look serious. 'Dessert?'

'Tiramisu. Can I tempt you?'

Tempt her?

Um yes, please. But it was never good to look too keen.

'Maybe just a taste.'

'It's Giuseppe's recipe.'

Sally shook her head unable to hold back her curiosity any longer. 'Okay, so tell me. A doctorate in psychology?'

'Almost.' His tone was modest.

'Commercial cooking?'

He nodded.

'Pastry chef?'

Another nod.

And veterinary science?'

'Another set of exams and then I qualify.' He shook his head. 'I will practise.' But Sally got the impression the words were for his benefit rather than hers.

'Anything else?' She leaned her head back and observed him. The smile playing around his lips as he put the bowl of dessert in front of her was beyond sexy. Or was that her looking at it through wine-soaked eyes?

'I did my pilot training before I left school.' He sat down and picked up his spoon. 'That's enough about me. Now tell me about you.'

'Pretty boring,' she said. 'Sonia and I were born on a farm on the other side of Wagga. Our parents were killed in an accident when we were only eighteen and we moved to Sydney to live with Dad's brother.' She tried a spoonful of the Tiramisu and closed her eyes.

Bliss.

'It didn't work out, and I'd met Rosie at college when I was getting my certificate'—she lifted her spoon into the air and waved it around—'my only certificate, I might add. She was looking for someone else to move into the house at Bondi and we jumped at it. When we both qualified, we started Divine Soul Sisters.'

'You were the yoga instructor?'

She nodded and almost inhaled the next spoonful of dessert. 'Sometimes I helped Rosie—she's a remedial massage therapist— with massage when she got too busy, but after a while, we all picked up our own clients and classes.'

'And Sonia? Is she a Divine Soul Sister too?'

'Sonia has her own special talents.' The wine gave her courage. 'How . . . um . . . open-minded are you?'

'Well, we've already established I believe in ghosts.' His smile came in for the kill and the butterflies had babies. 'Is she a medium?'

'Close. Sonia reads tea leaves and she's a clairvoyant.'

Sol shook his head. 'And you think I've got an interesting background? I love it. Makes my academic life seem so boring.'

'It's not as exotic as it sounds. Business has fallen away this winter, and it's been hard to—' She cut her words off. He didn't want to hear about the financial woes of the household.

All was quiet for a moment and Sally looked down at her bowl with surprise. The dessert was all gone, and Sol was looking at her with approval.

Otis moaned under the table and Sally lifted the tablecloth and peered underneath. The dog rolled over and lay on his back, his eyes closed, and his mouth opened as he snored. 'Don't tell me he had some Tiramisu too?'

Sol shook his head and his teeth flashed in a smile.

'No, dogs can't eat chocolate.' He stood and as he leaned forward to reach for the wine, he gasped, and his face went white.

Sally jumped up and took his arm. 'What's wrong?'

'My back just caught. I can't straighten up.'

She took his hand in hers and gently pulled him away from the table. 'Have you got a high bed in one of the bedrooms?'

He nodded as perspiration dotted his brow. 'In the main bedroom. Pearl had a bad back. There's a board under the mattress. And it's high.'

'You'll have to tell me which room.'

'Down the hall, past the bathroom and the last door on the right.' He hung onto her hand like grim death.

Once they got there, she sat him carefully on the edge of the high bed. Putting on her most professional voice, she said softly. 'Now can you lift your arms and take off your shirt?' Sally dug deep for professionalism as Sol lifted his shirt off, but her mouth still dried. The bed was high, and a gorgeous, smooth, tanned chest, lightly sprinkled with fine dark hair met her at eye level.

'Now while I go out to the car and get some oil, can you get over onto your stomach?' As she spoke, she went into the bathroom next to the bedroom and collected two towels. She rolled up one to put beneath his head and spread the other on the end of the bed.

'Oil?'

'Yes. I'm going to ease your back for you. If we can find the offending muscle, you'll feel much better within an hour.'

She backed out of the room as he lay down.

Chapter 11

Sol's back had given out on him several times over the past few years but he'd never been happy about it before. As he lay there with his eyes closed, and Sally's strong fingers ran up and down the backs of his legs, he thought about going to the butcher and buying Otis a year's supply of bones.

First time he'd ever been grateful to the damn dog.

His eyelids flickered open as he sensed the light change and soft music surrounding him.

'Have you ever had a massage before?' Sally's voice was soft.

'No.'

'Not even for relaxation?'

He shook his head; it was hard to speak with his face in the rolled-up towel. Firm hands pressed on his shoulders.

'Keep your head still.

He obliged. He wasn't going to move at all and he hoped and prayed that he didn't have to turn over at any point soon.

'It was lucky I always carry my gear in the car.' A light chuckle came from just near his ear. 'Even luckier for you that Otis didn't get into the back seat and find the massage oil and my CD player.'

Warm fingers stroked from his neck down to his waist, and Sol was hard-pressed not to groan. It was even harder when she hooked her fingers under the waistband of his track pants and pulled them down over his butt. As the cool air hit his bare skin, she placed a towel over his back.

'Lift your hips a little if you can. I'm just going to slip another rolled-up towel under your groin.'

Managing that was a miracle but he did.

Sally's voice blended with the music as her fingers

moved up and down the backs of his legs. The smell of the oil was unusual but pleasant.

'Like I told you the other day, I did some courses with Rosie when I was at college before I followed the yoga path. Now there are two types of massage: relaxation and remedial. First off, I'll relax you with long flowing strokes, kneading and some gentle manipulations of your muscles. A relaxation massage is to de-stress you and loosen your body. Once you're relaxed, I'll look for that pesky muscle and find the trigger points, but it might hurt a bit.'

The pesky muscle that he'd pulled when he'd tackled Otis wasn't the one that was misbehaving at the moment. Sol gulped, trying to think of something that would take his mind off the gentle fingers caressing the backs of his thighs.

Getting the pages in order for his thesis. He worked his way through the chapters in his head, and by the time he had his physical reaction under control, Sally's hands had moved to his feet, and Sol tried not to chuckle. His feet were ticklish. Her hands went around his ankle and she tugged at his legs.

'Hmm,' she said.

'Hmm, what,' he murmured.

'Your left leg is about four centimetres shorter than your right at the moment. It's the right side of your back that's sore, isn't it?'

'Yep.' He jerked as she tugged at his leg and the pain shot through his back. 'Ow.'

'Good. I know where to work now.'

Sol wanted to say that she'd been doing just fine where she'd been before but he kept his mouth shut.

'I'm going to work on the trigger point now. Do you know what that is?'

He went to shake his head but thought better of it. 'No.'

'The injured muscle's taut and your other muscles are

compensating. That contributes to the pain. I'll palpate the muscle that's not performing—'

God give me strength, he thought.

'I'll apply compression to quite precise points and the pain you feel will be intense to start with, but I'll tell you to breathe it out for thirty to ninety seconds. The longer you can bear it, the quicker it will heal.'

'Sounds good to me.'

Not.

'Okay. you ready?'

When Sally climbed up on the bed and put her knees on either side of his back, Sol headed straight back to chapter counting. The fabric of her jeans was soft against his hips, and each time she leaned forward and deepened the strokes on his back, it swished against his bare skin.

'Now, Sol. Breathe in and hold it until I tell you to let go.' Her knees gripped his hips.

'Fuck!' he couldn't help the expletive as excruciating pain radiated across his back and down his right hip. It felt like she'd sliced a knife through his muscle.

Sally leaned down and her hair brushed his cheek as she spoke softly into his ear. 'No talking, no yelling. Just breathe in. We'll start again.'

This time he was ready. He took in a deep breath and held it as the pain built in intensity.

'Okay. Let it out slowly.'

As he let the breath out, the pain eased as the air left his lips.

'Good.' Her voice was louder and brisk as she straightened up.

'Ready for the next one?'

Another ten minutes of torture and Sol didn't need to worry about being embarrassed, turning over or even getting off the bed. He breathed in and out as she told him to, and waited for the welcome gaps between the pressure she placed on each trigger point. How strong was she? When he didn't think he could take any more, her fingers slid smooth and warm up over his shoulder blades.

'Now I'll get you back to a relaxation state. And if you'd like I'll tell you a little bit about the chakras in Ayurvedic massage as we cool you down?'

'Yes, please.' Anything except for trigger points again.

'There are more than one hundred chakras in the body, but we focus on seven.' Her fingers were firm at the base of his back again and Sol braced himself. 'The root chakra is near your tailbone at the back and opposite at the front.' Sally sounded uncomfortable for the first time and Sol grinned into the towel.

'They say if this chakra is blocked you might feel restless, unable to settle to a path.'

What was she trying to tell him? Or was he being sensitive?

'Its colour is red. Last night in my notes, it was this chakra that we spoke about being associated with sexual energy, and utilised in Tantric massage.' She paused and cleared her throat.

Sol swallowed deep and hard as Sally's fingers moved around to his stomach beneath the towel.

Chapter Six. Think of Chapter Six. Bloody heck, what was it again? Focus. He fought the immediate physical response as her fingers brushed lightly and briefly—oh so briefly— on his skin a couple of centimetres below his belly button.

'This is the second chakra.' Her voice was low. 'Balance here means that your emotions will flow freely and the emotion associated with it is passion. Can you remember what else I read out to you in my notes last night? It'll relate directly to your research.

Sol was having trouble remembering what day it was as her fingers moved up to his chest. 'Um. Remind me.'

'It can be affected by inherited emotional patterns, or even by emotions repressed in childhood.'

Sol nodded or moved his head as best he could on the rolled-up towel.

As Sally worked her way through the rest of the chakras, her fingers brushing and caressing, her voice low and melodic, and the background music soothing, Sol finally found himself in a total state of relaxation. He was awake but he wasn't. His eyes were closed, his face pressed into the towel, and after she ran her fingers lightly through his hair, saying, 'The crown is the centre of spirituality, enlightenment and energy, and it allows for the inward flow of wisdom,' he took a deep breath.

Strangely Sol felt as though he was almost floating when Sally stopped speaking. He kept his eyes closed as he listened to her moving quietly about the room. Finally, the music stopped followed by the door clicking shut and he drifted off to sleep.

Chapter 12

Sally closed the door of the guest room behind her. She knew that Sol was almost asleep, and it wouldn't hurt him to sleep off the remedial work she'd done. Leaning with her back against the door, she closed her eyes and stood in the dark room.

Never before had she had such a reaction to the body of a client—or indeed to the body of a lover, not that there'd been many of them. The feel of Sol's warm skin, the whipcord toughness of his muscles, and the long smooth plane of his bare back beneath her fingers had sent exquisite warmth to her lower belly. She'd almost not been able to finish the massage because her legs had been shaking so much. The temptation to climb up onto the bed and press herself against him had been strong, but she'd talked herself down by going through the chakras. It had knocked some much-needed sense into her.

Never before had she been so aware of a man.

He was beautiful.

In every way. He was a good man, he had a sensitive soul, and once you got past that shaggy haircut and the old-fashioned clothes, he oozed sex appeal.

Sally swallowed and went into the small bathroom that was off the guest room. She ran the cold water tap and after running cool water over her wrists, she filled her hands and sluiced her face. As she reached for a towel she looked into the mirror. Her eyes were bright, her cheeks were pink and she could see the pulse beating in her neck, as her heart beat in time with the nerve endings that were firing right through her body.

She pressed the towel to her face and shook her head. All she wanted to do was go back into the bedroom next door.

No. It wasn't the right thing to do.

With a sigh, she pulled back the bedspread on the single bed, plumped up the pillow and tried to ignore the overwhelming fragrance of mothballs as she sank onto the soft mattress. She lay on her back and closed her eyes. There was no sound from the room next door so she assumed that Sol was fast asleep. She rolled over and thumped the pillow and buried her head.

Three hours of tossing and turning did nothing to ease her frustration. In the early hours, she drifted off and dreamed of Sol. They were in a meadow with flowers and soft green grass. His head came closer, and the warmth of his breath tickled her cheek. She could smell flowers . . . *and fish.*

Sally's eyes flew open.

A slimy dollop of dog slobber landed on her cheek seconds before a huge silver body snuggled onto the pillow next to her head.

'Oh. yuk.' She sat up and pushed Otis off the bed. 'Get off. Beds are for humans. Not dogs.'

He put his paws on the side of the bed and licked her cheek.

'Okay, you're gorgeous but you have to go out while I have a wash.' She climbed out of bed and padded across to the door, with Otis beside her. When she opened the door, he backed away, but she grabbed his collar and pushed him into the hall before shutting the door firmly. After finishing in the bathroom, she smoothed her hands down her T-shirt and jeans; maybe sleeping in her clothes hadn't been such a great idea after all.

The house was quiet. She peeked in the main bedroom on the way past but Sol wasn't in there. Otis was waiting for her on the mat in front of the fire, and the smell of coffee tickled her nose. As she reached for a cup, she heard a car engine and walked across to the back door and opened it.

Mac's work truck was in the driveway and Sol was sitting in the front of his car. As she watched, she saw him give a thumbs up to Mac, and a cloud of grey smoke puffed from the exhaust.

When Sol came inside with a grin on his face, she was sitting at the table hugging her coffee.

'All good. Gertie's got a new battery so we can head off whenever you're ready.' He went over to the sink.

'How's your back?' she asked.

'You're a miracle worker. You'd never know that I'd hurt it.' He half-turned his head as she scrubbed his hands. 'Ever thought about giving away the yoga instruction and taking up massage?'

Heat ran into her cheeks as she shook her head. The few massages she'd done when she'd been at college, she hadn't enjoyed. She's always felt self-conscious touching another person so intimately. But last night, she'd enjoyed every minute of smoothing her hands over his skin.

'Um no. I prefer yoga.' She fanned herself with one hand. 'The coffee's hot.'

'Well, you're good at it. I slept like a baby. Did you sleep okay? '

'Like a charm,' she lied. The last thing she wanted was for him to know that she'd stayed awake half the night resisting the temptation to go back to his room. 'I'll just gather up my notes and I'm ready to go.'

'Okay. I'll feed Otis and grab my computer.' He frowned and crossed to the back door as the sound of a car reached them.

'Great! Dave's home. I wasn't expecting him until the weekend.' He opened the door and let Otis out. 'Means I won't have to drive back up here tonight.'

'Have you got somewhere to stay?'

'I can always go home.' His eyes danced. 'Unless I get

a better offer. Do you know when your sister's due home and you want me to come and stay?'

'No. I haven't heard from her yet. I tried to call a couple of times but she's not answering her phone.'

'Would she be on the way back yet?'

'No, she's got a few more days yet.' Sally shook her head, but her lips twitched into a grin. Knowing Sonia she would have found a man by now; that's why she wouldn't be answering her phone.

Half her luck, she thought.

She tipped her head to the side. 'If you want to stay while you get your thesis sorted, you're quite welcome. 'There's plenty of room there.'

'Really, are you sure? That's a way better option than going home to my parents' place.'

'Is that where you live? You don't have a place of your own.' She stood and put her hand on his arm as he stood by the door. 'I'm sorry. That sounded rude and it's none of my business where you live.'

He put his hand on hers and those damn butterflies headed straight to her belly. 'No, you're right. It's way past time that I found myself a place of my own.'

'Don't do that. I need you up here.' The man who stepped through the back door grinned sheepishly at Sally. 'Hi, I'm Dave. I hope that's not your car out there?'

She nodded. 'It is. I'm going to have to sort something out.'

She bit her lip. If the insurance didn't accept the dog ate my car, she and Sonia were going to be catching buses for a while.

'Let me know if I can help,' Dave said before he enfolded Sol in a man hug. 'Hey, bro. Sorry I didn't call. I got an earlier flight out of Tokyo, and the meeting in Taiwan was cancelled so I came straight back to Sydney.' Sally watched the exchange with interest. Dave was certainly an interesting character—way removed from the farm owner she'd expected. His hair was swept up into a ponytail on one side of his head, and on the other side of his head, his hair was short and dyed purple. He wore some sort of Japanese kimono in red, over skin-tight black jeans with high-heeled boots.

'No problem. I have to take Sally back to Sydney this morning, so at least Otis will have company now.'

Dave looked at her curiously, but Sol didn't say why she'd been staying up here.

'We'll head off now. When do you need me next? I've got a commitment for the next week or so.' Sol turned to Sally. 'Will a week be enough time for the . . . er . . . favour?'

She nodded. 'Yes. Sonia will be home by next weekend.' She picked up her bag and notes off the table. She'd put the massage oil and CD player in there last night.

Sol held open the door and followed her out to his car. 'See ya, mate.'

Dave held onto Otis. 'Nice to meet you, Sally.'

As she turned, she caught the wink he directed at Sol.

***

When Sol started the Land Rover, he glanced over at Sally as she put her head back on the seat and closed her eyes. By the time they reached the turn-off at the road to the farm, she was fast asleep. Despite the rough road she slept quietly, all the way to the motorway. Her head rested in the space between the seat and the window, and her hands rested in her lap.

Sol chewed his lip as he turned onto the M1, lost in thought. Even though he'd had trouble sleeping once Sally had left the room, he'd woken up feeling refreshed, and he'd bounded out of bed feeling guilty that he hadn't even shown her to the guest room last night. He'd tapped on the door but there'd been no answer, and when he'd pushed it open, he'd stood there looking at her for a moment.

She'd been fast asleep, one hand tucked beneath her cheek. Her lips were slightly parted, and he watched her sleep before he felt a bit guilty. If she woke up and caught him, she'd probably think he was overstepping the mark. He'd left the door slightly ajar, hoping that the smell of brewing coffee might wake her.

Last night had been amazing. He could still feel her fingers on his skin and the slide of her firm hands up his back.

He wondered what she'd been thinking; a couple of times her voice had been a bit shaky, and he'd wondered if the massage was having the same effect on her as it was on him.

He was in trouble here. And he didn't know how to handle the situation. She wasn't his type. The women he'd taken out before had all been university colleagues. He liked them because they were smart and could talk to him about the things he was interested in. They were busy with their studies and didn't expect him to take time out of his life for them. Sometimes, he'd spent a night with them, but he'd never experienced anything like the sensual feelings that Sally's touch had raised in him last night. He'd always accepted he was meant to be a loner.

Sally was whip-smart; there was no doubt about that. He grinned as he thought about what his family would say if he turned up with an alternate yoga instructor to a family dinner.

She was beautiful, inside and out; he couldn't get her out of his head.

He drove while she slept. Through the outer suburbs of Sydney and across the Harbour Bridge, and still, she didn't wake. The day was clear and bright, and the harbour was a deep blue, contrasting with the white sails of the yachts that dotted the bays. By the time they were on Oxford Street, Sally began to stir, and he smiled as she yawned and rubbed her eyes.

'Good morning again,' he said cheerily as she stared at him through bleary eyes.

'Sorry, I didn't mean to fall asleep. She turned to the window. 'I must have been asleep for ages.'

'An hour and a half, and you didn't move once.' He changed back a gear as the lights turned red. 'Fixing my back must have worn you out. And I haven't said thank you yet. I really do owe you. You've saved my skin with the interviews for my thesis, and you've fixed my back.'

'Don't worry. You're probably going to be sorry you agreed to my favour when you meet Sonia.'

'Are you identical twins?'

'Oh, God. No.' Sally turned to him and tucked one leg under her on the seat. 'We don't look alike. We don't think alike. We don't have any common interests.'

'Interesting. I have a friend at the uni who was doing a longitudinal study of twins over a lifetime. Behavioural genetics. For a while, I thought about studying in that field, but psychology won out.'

Temporarily, he thought.

'You've done so much study you must have a great repertoire of dinner conversation.'

'Nuh, I'm pretty boring.' He flashed a grin as he let the clutch out and Gertie jerked forward.

'No, you're not! Sonia is going to love you.'

He wondered if that meant that Sally found him a little bit interesting. He doubted it.

'How long do you want to string her along for?'

'Oh, only a day or two.' Sally smiled back at him and his heart did a little flip as her dark eyes held his. 'I can't impose on you for much longer.'

He lifted one hand off the wheel and waved it. 'I'm not

in a rush. As soon as this thesis is bound, I'm giving myself some time off. I might even take a holiday.'

'Where to?'

He shrugged. 'I don't know. I haven't travelled much. Where would you suggest for a good relaxing holiday?'

Sally shook her head. 'You're asking the wrong person here. I haven't taken a holiday since I left school.'

He looked at her curiously. 'I thought we were different, you know. But really we're not.'

She sat up straight and folded her arms. Sol knew straight away he'd said the wrong thing.

'What do you mean different? You mean because I haven't been to university.'

'No. I didn't mean that at all. I mean because we . . . because—'

'Because we come from different backgrounds, and I have a boring life compared to your interesting one.'

'No.' Sol frowned. For a moment he considered pulling over. It was hard to talk when he was focused on the traffic, but the road was busy and there was nowhere to pull up. 'Hold that thought. I want to talk about that in a while.' He glanced over at her, and his heart clenched because she looked so sad. 'Please don't look like that, it's all good.'

With a shrug, Sally turned and looked out the window as they headed through Bondi Junction, and kept looking out until they reached the beach.

Chapter 13

Gertie chugged up the steep road to the house on top of the hill. The sky was a soft winter blue, and the crest of white foam on the breaking waves contrasted with the azure blue of the ocean. Surfers rode the long line of swells into the shore, catching the waves before they broke. People walked on the beach in the warm winter sunshine and as he parked the car, the sound of children playing on the sand carried up the hill. Sol closed his eyes and let the serenity fill him; he could spend the rest of his life here. A study on the top floor of the house, he could research—

'Are we going to sit here all day?' Sally's voice interrupted his daydreaming.

'Ah, I was just enjoying the view.' Sol gestured out the window to the ocean.

'You had your eyes closed.' Even though her voice was dry, it held amusement.

'Caught out. I was thinking about that gorgeous house. You're so lucky to live and work here.'

'I know. I should appreciate it more. Like everything, you take things for granted after a while.

Sol parked the car on the road outside the house. There was no driveway. He guessed it had been built in the days before there was a need for driveways and garages to house a modern car.

Hmm… the history of architecture in Sydney. He wondered how much research had been done on that.

'Um, are we going to sit here all day?" This time her voice held a giggle, and it made him smile.'

'No, we're going go into that gorgeous house and I'm going to talk to you.'

***

Talk to me?

What was there to talk about?

When Sol had said that they were different, it had cut straight to Sally's heart. Sonia had told her often enough over the past few years that she was boring, and Sol's words had brought home to her how boring she was.

He was different. He'd studied, explored so many different avenues, and had interesting friends—if Dave was any indication. He'd also hinted about a difficult family, but that would make life even more interesting. A little bit of conflict spiced up life.

My life is dull.

And it was no one's fault but her own. Blake could take a bit of the blame for starting it off, but she was the one who'd indulged in a pity party for too long.

Way too long.

She spent her days—and nights—in this house, with the occasional trip across town to her classes. She didn't really mix with anyone after her working day and was—had been anyway—quite happy with her own company, but since the Blake dumping, her self-confidence had been shot.

Sally knew she had to remember what she'd promised herself on the way up to Peats Ridge yesterday.

From now on, life was going to be fun, and she'd make an all-out effort to be a part of it again. She was going to loosen up and lighten her attitude.

She was going to write an affirmation and put it on the fridge door.

I will do something fun every day.

Sonia was about to get the biggest shock of her life.

Sally looked sideways at Sol as he lifted his bag from the car.

And if it meant that Sol might end up in her bed, she wasn't going to complain.

She put the key in the door, and it creaked open. Paws pounded on the stairs, and Muggins came flying along the hall and spun out on the tiles.

'Hey, baby.' Sally leaned down and picked him up. 'Were you a lonely little pussy cat?'

His little motor purred as she snuggled him against her. She looked up at Sol, and he was standing there staring at her with the strangest look on his face.

'Bring your bag in and I'll sort out a room for you. Heaven knows there's plenty to pick from.' Sally put the kitten down. 'I'll just top up his food bowl and I'll take you upstairs.'

She was surprised when Sol followed her through the kitchen and into the laundry. He looked around as they walked in. 'Gosh, this house is amazing.'

Sally shrugged. 'Again, because I've lived here so long, I'm used to it.'

'It's got so much character. You can feel the memories in it.'

There was a loud bang from upstairs. She turned and smiled at him after she poured the dry cat food into the bowl. 'You can often hear them too.'

He shook his head. 'I love it.'

'Come on, we'll get you a room sorted.'

'Not yet.' Sol reached out and gently took her hand as she turned for the door.

She looked down at their joined hands and her heart rate kicked up a notch. 'Why, not yet.'

'Because we need to talk.'

'About the favour? I really do appreciate—'

'No, about what you said in the car.'

Heat flooded into her cheeks. 'Oh don't worry about me. I was a bit tired and cranky.'

He put his other hand on the side of Sally's neck and

pulled her closer to him.

'No. Your feelings were hurt, but you misunderstood what I meant. You made assumptions. Hell Sally, if anyone is the boring person in this relationship—'

'Relationship?'

'We do have a relationship. I don't know what it is yet, but we have one. It could be friendship, it could be business, but it could simply be this.'

Her eyes widened as he let go of her fingers and lifted his hand to cup her other cheek. Both his hands were warm on her face as he held it gently and lowered his head.

'I'm not very good at this, but all I know is that I've wanted to do it since you answered the door like a little spitfire the other night.'

Sally widened her eyes as the light was blocked by his head and her mouth opened as surprise flooded through her.

Surprise that flew out the window as his lips gently brushed against hers.

'Sol,' she murmured.

He raised his head. 'You're not different and you're not boring.'

Her heart kicked again, and it had a lot to do with those butterflies that were beating their wings harder. 'I am, but I'm going to do something about it. I decided that on the way up to Dave's farm yesterday. I've been wallowing in self-pity for way too long. I've made up my mind. There's going to be a much more exciting Sally Smith from now on.'

His lips brushed against hers again. 'What if I said I'm interested in the one I met?'

'Um, I don't know. There's really not a lot to be interested in.'

He shook his head but kept his lips hovering above hers. 'Oh yes, there is.'

She found it hard to take a breath, and the room spun a

little bit as she looked up at him. She hadn't felt like this for a long time.

If ever.

The emotion was so sudden her cheeks burned when his lips took hers. Sensation flooded through her as she was swept into the moment. Her hands went around his neck and she clung to him as his lips burned against hers.

Hot and hungry.

A sensual shaft of desire speared through her as his hands went beneath her T-shirt. 'Let's take this out of the laundry,' she said as she managed to get her breath back.

He chuckled and lifted his head. 'Not the most romantic setting. Where will we go?' His voice was low and deep.

'Maybe I could show you the different bedrooms and you can choose which one you'd like to stay in.' She looked up at him and shyness flooded through her. 'The beds are all comfortable. It's one thing Aunt Aggie insisted on.'

'More comfortable than the one I slept in last night? I'll swear I could feel the board under it.'

'You told me you slept well!' Sally turned away from him, but Sol held her hand as they walked down the hall towards the sweeping staircase that led up to the bedrooms.

'How could a man sleep after you'd trailed your fingers over him for an hour? And all I could think about was you asleep in the room close by.'

She laughed. 'I didn't get a wink either. All I could think about was you in the next room.' She paused at the bottom of the stairs. 'Do you want to bring your bag up?'

'Not yet.' He held her gaze and she tried not to react too obviously as she stared into his dark eyes. Warm shivers ignited a fire in her lower belly as his hand settled in the small of her back.

'Let's check out these rooms,' he said.

'Follow me.'

They reached the top of the stairs and Sally stood back. She gestured to the spare rooms up the hall from hers. 'Sir, you have a selection.'

Sol smiled. A slow, lazy smile that curled her toes. 'A single or a double? What would you recommend?'

'Depends on what sir wants,' she said with a giggle.

His eyes were dancing as Sol held his arms open. 'Definitely a double.'

His arms came around her and he lowered his lips to hers again. Sally closed her eyes as his soft groan matched hers.

'Are you happy to share?'

'I am. It's about time I tried a new bedroom.' She giggled. 'Another way to show Sonia I'm not boring anymore.'

'Oh sweetheart, boring is the last word I'd ever apply to you.' His words vibrated against her lips and for a moment she forgot everything else as Sol explored her mouth. She sighed when he moved down to kiss the soft skin of her neck, and his hands explored the bare skin under her T-shirt.

Chapter 14

Two hours later, a hot breath stirred against her cheek and Sally kept her eyes closed as she murmured against Sol's mouth.

'Not again?' She parted her lips to take his kiss. 'I think I need to find some energy.'

Sol chuckled and ran his hand down her bare thigh. 'No. I thought I heard someone at the door.'

Sally frowned and sat up clutching the sheet to her chest. 'I don't have any appointments until tonight.'

'Maybe it was Aunt Aggie,' he said as he sat up beside her.

'She usually stays upstairs.'

Sol chuckled. 'As long as she respects people's privacy.'

Sally frowned as there was a sound in the hall outside. 'Muggins must be hungry again.'

'Speaking of hungry again. . .' She leaned into Sol as she put his arm around her.

'You are the most energetic . . .' Her words ended with a gasp as the bedroom door opened.

'Sal, are you in here? Where's our car? There's a strange car outside and a bag at the . . . Oh. My. God.' Sonia stood in the doorway; her eyes as wide as the multi-coloured stripes on her dress.

Sally giggled, but Sol tensed beside her.

'Relax,' she whispered. 'Just follow my lead.'

She stretched and pulled the sheet up over Sol's bare legs as she did.

A man had to have a bit of privacy.

'Sonia,' she said loudly. 'When did you get back?'

'Sally Smith. Just want do you think you're doing!'

Sonia's voice was indignant.

'Just following your instructions, sweets. Oh, this is Sol. You spoke to him on the phone the other night.'

'What instructions?' Sonia's hands went onto her hips. This is so out of character for you, Sally.'

'I'm getting out of my comfort zone like you told me to.' Sally glanced at Sol and saw his lips twitch. 'And Sol's been helping me out.' She nudged him. 'Haven't you, Sol.'

'Sally's taught me about chakras and Tantric sex, and I taught her about—'

'No. I don't want to know! That's my twin sister's bed you're in!' Sonia's hands went up and she backed out of the room.

The door closed behind her, and Sally stifled her giggles until Sonia's footsteps pounded to the bottom of the stairs. At the same time, there was a loud crash from the floor above.

Sols' shoulders were shaking beside her. 'Aunt Aggie approves?'

'I think she must.' Sally tried to stop laughing but her eyes were filled with tears of mirth. 'Oh, that was so good. We couldn't have done it better if we'd planned it. Fancy Sonia coming home early. And what fabulous timing.' She picked up the sheet and wiped her eyes. I can guarantee she'll be on the phone to Rosie by now.'

Sol rolled over onto his back. Sally looked down at him and his eyes were shadowed.

'So we're square. I've done your favour for you. What now?'

For a moment uncertainty ran through her and the old Sally kicked in but she swallowed.

Self-confidence. She had it. The pity party was over. There was no way she was going to stuff this up.

She twisted sideways and moved across, so her chest

was on his. He stilled as she put her face close to his.

'Well, I don't know about you. But I know what I want and I'm going to go for it. We might have only known each other a few days, but they've been the best days I've spent for a very long time.' She closed her eyes and took a deep breath. 'I don't want to see it end. Unless that's what you want. I know you'll be busy, and I know—'

'Yes.'

With that one word joy stomped through her as loudly as Sonia had gone downstairs, and as loud and strong as Aunt Aggie had shown her approval. Sally shifted so that she was lying on top of Sol.

'Do you think we should lock the door?' he asked.

Epilogue
Six months later

'Sally!'

Sally said goodbye to the last client in her class as a cry came from the kitchen. 'Bye, Mrs Tonks. I'll see you next week.' Sally closed the front door when the elderly lady reached the gate.

'Sally!' The voice was getting louder each time, and it sounded as those there was a good dose of frustration—or temper— mixed in there as well.

She wandered into the kitchen. Sonia was standing at the table; her hair damp with perspiration, her cheeks bright red and her hands out of sight in the cavity of the biggest turkey Sally had ever seen.

'What are you trying to do?' She tried not to laugh. Sometimes Sonia got a bit cross with the new light-hearted Sally. Since Sol had moved in, Sally had laughed every day. There had been no need for an affirmation on the fridge door.

'I'm trying to stuff the frigging turkey. What does it look like I'm doing?'

Sally burst out laughing but the grumpy look stayed on her sister's face.

'It's all right for you, Mrs Happiness and Light. I've had to do most of the shopping and cooking for Christmas dinner while you've had your yoga classes and his nibs has been stuck up in his study.'

Sol shared her bedroom, but when he'd moved in, Sally had found a study space for him in the small room off the widow's walk on the top floor of the rambling old mansion. It had been perfect for his needs. He'd almost completed the last work towards his qualification, and he was thinking of opening a vet surgery somewhere at the beach.

'Sorry. Just let me have a wash, and I'll help you.'

'Rosie and Taj and the kids are arriving at four. Aren't you going to the airport to pick them up?'

'Sol offered. He has to pick his mate up at the airport too, and they'll all fit in Gertie.' Sally wiped her hands and took one of Aunt Aggie's floral aprons from the bottom drawer.

'Did I tell you his mate, Dave was coming for Christmas dinner too?'

Sonia nodded. 'Sol did. But I'd already seen it in the tea leaves. A tall, dark and handsome stranger is coming into my life.'

Sally spluttered. 'I don't think we could call Dave tall, dark and handsome. Besides, Sonia, I think he's gay so don't go getting your hopes up.'

***

Sol parked the car up the road while Dave and Taj took the suitcases inside. Rosie and the kids had run inside to see Sonia and Sally. They'd welcomed him, and as soon as Taj and Sol had shaken hands they'd looked at each other.

'We used to go to Christmas parties at your house when I was a kid,' Taj said.

'I remember.' Sol put his head to one side. 'I wonder if that means I'm related to Aggie too. I must ask my mother next time I call in.' Since he'd moved in with Sally—his mother had taken to her straight away and was even going to a yoga class once a week—and he'd picked up his vet science, the attitude of his family had done an about-turn.

Dave was waiting for him on the footpath outside the house. 'Not a bad place, mate. You've fallen on your feet here.'

'I've fallen in love here.'

Dave rolled his eyes. 'Pathetic. I think I preferred the old vague Solomon Brown.'

Sol looked at him. 'And I definitely prefer the old

Dave Walker. The one who used to wear things resembling clothes. What the hell are you wearing?'

Heads had turned at the arrivals hall as Dave had walked down the ramp. His three-piece suit was hot pink and patterned with large purple flowers.

'One of my designs, and before you say anything, it was on the catwalk in Milan last week.'

'Different.'

Sol held the door open. He was part of the house on the hill now, although Sally had assured him she would move anywhere he had to go. 'Come on in. I think you've met everyone except Sonia, Sally's twin.'

Dave's eyebrows lifted hopefully. 'Identical? Sally is a stunner. I can see her modelling some of my designs.'

Sol hid a smile. 'I can't see Sally being interested in that, but Sonia certainly loves her fashion.'

The smells coming from the kitchen were divine. They walked past a huge Christmas tree in the front living room and the fragrance of the pine needles mingled with the smell of roast turkey.

'Sit down, Dave. I'll see where the girls are.' Before he could leave the room, the door burst open.

Sonia struck a pose in the doorway and Sol grinned. Sally stood behind her and caught his eyes and winked.

Sonia was wearing a purple, pink and yellow striped dress—one of her signature tent dresses—and a matching turban. Her feet were bare and each toe had a different ring on it. Bangles jangled on her arm and her lipstick was the same purple as the stripes in her dress.

Sol stiffened as Dave chuckled beside him and stepped forward.

'You must be Sonia.' Dave held his hand out. 'Is this for my benefit, darling? All you need is a bowl of fruit on your head, and you'd be perfect.'

Ice dripped from Sonia's words. 'Perfect for what?'

'For the Mardi Gras parade.'

Sally stepped forward and nudged Sonia. 'Be polite, he's Sol's guest.'

Sol sat back and waited for the fireworks. This was going to be one hell of a Christmas dinner.

***

Once Dave and Sonia had stopped circling each other like cats on a hot tin roof, Christmas dinner had been fun. Taj had kept them entertained with stories of his year on the circuit, and the kids had pulled all the bonbons to get the jokes out.

Sally looked up at Sol as he stood behind her and held out a champagne glass. 'Oh, I couldn't. I've eaten way too much.'

Her eyes widened when he reached below the table and lifted a bottle of Moët.

'You have to. Just one. I hope we have something to celebrate.'

Her eyes widened when he put the glass on the table and handed the bottle to Taj.

Sol took Sally's hands and led her to the bottom of the stairs, followed by the rest of the dinner guests who seemed to know what was happening. Sonia even smiled at Dave when Sol reached into his pocket and pulled out a pendant on a chain.

'May I?' He held her gaze as he held it up. Sally reached for the pink stone dangling in front of her.

Sol's voice was low. 'Sally, wearing this rose quartz pendant will activate your heart chakra and bind you to me, your soul mate. If you accept it, this stone will protect our unbreakable vows from all that life might put in our way.'

Sally smiled as tears filled her eyes.

Happy tears.

'Rose quartz is a stone of the heart, the crystal of unconditional love,' she said. 'You've chosen well.'

'Will you marry me, Sal? Will you fill my heart with love, and let me love you back?'

She nodded and threw her arms around Sol's neck. As his lips met hers, the promise of a blissful future was set in stone.

Sonia's story

Beach Walk

Annie Seaton

Dedication

*This book is dedicated to my fabulous friends, Kristen and Dianne.
Great friends, fun times!*

Prologue

Christmas Day 2017

Sol parked the car up the road while Dave and Taj carried the suitcases inside. Rosie and the kids had run inside to see Sonia and Sally. When Taj and Sol had shaken hands, they'd looked at each other.

'We used to go to Christmas parties at your house when I was a kid,' Taj said.

'I remember.' Sol put his head to one side. 'I wonder if that means I'm related to Aggie too. I must ask my mother next time I call in.' Since he'd moved in with Sally—his mother had taken to her straight away and was even going to a yoga class once a week—and he'd picked up his vet science, the attitude of his family had done an about-face.

Dave was waiting for him on the footpath outside the house. 'Not a bad place, mate. You've fallen on your feet here.'

'I've fallen in love here.'

Dave rolled his eyes. 'Pathetic. I think I preferred the old vague Solomon Brown.'

Sol looked at him. 'And I definitely prefer the old Dave Walker. The one who used to wear things resembling clothes and not have a stupid haircut. What the hell are you wearing and what's with the hair?'

Heads had turned at the arrivals hall as Dave had walked down the ramp. His three-piece suit was hot pink and patterned with large purple flowers.

'One of my designs, and before you say anything, it was on the catwalk in Milan last week.'

'Different.'

'I've got an image I have to project.'

'If you say so.' Sol held the door open. He was part of the beach house on the hill now, although Sally had assured him, she would move anywhere he had to go. 'Come on in. I think you've met everyone except Sonia, Sally's twin.'

Dave's eyebrows lifted hopefully. 'Identical? Sally is a stunner. I can see her modelling some of my designs.'

Sol hid a smile. 'I can't see Sally being interested in that, but Sonia certainly loves her fashion. I think she studied it for a while.'

The aromas coming from the kitchen were divine. Roast pork and turkey, baked vegetables and apple sauce were heading for the table on platters. Dave and Sol walked past a huge real Christmas tree in the front living room and the fragrance of the pine needles mingled with the smell from the kitchen.

'Sit down, Dave. I'll see where the girls are.' Before he could leave the room, the door burst open.

Sonia struck a pose in the doorway and Sol grinned. Sally stood behind her and caught his eye and winked.

Sonia was wearing a purple, pink and yellow striped dress—one of her signature tent dresses—and a matching turban. Her feet were bare, and each toe had a different ring on it. Bangles jangled on her arm and her lipstick was the same purple as the stripes in her dress. Blonde curls puffed out around her face and down to her waist in a tangle.

Sol stiffened as Dave chuckled beside him and stepped forward. Dave was not known for his tact.

'You must be Sonia.' Dave held his hand out. 'Is this for my benefit, darling? All you need is a bowl of fruit on your head, and you'd be perfect.'

Ice dripped from Sonia's words. 'Perfect for what?'

'For the Mardi Gras parade.'

Sally stepped forward and nudged Sonia as she whispered. 'Be polite, he's Sol's guest.'

Sol sat back and waited for the fireworks. This was going to be one hell of a Christmas dinner.

##

The conversation over Christmas dinner was lively. At the end of the table where Sol and Sally were sitting, the mood was festive and happy as they caught up with Rosie and Taj's news, and enjoyed the children's excitement as they pulled the bonbons and played with the party favours inside.

'Ooh, look I've got two frogs now,' Lily said. 'Aunty Sally, if you get a frog in yours, can I have it?'

'Please,' her mother added.

'Please,' Lily said. 'I love frogs!'

Smiles and laughter drifted across the room.

The same couldn't be said for the conversation at the other end of the long table. Every so often Sol and Sally would exchange a worried glance and try to interrupt with a comment or question to lighten the mood, but the two conversationalists were going at it hammer and tongs.

'A clairvoyant?' Dave's lip almost curled and Sally flinched when Sonia bristled. 'Is there much call for that in Bondi Beach?' he asked.

'Oh David, you would be very surprised.' Sonia's voice was saccharine sweet.

'Dave,' he said.

Sally stifled a giggle, wondering if either of them realised how silly they looked with the paper hats on their heads as they argued so seriously.

'Do you have a business plan,' he persisted.

'I do.' Sonia nodded. 'Perhaps you'd like to see it.'

Sally bit back a grin. It would be a first if Dave bested Sonia. No one ever got the better of her sister. If it looked like things weren't going her way, she'd retreat into her crazy persona, and confuse the issue with zany behaviour.

'I could probably help you improve it a bit. Doesn't matter what profession you're in. Bricklaying, building, fashion, psychic stuff' —this time his lip did curl and Sally waited for the fiery retort that was sure to come from her twin—'a good plan will see an increase in profits, and let you reinvest to make more money.'

Sonia leaned forward and fluttered her eyelashes.

'Uh oh,' Sally thought. Dave leaned forward and the one-sided ponytail dropped across his face.

'So what would you suggest?' Sonia said moving in close and reaching up to lift the hair from his face.

'Well, I suppose you have to incorporate ways to get prospective clients to come to you.'

Sonia's voice was so, so sweet and Sally held her breath. 'But I know who's going to come, don't I? I'm a clairvoyant!'

Chapter 1

'Please, please, please, Aunty Sonia.'

The children's voices got louder as they tried to outdo each other.

Four-year-old Lily Brown folded her arms and stared at her surrogate aunt. 'You have to come to the beach because we need to be looked after.'

Sonia looked down at her as her goddaughter's cute little lips pursed in disapproval.

'And you have to get your swimmers and a towel,' Theo, her twin, chipped in. 'If we go into the water and go over our heads, you'll have to rescue us, 'cause if you wear a dress you won't be able to save us.'

'And we'll get *drownded*!' Lily piped up, seeing another way to convince Sonia to come with them.

Sonia folded her arms and looked to her sister, Sally, for help. 'Maybe Aunty Sally could go instead? She could have a turn.'

'No, we want you to come. Like you did when you came to visit us at our beach at home. We built that sandcastle, remember?'

'It's okay, Son. Kids, leave Aunty Sonia to eat her brekkie in peace.' Rosie pointed to the two empty chairs beside her in the café overlooking the southern end of Bondi Beach. 'Come and finish your eggs and then we'll worry about what we're going to do today.'

Even though it was still early, not yet eight o'clock, the world-famous beach beneath them was already getting busy. The early summer sunshine glistened on the small surf as it crested in a wavy lace of foam before pushing its way to the wide expanse of sand. The tide was low and already small groups of children were playing in the shallows as the water receded. Seagulls squawked overhead before they settled on the footpath, squabbling over food scraps that unwary diners threw to them.

'Rats with wings,' Sonia muttered as she tried to think of a way out of going to the beach. She lifted the edge of the top pancake on her triple stack and let the maple syrup drizzle onto the berries, bananas, pistachios and ricotta cheese.

'That looks yummy,' Sally said. 'But huge. I don't think I could get through it.'

Sonia frowned, hearing implied criticism in her sister's words. 'I'll need the energy to get through the day looking after this pair.'

'I wasn't having a go at you, love.' Sally lifted her coffee cup to her lips. 'Come on, Sonia. The kids would love you to go to the beach with them.' She lowered her voice and stared at her. 'You went to the beach in Hawaii, didn't you? Why can't you take them now?'

Sonia whispered as the children sat at the other side of the table. 'You take them for a swim.'

'I have a busy—and stressful— day ahead. Sol and I are going to his parents' house for a visit.' Sally narrowed her eyes and stared at her twin. 'Why don't you want to go to the beach here anyway?'

'I didn't know anyone on the beach in Hawaii, so it didn't matter there.'

'What didn't matter?'

Sonia rolled her eyes at Sally.

Honestly, weren't twins supposed to have some connection where they knew what the other one was thinking or feeling?

Ignoring Sally's question, Sonia smiled brightly and looked across at her godchildren. 'How about we do something different? Something really, really special.'

'Like what? Not girly stuff.' Theo's voice was laced

with a healthy dose of suspicion. His chin was equally laced with egg yolk, and Rosie leaned over and scrubbed at it with her napkin.

Sonia grinned at him and thought quickly. 'How about the movies?'

'Nope, we want to go to the beach,' he said. 'It's hot and sunny. It's a perfect day for swimming.'

'Yes, it's hot.' Lily picked up a napkin and fanned herself reminding Sonia of dear old Aunt Aggie. 'I want to have a swim too. With Aunty Sonia.'

'No one is going anywhere on an empty stomach.' Rosie wagged her finger and the two small children picked up their forks and continued eating.

Sonia put her head down, and focused on her meal, trying to think of a way of getting out of going down onto Bondi Beach with the kids.

'Just like the old days, isn't it girls?' Sally looked at the buff tanned surfers walking past the open-air café heading for the rocks where they'd jump into the water with their boards, paddle out and catch the waves.

'The old days sans kids,' Rosie said with a wry smile.

'You wouldn't have it any other way, Rosie.' Sally looked at the children with a smile and Sonia could read her thoughts. She was thinking about the children that she and Sol would have, and Sonia suspected it wouldn't be long after their planned Easter wedding.

Rosie and her husband, Taj, had an appointment at the solicitor's office mid-morning. Sonia had agreed to look after the twins when Rosie had asked her last night. When she'd been in Hawaii last month, she'd had a great time with them but fought the maternal feelings that had risen.

She would be a godmother, and an aunt to her twin's children one day, but Sonia doubted that she'd ever be a mother herself, as much as she would love to be. She pushed the thoughts away; it was times like that she was pleased that Sally wasn't in tune with her mind. Sonia took great pride in how clever she was in creating the persona that she hid behind. Loud, confident Sonia, in her brightly coloured tent dresses with her jangly bracelets, multicoloured toenails and toe rings, and her ability to have fun wherever she went. Looking to get laid in Hawaii, she'd told Sally on the phone when she'd set her up with Sol.

If only they knew.

Up until a few years ago, she'd even changed her name every month or two to keep everyone on their toes, but since her last name change—Ocean Lily—at Aunt Aggie's funeral, she'd gone back to being plain old Sonia.

Yep, plain old Sonia, she thought.

'What are you thinking about, Son?' Rosie leaned over and touched her arm. 'You look sad.'

'No, not sad.' She flashed a wide smile around the table. 'I was just thinking about dear Old Aunt Aggie. And it made me think, it's time to see what's coming up for us gals!'

As Sonia turned and called the waiter over, Sally glanced at her watch. 'I've only got half an hour. Sol's picking me up here soon.'

'Me too. Taj and I are going straight to Mr Pepper's office from here,' Rosie added.

'Half an hour gives us plenty of time to read the tea leaves,' Sonia said as the waiter came over. 'Could we please have a pot of tea—a large one and three teacups with saucers, Mitch?'

'Certainly, Madame. Anything else?' He looked around the table, but his gaze lingered on Sonia. Sally nudged Rosie and they giggled like the teenagers they'd been a decade ago.

Chapter 2

Probably wondering how such a plain Jane like me can be with two stunners like that pair, Sonia thought as she watched Sally and Rosie check Mitch out. Sonia had only been home from Hawaii for a couple of weeks, but the change in Sally since she had fallen in love with Sol Brown was amazing. The dark shadows had gone from beneath her sister's eyes, and she'd lost that intensity she'd always had. That's what love had done for Sally.

Love at first sight. And Sonia hadn't even seen it in the cards.

She smiled—if it hadn't been for her placing the ad in the local paper last month, Sol and Sally would never have met. Different as chalk and cheese, but they adored each other. It warmed Sonia's heart to see it, but she'd never admit it to Sally. They'd always had a strange relationship, never as close as people always said twins were. And over the past couple of years, Sonia had felt as though she had never quite measured up to her sister.

She sighed. Now that Sally and Sol were moving away, she was going to be lonely in the house on the hill.

True love at first sight.

Apparently, it did happen.

'A couple of small chocolate milkshakes please,' Rosie's words interrupted her musing. Mitch nodded before he walked away.

'That'll give you a bit of a break from the kids' nagging, Sonia,' Rosie added. 'If it's easier for you, we can take them with us.'

'No, no. I love spending time with them.' Sonia leaned forward and spoke to the kids. 'How about we get our bikes, guys, and we can go for a big bike ride along the beach walk to the playground at Marks Park?'

Lily put her finger to her lip as she considered the option. 'How about an ice cream too?'

'And then a swim when we get back?' Theo added.

'You strike a hard deal,' Sonia said, but she nodded. 'But it sounds good to me.' With a bit of luck, Taj and Rosie would be back in time for the beach end of the activities, and she could opt out.

Mitch placed a fine china teapot on the table, and then carefully put a teacup and saucer in front of each of the three women.

Sonia chuckled as he winked at her.

'That should be right, Sonia,' he said.

'Do you know him?' Sally asked suspiciously.

She nodded. 'I read the leaves for Mitch and his partner a couple of weeks ago.'

'Damn,' said Sally. 'He's a good looker. I thought he was checking you out.'

'Why damn, Sal?' Sonia's voice was surprisingly calm, considering how cross she was beginning to feel. 'Do you feel the need to hook me up with someone now that you're in lurve?'

Sally bristled, but Rosie put her hands up. 'Come on you pair, no fighting. You're grownups now.'

Sally touched Sonia's hand lightly. 'Sorry. I just want to see you as happy as I am.'

'I am happy.' Sonia picked up the teapot and poured Rosie's tea. 'What makes you think I need a man to be happy?' She turned to pour Sally's tea. 'Oh my God, Sal. Look.'

Sally put her hand over her mouth as she looked at her saucer. Two teaspoons were sitting together on the saucer.

'Twins!' Sonia and Rosie said in unison.

'Don't get carried away. Wait till you read the leaves.'

Sonia took a deep breath and closed her eyes to relax and gather her thoughts as Rosie took the teapot from her and poured the boiling hot tea into Sonia's teacup. 'You can read your leaves today too,' Rosie said.

Sonia's eyes flew open. 'Maybe.'

Rosie nodded. 'Not maybe. Yes.'

The girls chatted as they sipped at their tea and the conversation was happy. Rosie sent Theo and Lily over to the small outdoor chess set, and they all smiled as the children began to climb the pieces. Sally was the first to finish her drink and she swirled the tea leaves around three times in a clockwise direction before unending the cup in the saucer and letting the small amount of liquid drain out.

Her face broke into a smile and she quickly passed her cup to Sonia. 'Tell me later. Here's Sol.'

'Do you still want me to do the reading?'

'Yes, please.'

'Once she finishes hugging and kissing him, Sol might take the kids for a short walk.' Rosie said with an indulgent smile. 'It warms my heart to see Sally so happy.'

'It's been a long time coming,' Sonia said.

'It has,' Rosie replied. 'And what about you?'

'Me?' Sonia laughed loudly and her eyes widened as she saw the man walking along next to Sol. She bit back the groan that was forming in her chest. The fun had just left the day.

Oh no! What's he doing here?

'I've already found my happy place. You know that,' she said looking back into her sister's teacup.

Rosie raised her eyebrows. 'Do I?' Her look was way too shrewd for Sonia's liking.

But now Sonia stared at the man who stepped to the side of the path and waited as Sally threw her arms around Sol.

Bloody Dave Walker. She didn't think she'd ever see him again.

She looked at the cups on the table and then back to him before tapping her finger against her lips.

Payback time, she thought, smiling widely as she stood up and spread her arms in welcome.

Chapter 3

Dave Walker was in a difficult place. So difficult, he was thinking about pulling the pin on his whole career, his fashion business, and starting over again.

A totally new career, in another direction.

Problem was he didn't know how to do anything else. And he didn't want to do anything else. About the only thing he could do was resurrect the orange orchard at Peat's Ridge that he'd inherited, but the thought of being outdoors and working with dirt and tractors and trees sent a shudder down his spine. There was no comparison to the feel of a silky piece of fabric flowing through his fingers as he thought of a garment to create. Or the moment when the visual came into his head and he sketched it and it became real.

The call from the police on Christmas Eve had rocked his world. His finances were now non-existent, the upcoming show in Japan had been cancelled and it looked like he was stuck on the farm for a while.

As he walked toward the table in the outdoor café at Bondi Beach with his best mate, Sol Brown, loud raucous laughter from that clairvoyant sister with the dreadful dress sense filled the air. For a moment he was sorry he'd agreed to come to breakfast with Sol before he went to town.

He would have been happier wallowing in his own misery.

And the problem was, Sol didn't see a change of career as a problem, because he'd changed direction so many times himself since he and Dave had left high school. Although it did appear he was now about to settle in his veterinary practice, up at Peat's Ridge, near Dave's farm. Dave had offered Sol the farm to rent—hell, he'd house-sat for him so many times as Dave travelled the world with his business, Sol had probably spent more time there over the past few years than Dave had.

And if Sol and Sally moved in there, Otis could stay; Sol was happy to look after him, despite the fact that the dog had totalled Sally's car last month. The thought of giving Otis away had been one of the "plus" reasons to go back to the farm. If he stayed home Otis didn't have to go.

But due to things out of his control, Dave had to find a job. He was embarrassingly, stony broke.

Five minutes ago Sol had even suggested they buy the fish and chip shop that was for sale near the beach house on the hill above Bondi Beach. 'I can be the silent partner, you can run the business, and I'll throw in the funds.'

Dave shuddered.

'No thanks, mate. Cooking in a confined space the size of that café would be worse than being on the tractor at the farm. I'd go stir-crazy. And I don't want another business loan. I've only just paid the other one off.'

'Well, you're going to have to come up with something. And fast,' Sol said.

'I know. You don't have to keep reminding me.'

The deal Dave had been about to sign in Japan supplying his label to a range of high-level boutiques in Tokyo had gone to shit. By the time he'd received the call that his assistant, Mitzi, had been doing the dirty on him, it had been too late. The contract dates hadn't been fulfilled, his trusted assistant had disappeared with the significant deposit that had been made at the beginning of contract negotiations, and his name was mud in the fashion world for not delivering the goods. Not only that, she'd helped herself to his working account when she'd left and cleaned that out too. And foolishly, because Dave had been so flat out, all of his funds had been in that one account.

If he could think of a way to redeem his good name, he

was willing to start again. If there was one thing, Dave was a hard worker, and he didn't care what it took to get his business up and running again. The problem was, it was so hard to escape the gossip and innuendo that was currently doing the rounds of the international fashion world, and, as far as he could see, no one was interested in looking at his new line.

'Sally!' Sol's face broke into a wide smile and Dave stood at the side of the path as Sol's fiancé flung her arms around Sol's neck and kissed him. Dave refrained from shaking his head, but he knew his expression was probably a bit cynical. Honesty, Sol had only left Sally a short time ago, before he'd met Dave at the car park.

Dave had driven down from the farm, agreeing to meet Sol for a quick breakfast, but if he'd known Sol was out with the crowd from the house on the hill, he probably would have gone straight to the city to his business meetings.

Especially that brassy, Amazonian sister he'd met at Christmas lunch.

The meetings were to come up with suggestions to dig him out of the hole that he'd found himself him—through no fault of his own. The financial hole, and the career future hole, were the two immediate problems that were currently staring back at him. He wasn't in the mood for socialising. Meeting with his financial adviser was filling his thoughts.

'Earth to David. Helloooo....'

Dave jumped and turned to face the woman who was standing in front of him, waggling her fingers in his face. Jesus, it wasn't his problems that were staring him in the face, it was a statuesque woman in a . . . in a . . .

My God, what is she wearing?

Again he regretted agreeing to meet Sol.

A walk along Bondi Beach had appealed, but if he'd known that the Carmen Miranda of the house on the hill was going to be at the cafe, he would have declined the invite. The woman had no sense of humour. Since he'd quipped about the bowl of fruit on Sonia's head on Christmas Day, she'd totally ignored him the couple of times he'd called in to see Sol. It hadn't been his fault that he'd thought she was in some sort of fancy dress for the kids' amusement. Any normal person would have thought the same.

And when he tried to talk to her about business over lunch, she'd treated him like a fool.

And now here she was greeting him like a long-lost friend. He narrowed his eyes as suspicion kicked in.

What did she want?

'Oh,' he said smoothly keeping his expression bland. 'Good morning, Sonia. How are you?' He looked past her to the table, but Rosie was busy with the children. It looked like there'd been some sort of spillage with a milkshake and Rosie was busy mopping up the table with a handful of paper napkins.

'Would you like to join us for a cup of tea?' Sonia's eyes were wide and innocent, but he sensed there was something behind the invitation. Trying to think of a reason to decline was unsuccessful, so Dave tried to inject some interest into his voice. He wasn't going to let on he was here for breakfast, even though the plate of pancakes on the table was enticing. If there was one thing Dave appreciated as much as fashion, it was his food.

'Sure. But I'll go for coffee instead of tea.'

She nodded and gestured to the chair beside her. 'Coffee's fine. I can do that too.'

'You can do it?' he asked with a frown as he sat down.

'Yeah. Tea, coffee, as long as there are leaves or grounds in the bottom of the cup.' Sonia called the waiter over. 'Mitch, a coffee, please. How do you take it?' she asked turning to Dave.

This was weird. After they'd left the dinner table on Christmas Day Sonia had barely exchanged more than one word with him, and from memory, that word had been "goodbye", and nothing more. Now she was chatting with him as though they were best friends.

Chapter 4

Sol and Sally were standing talking over on the path, Rosie was still busy with the kids, the waiter was blatantly checking him out, and Sonia was sitting there with a huge smile on her face. Dave felt like he'd entered some parallel universe.

'Just a short black, thanks,' he managed to say.

'Make sure there's some sludge, Mitch,' Sonia said.

Sludge?

Dave looked up at the waiter. 'Um, go easy on the sludge.'

The waiter shrugged at Sonia, shot a broad smile Dave's way, and then flicking the white linen napkin over his arm he headed to the kitchen.

'Hi, Dave.' Rosie's head appeared from beneath the level of the table on the other side, accompanied by an 'ouch, Mummy.'

'Hello, Rosie.'

'Sorry, children issues. I'll be ready in a couple of minutes. Sonia, do yours first.'

Dave frowned. 'Do what first?'

Sonia sat back and he blinked as the clashing purple and green stripes in the voluminous dress—if it could be called a dress— rippled.

It was more like a tent. Around her neck were three high rows of beads in lime green, yellow and red and they didn't match the large purple earrings hanging from her ears. Her unruly blonde curls were pulled up into a sort of topknot on one side of her head, and a red ribbon matching her lipstick was tied at the base in a floppy bow. She had the absolute worst dress sense of anyone he had ever met, and you didn't have to be in fashion to see how bad it was.

'Darling, my tea. But we'll wait till you've finished your coffee and do you first.' Sonia's voice didn't match her bizarre appearance at all. If Dave closed his eyes it had a low, sexy, husky tone that was quite appealing. Not that he was saying she wasn't attractive; she was just . . . just different. If he opened his eyes, all he could see was the overwhelming clashing of colours. Once you got past that, you could focus on the beautiful olive skin and the unusual tipped-up at-the-corner green cat's eyes. She had a really pretty mouth too.

Lush lips.

'Are you right there, David?'

Dave jumped as he lifted his eyes to Sonia's. For a brief moment, the smile left her face, and he knew he'd been caught checking her mouth out.

'Dave,' he said.

'You can go first, Dave.' She folded her arms and pointed to the cup as the waiter placed his coffee on the table. 'Drink it.' Now her voice wasn't quite so warm.

He wasn't in the mood for this. Gritting his teeth, Dave attempted to keep this voice polite. 'I'm sorry, Sonia. You've lost me. What am I going first at?'

Her laugh was a tinkle, but when she spoke there was a hint of steel beneath her words.

'I'm going to read your coffee. That's what I do. I'm not just a clairvoyant. You should have read my business plan.'

Unfortunately, just as she answered, Sol walked across to the table and he opened his big mouth.

'Great idea, Dave. Especially with the way things are for you at the moment. You could get all your answers here in one quick read from Sonia.'

Sonia put her hand on Dave's arm as he stared at Sol. Warmth fired in his nerve endings and the heat zinged up his arm. He looked down thinking that she'd hit him with something but only her fingers with the multi-coloured nails were on his wrist.

'Leave a small amount of liquid in the bottom of the cup,' she said. 'Then using your left hand, swirl the sludge three times that way.' She lifted her hand and gestured in a clockwise direction. 'Then put the cup in the saucer upside down and let the liquid drain away.'

He had her now. 'I don't have a saucer. He lifted the mug in his hand, but she came back quickly.

'Use this one,' she said as she passed a bread-and-butter plate across to him.

Hmm. For some reason, he did as she instructed—the coffee had been only lukewarm anyway, but it had given him a good buzz as he'd downed it quickly. He lifted the cup and twirled it around but before he could put it on the plate she took it from him.

Sol and Sally sat opposite him at the table, and four heads—including his—turned to Sonia as she looked down at the sludge of coffee in the cup. The only difference was that Sol, Sally and Rosie looked serious, and Dave was fighting the urge to laugh. Sonia lifted her eyes from the sludge and held his gaze intently.

Hocus pocus, mumbo jumbo. He'd seen so much of it when he was growing up. His mother, Pearl, had been a new-age hippy, and he could still remember his dad's words before Mum had left him Dave had been about fifteen. It was a miracle she'd stayed that long.

'A hotch-potch of beliefs and stupid trendy practices,' Dad had yelled the night Mum had set the kitchen curtains on fire with a burning candle as she'd meditated. 'When you get some sense into you and forget all this hocus pocus, woman, maybe you can have a go at being a proper farmer's wife.'

They'd moved out soon after the curtains had burned.

The house had survived.

No, it hadn't been pretty. But he and Mum had been happy enough as they'd lived in various bedsits with her alternate friends around the city, and there Dave had discovered his love for fabric and design. The biggest surprise had come when Dad had passed away and left the farm to him. Guilt had hit Dave hard; he hadn't seen his father since the day they'd left. The letter from the solicitor that had come out of the blue when he was at Fashion College had been a shock, but Mum had been pleased for him.

'It was never about you, darling,' she'd said when the will was read, waving her hand at him. 'It was my fault. I should never have married your poor father, but the thought of baking bread and sitting in a wooden rocking chair on a verandah watching the sunset appealed at the time. But look what we made together. A gorgeous boy!'

Maybe he'd inherited a bit of the drama queen stuff from his mother.

Dave sat back and returned Sonia's hard stare.

Chapter 5

The look on Dave's face was strange, and Sonia felt a bit mean that she'd been stringing him along. And then she thought of Christmas Day and the rude comment he'd made about her dress.

'All you need is a bowl of fruit on your head, and you'd be perfect!' he'd said.

But now when Sonia lifted her eyes from the coffee dregs and held Dave's, an unfamiliar feeling coursed through her. She thought carefully before she spoke. It was the most interesting read she'd ever done, and the most unexpected.

She'd thought she had Dave pegged. Pompous, full of himself, judgemental, and cynical, but the leaves—or the coffee dregs in his case—had taken a different turn.

'So?' The voice was still definitely cynical, but there was a glimmer of something in his eyes.

Something soft.

Something curious.

Something . . . nice. Maybe he wasn't as much of a non-believer as he was making out.

'Yes, hurry up, Son. Sol and I have to go soon.' Sally was obviously picking up on her vibes because she raised her eyebrows as she glanced at her.

That'd be right.

'Interesting. Very interesting.' She put the cup down gently and bit her lip, aware of Dave's eyes dropping to her mouth again. An unexpected heat ran through Sonia and she knew her cheeks were pink. She didn't like this feeling. It had been a stupid idea to get back at Dave for being rude to her on Christmas Day, and she regretted ever starting it.

'In what way?' he asked. His voice was soft, and it was as though they were alone at the table as she kept her gaze on his.

Oh dear! What to say? What to say? She went to bite her lip again and then remembered he was watching her closely. Instead, she ran her tongue over her lips and lifted her arm until her bangles jangled all the way to her elbow.

It broke the intense moment; Sonia sat back and straightened her shoulders. Dave watched and then he sat straight in his chair too. Rosie, Sol and Sally were watching every movement and not saying a word. The kids were playing happily over on the chess pieces.

'Well . . .' Sonia said.

'Yes?' Dave asked leaning forward, his dark brown eyes fixed on hers. It was funny, when she'd met him at Christmas, she hadn't thought much of his looks, but today, there was something different about him. Intensity, but intensity tinged with sadness or a preoccupation about something that was not quite right in his world. He still had the weird haircut, but hey, who was she to judge? Sonia knew all about hiding behind a crazy out-there look.

'Your anchor is obscured by an alligator.' She narrowed her eyes when Dave chuckled.

'Surely you mean a crocodile?' His eyes were dancing with mirth and she bit back the slow fire of temper that burned in her stomach.

'No, I meant an alligator.' She cleared her throat. 'Okay, let's forget the symbols. I'll just tell you what it means and then I can move on to Sally and Rosie's readings.'

Dave shrugged and the man she'd disliked on Christmas Day was back in full force.

Good, I can deal with that.

'Okay, in a nutshell. You've experienced treachery. You've been let down by someone you trusted. Right?'

Dave frowned and glanced at Sol, but Sol raised his hands palms up and shook his head. 'Your private business,

Dave. I've said nothing. Not my place, mate.'

Sonia stared down at the dregs and spoke slowly. 'You've made new friends, but you still have to be careful because the treachery isn't far away. I see one friendship coming that is very close but you'll fight it. But you need to embrace it because this will be your path back to what you desire most in life.'

She slumped back in the chair, exhausted by the emotion that had grabbed at her throat as she read the symbols. Never before had she had such an intense reading. Or such a physical response. Her heart was beating hard, and her face was burning.

If Dave came back with a sarcastic response, she'd be disappointed. She honestly wouldn't have the energy to retort; it was the strangest thing that had ever happened to her.

Sally caught her eye across the table and nodded in support. Sonia took a deep breath as she waited for him to reply.

'Thank you.' His voice was calm. 'That was very . . . um . . . shall I say . . . yes, interesting.'

Sonia nodded, unable to meet his eye. There was some strange energy spinning around them. His aura was glowing so brightly, she had to look away. It was hot pink, and she shook her head.

No, not going there. No way.

Enticing and vivid, his sexual aura just about jumped out and literally grabbed her by the throat.

The restaurant was full of chatting voices, the seagulls were squawking outside, and the waves were crashing onto the rocks. Theo and Lily were squealing, but it was as though she was in a world of her own.

Locked into a world with Dave Walker.

'Um, my pleasure,' she managed to get out without looking at him.

She swallowed, focused on Sally, who was holding her teacup out to her and turned away from Dave who was sitting quietly on her right.

Trying to make her voice brisk, she leaned over and held out her hand for Sally's teacup. With a casual glance back at Dave, she added. 'Oh, and just watch out for a temptation that seems too good to be true. An offer that's not really what it seems.

His eyes narrowed as he looked at her. 'You're covering all bases pretty much then.'

Her temper fired and this time she welcomed the surge of feeling. 'I don't cover anything. I see what I see, and I say what I see. Honestly, Dave. I couldn't give two hoots about what you think about me. You're obviously not a believer.'
As she tilted Sally's cup and looked at the leaves, she flicked him a dismissive glance. 'Your loss, your problem.'

Dave folded his arms and the table was quiet as Sonia examined the leaves in Sally's cup.

##

Half an hour later, Sonia was shattered. Tiredness tugged at her limbs, and she took a deep breath, widening her eyes as she fought eyelids that wanted to close. She'd been reading tea leaves in the house on the hill for five years, and had had all manner of clients, but never before had she had such a close and personal encounter with one person through a reading. Trying to keep up a confident persona in front of Dave, dealing with what the leaves had said about Rosie and Sally, and then finding the energy to take Lily and Theo for the bike ride she'd promised had Sonia digging deep for some more oomph.

Reading Rosie's leaves had left her unsettled. Change was coming and she knew it was going to affect her.

Reading Dave's coffee dregs . . . well she wasn't going back there.

She had started his reading as a joke so she knew she deserved everything she'd got in return.

Payback from the universe for being flippant.

As the others prepared to leave and began to say their goodbyes, she caught Mitch's eye. He came over and leaned down beside her and she was conscious of Dave watching. 'Want another coffee, sweets?'

'A double shot, large, please Mitch, to take away.'

'Sure, sweetie and this one's on the house. I can see how hard you've worked.' Mitch put his hand on her arm. 'Who's the good-looking man,' he whispered as he leaned closer. 'We haven't seen him here before.'

'He's Sol's friend,' Sonia whispered back.

'If only I was single. . .' Mitch fluttered his eyelashes at her.

Sonia laughed. 'You're naughty. Now go and make me that coffee so I can stagger through the rest of the day.'

As Mitch hurried off, she stood and smoothed her hands down the front of her caftan. 'You kiddos ready for a bike ride?'

Lily and Theo ran around the table to her. 'Yes, please!'

'Come on then, I have to go and get changed and then dig my bike out of the woodshed.' She grinned at the kids. 'Who wants to fight the spiders and the cobwebs?'

Chapter 6

Dave lingered on the walk above the beach after the others had left. The bank had called and postponed his eleven o'clock appointment. As he decided where to go next, he'd watched Sonia walk up the hill to the house with a child holding each of her hands.

Somehow, she'd found out about his business problems and he wanted to know how. If Sol had said he hadn't shared the information, then he was speaking the truth. Dave would trust Sol with his life. He might be a bit vague, but he was a good and loyal friend, and they'd been through some good and bad times together over the years.

So the first thing he needed to know was how she had known what had happened to him. He hadn't seen it in any of the papers yet, or online, so he was perplexed as to how Sonia how heard about his dramas.

Dave leaned back on the fence beneath the shade of a small tree. Perspiration ran down his neck and he ran a finger around the collar of his button-up shirt. He garnered a few looks; most of those walking by were in beach clothes and wet suits. The business crowd dressed in business clothes like his had downed their coffees quickly and run for the buses trundling down Campbell Street ready for their nine o'clock starts. For a few minutes, he sat there and let relaxation fill him. Sol and Sally had left, and Rosie had run across to the road when her husband had pulled up in a bright red Jeep. Now that he didn't have to rush to the city, he would enjoy the summer sunshine.

And talk to Sonia, the tea leaf reader.

Dave shook his head. He didn't know how to take her any more. On Christmas Day when Sol had invited him to the beach house for lunch, she'd been rude and aloof. Today, when she'd looked into that stupid cup, her whole manner had softened, and he'd found himself responding.

And in front of a crowd too.

Dave waited for half an hour and wondered if she'd changed her mind about the bike ride. He looked at his watch and considered whether to leave or grab another coffee. The coffee won out, but as he began to walk towards the café, a jangle of bike bells sounded behind him and he turned.

Three bikes were heading along the path to the south. The children were in front, on small push bikes and Sonia was bringing up the rear. He stood and stared as they approached him. She was wearing purple Lycra tights—the same colour as the earrings—and a huge loose over shirt in yet another myriad of stripes. The ensemble was completed by the hot pink Converse sneakers on her feet that were currently pushing the pedals hard and fast.

As they reached Dave he stepped to the side of the path. Sonia reached into the basket on the front of her bike and pulled out a small towel and wiped the perspiration that was already forming on her brow.

Dave frowned. 'A bit hot to be riding at this time of day, isn't it?'

'I promised the kids we'd ride to the playground.' Even though Sonia looked hot she wasn't out of breath.

'And then we're having an ice cream,' Lily said.

'And then we'll be ready for our swim,' the little boy added.

'I was hoping to have a word with you,' Dave asked.

Her expression closed as her eyes narrowed. 'About?'

Dave glanced at the kids. 'Probably not the right time now. Are you free for a coffee or a drink later this afternoon?' He wasn't sure what prompted his next words, but they came tumbling out. 'Maybe even dinner?'

This time the suspicion on her face was clear. Her lips pursed and her chin lifted. 'Why?'

He shrugged. 'Seemed like a good idea.'

She sat there high on the seat of her bicycle as her hand gripped the fence to keep her balance. 'I was under the impression that you didn't particularly like me—and the feeling was mutual—so why would you want to have dinner with me?'

Was mutual, she said.Ized Dave sensed a sort of victory. 'All the more reason to have dinner and discuss your capitulation,' he said.

'My what?' But there was a glint of amusement in her eyes.

'The feeling was mutual? From that, I thought you might have softened your harsh opinion of me.'

'That Carmen Miranda crack will take a lot of making up for,' she said, but a smile was beginning to tilt her lips.

Lily tugged at Sonia's arm. 'Who's Carmen Miranda, Sonia? Is she coming to our place? It's a pretty name.'

The smile that lit up Sonia's face as she leaned down to Lily's bike sent a shimmer of warmth through Dave's nerve endings. 'She was a lady who always wore a basket of fruit on her head. A famous movie star.'

'Can we go now?" Theo wasn't at all interested in the conversation about fruit baskets and movie stars.

'Yes, come on, Lily." She flicked a glance at Dave. 'I'll think about dinner. Call in this afternoon, but only if you're back this way.'

With that, she rode off, head held high, the two children pedalling furiously to keep up with her. Dave couldn't help the smile that stayed on his face until they'd rounded the next bend and were out of sight. He was thoughtful as he walked to the car park, and the prospect of the meetings ahead was tempered by the unusual interactions and feelings that the morning had brought.

##

Sonia blinked in the fierce brilliance of the January sun as they rode along the beach walk; the water beneath the cliffs was dazzling. By the time they reached the playground, she was reconsidering her decision not to appear on Bondi Beach in a swimming costume. The way she was feeling she could probably fling off the Lycra pants and the T-shirt and jump into the surf in her undies. Her pants were sticking to her legs and the T-shirt was plastered to her back. A ring of perspiration had almost glued the bike helmet to her head. Of course, the two kids were as fresh as daisies and after putting their little helmets carefully on their bikes they ran to the swings.

She stood on the dizzily high cliff staring down at the water. The sight of the ocean, the soft shushing sound of the waves as they rolled into the base of the cliff, and the fresh salty air all combined to soothe her. Since Christmas Day, Sonia's self-confidence had hit an all-time low, and a persistent feeling of misery and a horrid premonition that something was about to happen, wouldn't leave her.

'Come and push me, Aunty Son,' Lily yelled as she jumped onto the swing next to the climbing frame. Sonia drew a quick breath and went to call out, but Theo was already at the top. As she watched heart-in-mouth, he swung from the top bar and dragged himself along to the other side by his hands. He jumped down and ran over to the swings. Perspiration was still trickling down Sonia's back. If she'd known it was going to be this hot out here, she would have suggested something else.

'I'll come over in a minute, Lily.' Checking that the twins were both occupied in a safe activity, she pulled out her phone and scrolled through to Sally's number and sent a quick text.

Can u talk?

The response was instant.

'Yep. What's up?
Okay to call?

A thumbs-up emoticon confirmed Sally's availability, and Sonia pressed the call button.

'What's wrong, Son? Kids okay?' Sally sounded worried.

'Yep, all good. We're at the playground. Are you at the in-laws yet?'

'No, we're just about to pull up.'

'I just wanted to ask you about Dave.' Sonia stared past the playground equipment out across Bondi Beach. The heat shimmered over the flat silvery water and the heat haze tinted the sky with a muted glow. From here, she could see Aunt Aggie's house on the hill, the elegant old mansion stood out amongst all of the modern high-rise apartments.

'Dave? Ask what?' Sally asked.

'I just wanted to know a bit about him.'

Sally's voice was cautious. 'He went to school with Sol. They've been friends for years, and he inherited a farm up at Peat's Ridge. I stayed there when you were in Hawaii.' Sally's laugh tinkled over the phone. 'And he has a car-eating dog from hell called Otis.'

'Yeah, I know all that. But what's he like? Really like.'

'He's a nice guy. A bit intense sometimes, but a good person. I know that because Sol thinks the world of him.'

'Okay. Thanks.'

'Why are you asking this all of a sudden?' Sally asked. 'Did he upset you this morning after you read his leaves? You seemed a bit . . . um . . . preoccupied, for want of a better word.'

'No, no. I'm fine.' Sonia wasn't going to share with anyone how much Dave had actually ruffled her usual composure. 'Just curious. You have a good day, and don't let

Sol's mother lord it over you.' She knew how nervous Sally was going to her prospective mother-in-law's fancy mansion. She'd talked about nothing else since they'd been invited over earlier in the week. Sol's mother had been to a few yoga classes but going to the family home had daunted Sally.

'Okay. I'll see you when we get home. Enjoy the kidlets.'

Sonia chewed her lip as she put the phone back in the basket. Dave asking her out for dinner had thrown her. She hadn't been out on any sort of date for over two years; her confidence had been shattered by the last guy she'd gone home with. She'd always been self-conscious about her size, but his 'Whoa, big Mama,' remark when he'd unbuttoned her shirt had Sonia picking up her bag and walking out. Up until that comment, they'd been getting on well. They'd exchanged a few kisses in the pub, and she'd found him attractive. The stunned look when she'd headed for the door had soon turned to nastiness, and a few mutterings about "a tease" had rung in her ears for hours after she'd driven herself home.

From that day on, her image of herself deteriorated in an ever-increasing spiral. She'd always been big-boned, and tall, but playing hockey at high school had kept her toned and fit. These days she tried to walk and ride her bike, but time or the weather, or an appointment always got in the way.

She hadn't gained weight, she just felt huge.

Hiding her size as best she could behind her multi-coloured caftans, and creating a crazy, ditzy persona to hide behind might have hidden how she was really feeling from the rest of the world, including those closest to her, but she couldn't pull the wool over her own eyes.

She was big. She was unattractive, and if Dave Walker wanted to have dinner with her, he must have an ulterior motive.

But the memory of his leaves wouldn't go away, and

she worried that if she said no, he would take it personally. Despite the loud, sassy image she presented to the world, Sonia knew she had a soft heart, and she hated hurting anyone's feelings.

Just one screwed-up mess, she thought.

Sonia smoothed back her damp hair and walked over to the swings.

She'd decide about dinner later.

Chapter 7

By the time Dave had listened to his financial advisers, spoken to his agent and endured a grilling at the head branch of the bank, his confidence—what little there had been left—was in tatters. All he wanted to do was go back to the farm—and that alone was an indication of the state he was in—and crawl into bed and pull the blankets over his head.

The fact that Mitzi had caused the whole bloody schmozzle seemed to bypass everyone's attention.

He felt like saying, 'Hello, I'm the one who's been shafted here. How about a break here, guys?'

But no one was interested.

The bottom line was he had no money behind him to fund another show, his contracts had been wiped, and he had a warehouse full of designs that couldn't be sold unless he could have a show.

He was going round and round in circles.

If he sold the clothes, he could afford a show, but he couldn't have a show unless he sold them and got some cold hard cash to get it organised.

Venue, catering, publicity. It all cost, and at the moment, he didn't have a spare cent to his name. He'd maxed out his credit card getting back to Australia. The only avenue open to him was to take out a loan against the farm, but at the moment, the orange trees were not in any condition to bear good fruit, and the house needed a great deal of renovation love. There'd be a bit of rent coming in from Sol soon, but he felt bad taking that.

Maybe he could take out a loan against the land? Dave frowned as he stepped off the bus. He'd decided to leave his car at Bondi and take public transport into town.

It was bullshit. Two months ago he'd thought nothing

of paying two hundred dollars for a bottle of champagne. Now he was catching buses to save a few dollars. And he'd invited Sonia out for dinner.

Maybe a hamburger on the beach would suit her? She didn't look the sort to expect a fancy restaurant.

He walked along the street from the bus stop towards the beach. And why the hell had he invited her out anyway. He stopped by the car park and got a pair of board shorts and a T-shirt from the car. An hour in the surf might clear his head.

But before he did that, he had one more stop to make.

***

By the time they rode from the park back along the length of the path at Bondi Beach to the house on the hill on the north side of the beach, and stopped for ice cream on the way, Sonia was dripping with perspiration. Running her hand through her damp hair as they put the bikes in the shed, she came to a decision. She didn't care about what she looked like now, all she could think of was sinking into the cool ocean.

'Come on, kids. Grab your swimmers and beach towels. We're going for a swim.' She looked at Theo and shrugged. There was no one else to see the chocolate ice cream all over his chin; it would wash off in the water. 'Wait in the living room when you're ready, guys.'

'Yay.' The kids ran up the stairs with a whoop, both ignoring the loud banging coming from the attic on the top floor.

So Aggie was commenting, was she?

Lily and Theo were used to the old house and the quirky noises, and in the way of children, accepted the presence of Aunt Aggie. Aggie had been gone over five years now, but she still was a presence in the old house on the hill. It had taken Taj and Sol a little bit longer to feel at ease, and

Sonia wondered idly what Dave would say about it.

Sonia frowned. Why did I think that?

Last time she'd been up in the attic, she'd gone through the old trunks up there and spotted a swimming costume. Obviously one of Aggie's from the 1950s. She hurried upstairs wiping herself down with a hand towel she'd grabbed from the laundry as she walked up to the top floor.

When she opened the attic door the room was warm and Lily of the Valley perfume wafted out. Sonia couldn't help the smile that tugged at her lips.

'You were reminding me about the trunk, weren't you, Aggie?' She kneeled in front of the old trunk and opened the lid. 'Thank you.'

Carefully lifting the layers of tissue, she placed the dresses on top neatly on the old timber floor and dug deep into the recesses of the trunk.

A ha. There they were. A retro shop would love all this stuff, but she and the girls had decided while ever Aggie was around keeping them company, her things would stay. Her crystal hair brush set was still on her dressing table, and sometimes when the girls went into the room to vacuum and straighten the embroidered white linen bedspread, it had moved to the other side of the antique Queen Anne dressing table.

Sonia lifted out the swimming costume and nodded. White with little clusters of pink roses on it, the strapless, skirted swim dress would hide a multitude of sins while she got from the sand to the water.

She slipped off her bike pants and T-shirt, followed by her undies and bra, and stepped into the costume. It fitted perfectly.

Sonia walked across to the old cheval mirror in the corner of the attic and looked at herself critically. She twisted and looked over her shoulder. There were no bulges apparent, and there was still no sign of the dreaded cellulite on her thighs.

She went back to the trunk and went to place the dresses back in, but a tap on the floor made her look further.

Yes!

A gorgeous white—well maybe off-white now after all the years it had been in here—towelling wrap was sitting at the base of the trunk. She lifted it out and slipped it on over the costume. It was as though it had been made for her.

As she walked from the attic, she put her fingers to her lips. 'Thank you, Aunty Aggie. You are a sweetheart.'

A rush of cool air and a fresh waft of Lily of the Valley surrounded her and the door closed with a bang before she could close it.

There was a smile on Sonia's face as she ran lightly down the stairs. For once she felt attractive. 'Are you ready, kidlets?' she called as she slipped her feet into the beach shoes that were by the front door.

Theo and Lily came out of the living room, clutching towels, boogie boards and a bucket and spade each.

Theo screwed up his nose. 'Why have you got your dressing gown on, Aunty Son?'

Sonia rolled her eyes. 'It's a beach robe and it belonged to Aunt Aggie.'

'Did she say you could wear it?' Lily whispered with wide eyes.

'She did.'

Sonia took their boogie boards and juggled them under her arms. She managed to hold the children's hands as they crossed the road to the path that led to the beach. Bondi Beach was always busy, but a brilliant day at the beginning of January had brought the crowds out in force. From up here on the hill, it looked like the sand was dotted with multicoloured ants scurrying in and out of the water. Dark heads bobbed in the gentle surf, and Sonia was pleased to see that the northern end of the beach barely had a wave. The quad bikes that the Bondi Beach Surf Rescue used were sitting idle next to the observation tower, but the jet skis were out behind the break ensuring that swimmers stayed safe.

'The water looks awesome.' Theo's footsteps quickened and he ran ahead once they were on the path. 'I hope Dad comes to the beach when they get home and brings his board. I can have a surf with him.'

Lily turned her nose up in a grimace. 'There's not enough waves. I'm going to have a swim and then build a sandcastle.'

They found a small patch of sand amongst other family groups not too far from the water. Sonia took a breath and tucked her hair into a bathing cap before undoing the tie on the robe as the two children ran to the water. 'Wait for me, you pair.'

She slipped the robe from her shoulders, dropped it onto the beach towel, put her head down and hurried to the water. No getting wet inch by inch for Sonia; she put her head down and plunged beneath the first small wave that approached. Surfacing, she looked over to the children; they were frolicking happily in the shallow pool created by the sandbar. The water was like cool silk as it caressed her skin, and she looked down to make sure that the swimming costume had survived getting wet.

All good. It hadn't stretched and was still covering her in all the right places. After standing in the waves for a few moments, she waded back to shore and floated in the shallow water with the twins as they tried to catch the tiny waves that made it over the sand bar. Eventually, they tired of it and headed back to the sand where they had left their buckets and spades.

Sonia looked around, there was no one looking. Only

one woman was standing at the water's edge watching a small child play in the water. Putting her head down, Sonia walked quickly through the shallow water to the sand.

'Excuse me?'

She ignored the voice the first time.

'Excuse me?' This time it was louder and she raised her head. The woman had walked across to where Sonia came out of the water. She flicked a longing glance to where her robe was waiting for her before she looked back at the woman.

'I'm sorry. Were you calling me?' Heat rushed up her neck as the woman nodded and pointed to her swimming costume.

'Yes. I just wanted to ask you where you bought your swim dress. It's divine.'

Sonia stood there feeling exposed as the woman looked at her costume intently.

Bare legs, bare thighs and her entire body on display for the whole world to see.

She cleared her throat as she removed the bathing cap and ran her fingers through her hair. 'Um . . . it's an original from the fifties that belonged to an aunt.' Technically Aggie wasn't her real aunt, but she didn't want to take the time to go into a longwinded explanation. All she wanted to do was cover up with the robe.

'Oh, it's absolutely gorgeous. You look stunning.'

Sonia's eyes widened and the heat crawled up to her face. She shook her head and gave a tight laugh. 'Me? I don't think so. But it is a nice suit.' Embarrassment overcame her and she nodded toward the children. 'Excuse me, I have to go and supervise.'

The woman smiled and turned away to look after her child as Sonia hurried up to where the children were. She slipped the beach robe on and her tension eased a little bit.

'Who's ready to build a sandcastle?'

Chapter 8

Dave knocked on the door of the beach house on the hill, but there was no answer. He waited for a few minutes and then crossed the busy road and stood at the top of the path that led down to the beach. Once he'd changed and visited the barber, he'd gone back to the car and left his business clothes there. Since he'd had his hair cut, and put his boardies on, he'd relaxed a little. There was no point worrying over something he couldn't fix. He'd forget about his problems for today—really, a change of career wouldn't be too bad—and he didn't care what the gossip mill said about him. He'd given the fashion design business his best shot, and what had happened was out of his control. He'd had a hard life lesson in trust. He'd loved his designer job; once he was back on his feet, maybe he'd build it up again.

But in the meantime, I have to find a job and somewhere to live.

He'd have to commute for a while until he got enough together for a rental bond and a month's rent in the city. He'd looked in a couple of real estate agency windows as he'd walked up to the beach house, but the rents here at Bondi were way beyond what he could afford.

Now.

A couple of months ago, he'd been cashed up enough to buy an apartment at the beach. He pushed back the anger that rose from his gut as he thought of Mitzi and what she'd taken. At least the police were taking it seriously, but they didn't hold much hope of finding her. A false name, a false address, and a false trail of references; he'd fallen for the scam.

Like several before him apparently.

When he'd called into the police station after they'd

called, the police sergeant had looked at him over the top of his glasses. 'So you gave this personal assistant authority to operate your business account?'

Dave had nodded. 'Yes. She'd organised a big fashion show in Japan for me, we were about to fulfil the orders the boutiques had placed after the previous show.'

The sergeant had looked at his trendy one-sided haircut and the purple spikes on the left side of his forehead.

'Hmm.'

Now he almost looked like a normal bloke. If he was going to get a job, Dave knew the purple trendy haircut had to go. The barber at Bondi had barely blinked as he'd cut out most of the purple and chopped the ponytail from the right side of Dave's head, before tidying up the leftovers.

The barber had stood back and observed the neat square cut short back and sides. 'You look like you've had a touch of magic silver white on one side, but it'll grow out in a week or two if you keep the shortcut.'

'Thanks.' Dave had broken his second last fifty dollar note to pay for the haircut and knew he had to find a job fast.

The breeze was refreshingly cool on his neck as he stood and looked down at the beach. A dozen or so young people leaned against the fence along the paths, music blaring from their phones. A game of volleyball was in full swing at the base of the concrete wall, but the majority of the crowd was in the water or lying on the sand. As his gaze scanned the edge of the water, a tall woman wearing a white swimming costume and a bathing cap came out of the water and stood next to another woman. Dave let his gaze linger.

Oh wow. She would be a perfect catwalk model. Tall and beautifully proportioned with legs that went forever. She reminded him of Megan Gale at the peak of her career.

Feminine with a womanly figure and curves in all the right places. As he watched the woman removed the bathing cap and shook her hair out and his eyes widened. A tangle of long blonde curls rippled down her back and Dave caught his breath.

It was Sonia. And she was drop-dead bloody gorgeous.

With a smile, Dave kicked off his shoes and headed across the sand to the edge of the water where they had set up camp. By the time he reached them, she'd put on a robe and was sitting on the sand beside the children.

'Hey, there. I found you all.'

Sonia looked up from the sandcastle that was under construction and the pink of her cheeks deepened into red, but her tone was casual. 'Oh hello, Dave. Did you finish your meetings?'

That low husky voice sent a ripple of something down his spine, settling low in his stomach.

'I did. Unfortunately, they didn't go my way.' He dropped to the sand and picked up the pink spade that was lying on the sand. 'Want a hand?'

'Yes, please,' Lily said.

Dave sat across from Sonia, and they both focused on digging the sand and piling it on top of the sandcastle.

'Can we go and get some shells for decoration, Aunty Son?' Lily asked.

'And a stick for the flag,' Theo chipped in.

Dave looked up as Sonia nodded. 'As long as you don't go out of my sight.'

'Aunty Son?' he asked once the children had scampered off. 'Not a real aunt?'

'No.' She shook her head. 'Rosie and I are like surrogate sisters. Taj calls the three of us Aunt Aggie's strays. She was a wonderful lady who fostered a lot of children over the years,' she explained. 'It was her house.' She gestured to the house up on the hill.

'You were a foster child?'

Sonia shook her head. 'No, Aggie took Rosie in when she was eight, and Sal and I were high school friends. After school when Aunty Aggie started to go downhill, we moved in to help with the costs. We've stayed. We had a great business going for a few years, the Divine Soul Sisters.'

Dave frowned. 'I thought Sol said the house was in Taj's family? Sol's always loved this place. We used to walk past it when we'd come to the beach and he'd almost drool with jealousy.' His hand brushed hers as they both dug at the same time, and he pulled his back.

'Lots of coincidences. Rosie and Taj met at Aunt Aggie's funeral—well not really, they'd met when they were kids when he'd visited— but they met for real at the funeral. She'd left the house to both of them on the condition that Taj moved in for three months. Aunt Aggie knew what she was doing; she was an old matchmaker.' She looked up and met his eyes pretty much for the first time since she'd read his leaves—or dregs or whatever—this morning. 'And look at them now. Married five years and gorgeous twins.' Her gaze dropped back to the sand almost instantly.

'And you and Sally stayed?'

'Yep, the three soul sisters became two. Sally does yoga, and I do the leaves and clairvoyant readings, as you know. When Taj is on the circuit, Rosie and the kids go with him, and they mainly live in Hawaii when they're not here. I visited them late last year. They have a gorgeous house on a couple of acres near the beach. Much quieter than this.' She lifted the spade and gestured to the traffic and the crowd around them. A clod of wet sand flew off and landed in the middle of his forehead.

'Oops, sorry.' Her smile was wide, and he got the impression she wasn't really sorry.

'You don't like me very much, do you, Sonia?'

Her face reddened even more, and she looked away with a lift of one shoulder. 'I barely know you.'

'I'm sorry I made that crack about the fruit basket for your head on Christmas Day. I wasn't in a good place and you wore my temper. Besides we've already had this conversation earlier and I believe it ended with me inviting you out for dinner?'

She bit her lip before looking around for the children.

'They're okay. I can see them over there at the base of the rocks.' Dave persisted. 'So dinner?'

'I guess I could.'

Dave swallowed as embarrassment kicked in. 'I was thinking something casual. Maybe a stroll along the beach walk first, and then fish and chips on the grass? Or we could go to the pub down on the corner?'

She nodded and kept digging. 'A walk and fish and chips sounds good.'

'Okay, it's a date. I'm meeting Sol for a bit of a chat when they get back, so I'll be around. So whenever you're ready.'

'I—'

He wasn't sure what she'd been going to say because the kids came back with their booty and the next half hour was spent decorating the sandcastle.

Finally, when it was done, Sonia sat back on her heels and seemed to relax for the first time.

'Absolutely super-duper special, guys. How about a photo?' She reached down to her beach bag and pulled out her phone.

'Pass it here, and you sit with Lily and Theo and I'll take it,' Dave said.

'Oh, no way.' She shook her head and clicked the photo as the kids posed behind the castle.

'Why not?'

She lifted her chin and stared at him. 'I don't do photos, especially . . .'

'Especially?'

'Nothing.'

Dave stood as Sonia got to her feet. She held the camera in one hand and pulled the old-fashioned beach robe around herself with the other. He sniffed as a strange aroma wafted around them.

'What's that smell?

'Probably mothballs.' Her whole face lit up when she smiled, and he couldn't take his eyes from her face. 'This was Aunt Aggie's beach robe. It's probably been a very long time since it was last on Bondi Beach.'

'And the fabulous swimsuit? Was that hers too? I thought it looked vintage.'

The smile disappeared instantly. 'When did you see the swimsuit?'

'When you came out of the water, I spotted you. When you were talking to your friend.'

'Oh.' Instantly her voice was cold.

'I was thinking what a great model you'd make before I even realised it was you.'

This time her eyes were as cold as her voice. 'No need to lay it on thick, Dave. I've already said yes to dinner.'

He raised his hands, sensing something deeper behind her words. For someone who came across with such confidence and sass, he was beginning to wonder.

Sonia gathered up her bag and the towels, and Dave bent down to pick up his shoes.

'Kids, you get the bucket and spades, and I'll bring the boards.'

'I'll get them.' Dave bent down and picked up the two boards. 'I'm coming back to the house anyway.'

She nodded and they set off across the sand. Dave

walked beside her because he didn't want Sonia to think he was checking her out. Her reaction to his comment had been strange.

He shrugged. He'd be extra nice to her at dinner until he got to the bottom of it.

Chapter 9

'What are you doing?' Sally poked her head around the door of Sonia's room, her eyes wide.

Just about every item of clothing that Sonia owned was on the bed, over the back of the dressing table chair, on the window seat, and over the top of the wardrobe door. Sonia was sitting on the floor in the middle of a pile of shoes and she looked up at her twin.

'Help,' she squeaked.

Sally came in and shut the door behind her.

'What's wrong? It looks like you're packing to go away again.'

Sonia shook her head mutely. 'I have a date.'

The smile that crossed Sally's face was almost evil. 'I heard.'

Sonia's head flew up and she frowned. 'What did you hear?'

'I heard Dave telling Sol that he was taking you out, and how hot you looked in your swimmers down at the beach. He didn't know I was in the kitchen when they were walking in. You've sure made an impression on him.' Sally put her head to the side. 'I didn't think you were taking the kids for a swim, and what swimmers was he talking about anyway?'

'We got hot on the bike ride, and I found a pair of Aggie's swimmers up in the attic. She told me about them.' Sonia smiled. 'Well, at least she was banging about as she does when she wants to get our attention and I thought of them.'

Sally pushed the pile of clothes aside and flopped on the bed. She leaned against the headboard. 'So what do you think of Dave? He's different to your usual type. You do know, he's not gay, don't you?'

Sonia burred up. 'My usual type? What's that? And yes, I knew that. When Mitch was checking him out I picked up the vibes. He's straight.'

Sally waved a dismissive hand. 'You know what I mean. Your usual. The ones who pose no threat to your solitary lifestyle. Honestly, Son, I do worry about you.'

Sonia pushed herself to her feet.' And now you've found yourself a man, you're an expert on what I need.' She picked up her pink Converse sneakers—her favourites—and put them near the door.

'No. I worry about you. I worry about what's going to happen when—' Sally put her hand to her mouth. 'Forget I said that.'

'When what?' Sonia narrowed her eyes and walked over to the bed. 'What do you mean, what's going to happen?'

Sally sighed. 'Taj and Rosie want to talk to us all tonight after you get home. They're thinking about selling the house.'

Dismay rushed through Sonia, so strong it hurt. 'They can't do that! What about Aggie? We can't leave her here by herself.'

'I know. But it's an expensive place to run, and when they go back to Hawaii, and I move out to Peat's Ridge with Sol, it's going to leave you here by yourself. It's not fair on them financially, and it's not fair to expect you to look after the old place by yourself. That's what they went to see Mr Pepper about today.'

'Oh shit.' Sonia dropped her head in her hands. "I understand where they're coming from, but I hate the idea.' She flopped onto the bed next to her sister. 'I hate change, Sal.'

'I know. I knew you'd be upset.'

'I wish I could afford to buy the house.'

'Me too. But an old house like this right on Bondi Beach? It'll go for millions. It'll be snapped up by a developer and demolished. You watch a block of high-rise apartments go up.'

Tears ached in Sonia's throat. 'Sal, we can't leave Aggie here by herself.'

'Come on, sweetie, we have to be realistic. We've made up a lot of stuff about a few bangs and creaks because we hated the thought of letting Aunt Aggie go. It's time to move on.' Sally put her arm around her.

Sonia rested her head on her sister's shoulder and stifled a sob. 'I knew this was coming when I read Rosie's leaves this morning. I've just blocked it all day. It's been the strangest day.'

'And now it's going to end nicely with a dinner out for you with a nice guy. And he is a nice guy.' Sally got up off the bed and held her hand out. 'I've got a feeling about this. Come on, let's find you something spectacular to wear. I guess that's what all this is about?' She gestured to the clothes littering the room.

Sonia laughed. 'It is. What does one wear out to a fish and chip walk with a fashion designer? And I'm the one who gets the feelings, not you.'

'I can feel too. You didn't get all the psychic ability, you know. You forget we shared a womb. Now come on, let's go knock his socks off.'

Sonia pursed her lips. 'I don't know if I want to.' All she could think of was the pink sexual aura that had surrounded Dave this morning.

She knew she was in trouble.

***

The afternoon sun was low, and a soft silvery sheen hovered over the still water. The wind and swell had dropped, and the waves had all but disappeared; the ocean was like a calm lake.

'Just as well I didn't plan to surf tomorrow,' Taj said.

Dave was sitting on the front porch having a beer with Taj and Sol, looking out over Bondi Beach. They'd offered him a bed for the night to save driving back to Peat's Ridge after dinner. He'd called Uncle Mac at the local garage and organised for him to check on Otis and feed him. Sitting there with the guys had added to his relaxed state until Sol asked him how he'd gone today.

Dave shook his head. 'I had a shocker, mate. Unless the police come good with catching up with my PA, and all my money, I'm pretty well stuffed.'

'What a bastard.' Sol shook his head. 'All that hard work, all gone.'

Taj was following the conversation with interest. 'So there's nothing you can do?'

'Not unless we find Ms Mitzi Renaldo, or whatever her real name is. I'm not the only one she conned; that's my only hope. She's scammed a few big companies and the police said a couple of them are determined to get her. Pulling out all the stops and they've hired a private investigation firm. They asked me if I wanted to go in with them, but I had to say no. She cleaned me out. All my money and my reputation along with it.'

Taj looked at Dave and tapped a finger on the beer bottle. 'So you're looking for a job?'

'I am. I'll start with the papers and the agencies tomorrow.'

'You might not have to. I'll be back in a minute. Don't go anywhere.' Taj put his beer on the low brick wall and went inside. Sol looked at Dave, and Dave looked back at Sol and shrugged.

A minute later Taj came back and held up his hand for a high-five. 'Dave, the company that does my surf gear is looking for a designer for a new range. My mate said he'd be happy to interview you. I think you'd have a great chance. I'll put in a good word for you too.'

Dave almost gawked. 'Are you for real?'

Taj nodded.

'I'd be really keen.' A glimmer of hope fired in Dave. 'When can I meet him?'

'That's the hard part. You'd have to go to Honolulu.'

'Okay. Let me see what I can organise.'

'I'll give you Mark's card.' Taj dug into his wallet and passed Dave a glossy business card. 'Give him a call and let him know when you can get over there.'

'Thanks. Will do.'

Taj lifted his beer bottle and clinked it against Dave's. 'I hope it works out. Be an honour to have the famous Dave Walker designing our comp gear.'

Dave bit back the groan that threatened and forced a grin to his face.

A job right up his alley, and no chance of getting to the interview.

He didn't mention that because he didn't want Taj to think he wasn't keen.

Dave was keen.

 Super keen. He just had to find a way to pay for a return flight to Honolulu. He was deep in thought when the front door opened. Sonia stood in the doorway and looked around at the three guys.

'You all look settled for the night. 'If you want to stay in, Dave, don't worry about a walk and dinner. It's cool,' she said.

Before he could answer, Taj and Sol stood and headed for the door.

'All good, Sonia. We've got plans with the kids.' Taj said.

'We have plans too. Enjoy your night.' Sol actually winked at Dave on the way past him.

Dave turned to Sonia with a smile. 'I'm looking forward to it. It's a great night to eat outdoors.'

She lifted her chin and stared at him. 'Are you sure you want to go out?'

'Yeah. I am.' He stared back. 'You got cold feet?'

'Why would I have cold feet?'

He shrugged. 'You haven't seemed comfortable around me since this morning.'

'I'm fine.' She wriggled and hitched her skirt down a bit, and he lowered his gaze. A grin crossed Dave's face as he took in the hooped skirt that sat just below her knees at the front and was longer at the back. For once Sonia had shed the tent dress in all the primary colours. She'd teamed the white broderie-anglaise skirt with a loose pink T-shirt that had a big white heart on the front. Her pink Converse sneakers matched the pink of the shirt.

'You look . . . fabulous,' he said.

'Don't think I need a bowl of fruit?' Her mouth quirked in a little smile.

'A wedding veil would finish your outfit perfectly.' Dave shook his head. 'Have you ever thought about going into the fashion industry?'

She nodded. 'I did for a while. I went to design college in Ultimo before we started the Divine Soul Sisters. I was two years into my degree when I left.'

'You certainly have the knack. That certain je ne sais quoi.'

'That's high praise indeed from someone who's made the big time. Thank you.' Her cheeks flushed a pretty pink that matched the shoes and shirt.

Dave held out one arm. 'Ready to go for a stroll?'

Sonia hesitated for a moment and then slipped her arm

through his. 'Where to?

He tipped his head to the side. 'How about a bit of a progressive dinner and drink?'

Her laugh was as pretty as her skirt. 'Like a pub crawl?'

'Not exactly, but if that's what you want—'

She shook her head. 'Something quiet would be nice.'

Her arm stayed tucked into the crook of his elbow as they walked to the front gate. Dusk was falling quickly, and the sea held a deep purple hue. On the eastern horizon, the high clouds were picking up the last rays of the sun from the west and were bathed in soft golden light. The walk was filled with noisy young people as they headed out for a night at the beach pubs. The lazy chatter of the groups walking past them mixed with the crashing of the waves. A southerly buster had blown in mid-afternoon as they'd left the beach, and the swell was picking up quickly. A lone surfer hung behind the break waiting to pick up a wave. The other surfers, tanned and sun-bleached, were heading home along the sand, their boards under their arms.

'I'll miss this,' she said softly.

Dave turned to her with a frown 'Where are you going?'

Her answer was a shrug. 'I'm not supposed to know yet, but Taj and Rosie are selling the beach house.'

'That's a shame.'

'Life changes and we have to adjust.'

'Ain't that the truth?' Dave tried to keep the bitterness out of his voice.

Chapter 10

Dave was quiet as they strolled down the hill to the restaurant precinct opposite the beach, and Sonia tried to think of something to fill the awkward silence, but Dave spoke before she could make an inane comment about the weather.

'When you read my cup this morning . . .' he began.

'Yes?' she said cautiously.

'Do you really believe that, or do you just come out with a few stock lines?'

She pulled her arm out of his and stopped walking. 'Are you accusing me of being a fraud?'

'No. Not at all. My mother would have loved you. I've had a lot of alternative stuff in my life. I guess I've just got a bit more cynical lately.' He stood and they were almost eye to eye. He was a fraction taller than Sonia's just under six feet. Another thing she hated about the way she looked. Sally was petite and Sonia grew into the big gawky ugly sister in her early teens.

Twins? How many times had she heard the disbelief in people's voices when they heard that she and Sonia were twins? After a while, they stopped saying it, because Sonia got so upset by the looks and the disbelieving comments.

Dave crossed the path and rested his hands on the fence as he looked out over the ocean. 'I'm in a bit of a situation, and I've got to find a way out of it. Like you, I have to find somewhere to live.' He shook his head and looked down as Sonia's hands rested next to his. Her fingernails were long, and each was painted a different shade of pink. 'And I have to find a job. Soon.'

His voice was clipped and when she looked up at him his expression was set. 'How hard will that be? You're so well known. I'd already heard about you a couple of years ago. You set the fashion world on fire.' She laughed. 'I just couldn't afford to buy your label. But why do you need to find a job?'

'That treachery you mentioned today? You were spot on.'

Sonia's eyes widened as Dave outlined how he'd been fleeced by his assistant.

'So the bottom line is I've lost my contract and I've got a warehouse full of clothes that I can't afford to pay the rent on. And then to top it all off, Taj told me about an opportunity for a great job designing for his company, but I can't afford the airfare to go for the interview in Honolulu.'

Sonia thought back to his reading. 'But remember what else I said?'

'I do. Word for word.' A strange feeling gripped her as he held her gaze. 'The treachery hasn't left me. And I'm going to have a new friendship and that will help me get what I want.' He pushed away from the fence and started walking again and she caught up to him. 'All that sounds well and good, but I've lost my career and my last hope to keep any of my credibility was with the second big show that I had ready to go in Japan.'

'So what happens to the clothes that are in the warehouse? How would you normally sell them to stores? By having a show here?' Sonia put her arm through Dave's again and kept pace with him.

'Yep, that's how it works.'

'So what's stopping you from having a local show and getting your garments into Sydney stores? You've got a big name, Dave. That would set you on your feet again, surely?'

'Because I'm stony broke. I can't afford to hire a venue, I can't afford to pay the models, and I can't afford—'

'Oh for goodness sake, stop wallowing. If there's one

thing I've learned that no matter how bad you feel, you have to be positive. If you put across a negative persona, the world will believe it. So no matter how crappy or pissed off you feel, rise above it. Smile. Beam at the world.'

He stood still and looked at her without saying a word.

Her voice was a bit softer now and her cheeks were very pink. 'What if someone was to organise it for you and it didn't cost anything to put on?'

'That's not going to happen. Shows cost thousands to put on. And who would organise it for me anyway?'

'I could,' she said quietly. Ever since this morning, she knew that she had met Dave for a reason. And now she knew what it was. It didn't have anything to do with that sexual aura, thank God. She'd been put there to help him out.

The look on his face was comical. 'I don't mean to be rude but how—'

'Trust me,' she said simply.

He shook his head slowly. 'I'm sorry, Sonia. I can't. That's what got me into the situation I'm in. Misplaced trust.'

'Dave. I want to help. I have to help. That's what's brought us together.'

He screwed his face up. 'Are you for real? You think we've been brought together by some psychic force so you can help me organise a fashion show?'

'Yes. I do.' Sonia fought back the hurt that stuck in her throat. She lifted her chin and jutted her chin out stubbornly. 'So what have you got to lose? Nothing from what you told me, and everything to gain.'

He shook his head. 'Come on, let's go and find that fish and chip shop that Sol's been raving about.

'You don't want to listen to my idea?'

'No.' He shook his head mulishly. 'I don't want to listen to your idea.'

Sonia muttered under her breath as she strode ahead.

The hurt had been replaced by temper. Why did she bother? Sometimes it was easier to just be the big fat bimbo.

If she'd been a svelte-looking businesswoman in a sexy suit, he would have snapped up her offer to help. She would have had some credibility.

Well then, Dave Bloody Walker could take a flying leap. She didn't care what the leaves said.

For a moment, she considered turning around and marching back up the hill to the house, but she refused to give him the satisfaction of seeing that he'd upset her.

Beam at the world, she'd told him. Well, her eyes were on high beam and the smile on her face was about to blind him.

'Okay, McDuff. I'm starving. Lead me to the chips.'

Chapter 11

Dave felt bad at being so dismissive of Sonia's offer, but it hadn't seemed to bother her. Her smile was wide, and she hadn't stopped chatting the whole time they'd stood in the queue at the fish and chip shop. Or since they'd found a vacant square metre of grass above the beach. A couple of buskers were strumming guitars, and she finally stopped talking and listened to the music as they ate their takeaway meal.

Dave looked past Sonia to the busy street, and the nonstop traffic and blaring of horns reminded him of Tokyo.

How could he have been so stupid to let everything be taken from him? He turned back to Sonia. Her eyes were wide as she watched the two guitarists.

'So . . .' He was about to swallow his pride here. 'Were you serious before?'

Her eyes lit up, and this time her words seemed more genuine than the casual conversation they'd been having since he'd knocked back her offer.

'About organising the show?' Her expression was still wary though. 'Of course, I was. I have no doubt I can do it for you. All you'd have to do would be put together a list of boutiques and buyers to invite. I've still got heaps of contacts from the college. We've all stayed in touch.'

'And a venue?'

She shook her head. 'I've got some ideas, but I won't say until I check them out. So does this mean you might let me suss it for you?'

Despite his original doubt, Dave nodded. 'Do a bit of research, and when I can afford to pay you back, I will.'

She jumped to her feet and the hooped skirt swung perilously close to his head. 'I don't expect to be paid. It will be enough to see you out of your troubles. One day, you can pay me back when I need a favour.'

Dave wasn't used to such open generosity. Although he'd loved his job and had enjoyed every minute of the cut and thrust of the fashion business, it had been pretty much dog-eat-dog. Everyone was in it for their own benefit. He put his head down and rolled up the white paper that their dinner had been wrapped in. He pushed himself to his feet, and holding out his free hand, he said quietly. 'Thank you. I'm sorry I snapped so quickly before.'

Sonia slipped her hand into his; it was warm and soft and he tugged it until she was closer to him—or as close as that damned skirt would let her be. 'I think we need to celebrate with a drink. What do you think?'

'Sounds good. The local watering hole?' She nodded towards the pub on the corner.

'Maybe a quieter bar?'

'There's a secluded bar at the back of the arcade just off Campbell Street. Food's downstairs where the music is, but it's quiet and intimate upstairs.' Her face went pink again.

'Intimate sounds good.' Dave kept hold of her hand as they crossed the street.

***

Two hours and three drinks each later, Sonia put her hand to her mouth as Dave caught her in a wide yawn.

'I must be riveting company,' he joked. 'Time to head up the hill, I think. You've had a big day. Tea leaf readings, a bike ride, a swim, and a night out on the town.'

Sonia bumped his shoulder as he pulled her to her feet off the stool. 'You've been great company. That's the most fun I've had for ages.'

Once he'd agreed to let her investigate setting up a show, he'd relaxed and readily answered her questions. Sonia had learned a lot about his childhood on the farm and losing both his parents when he'd been in his late teens.

'Me too,' she said. But I had Sally . . . and Rosie.' She'd stared past him for a moment. 'And Aunt Aggie for a while.' As usual, she said too much and before too long, he knew most of her twenty-five-year history.

He held her hand as they strolled up the hill and contentment filled her. Just for one night, she felt good. She wasn't worried about what she looked like, or who was looking critically at her height or her size.

As they reached the gate, they could hear voices and laughter coming from inside the house. Dave pulled her back as he closed the gate behind them. The moon had just risen and a path of golden light stretched across the water. She opened her lips a little as he pulled her close and slipped his arms around her back. The hoop on her skirt pushed away at the back and he gathered her even closer.

Dave's voice was soft, and his warm breath puffed across her cheek. 'I'm leaving early in the morning, and I wanted to say thank you now.'

'Thank you?' Sonia tipped her head back and looked at him. 'For what?'

'For being such a kind and lovely person and letting me spend a most enjoyable evening with you.' His lips got closer to her mouth and she closed her eyes. 'Next time, I'll take you to a real restaurant and we'll drink real champagne.' His voice was low and husky, and his words vibrated against her lips as his mouth touched hers. A spark of mutual need passed between them and her heart pounded against his chest. She leaned against him for a moment and then lifted her head and smiled up at him as he lowered his mouth to hers again. Dave's lips were gentle, and she could feel herself blossoming beneath them. Even though her eyes were closed she could see the soft pink of his aura as he held her close. His energy surrounded her, cocooned her and warmed her.

She focused on her breathing and the feel of his skin beneath her hands. Without being aware of what she was doing, Sonia's hands crept beneath his shirt and her fingers caressed the smooth skin of his back. He deepened the kiss and she opened her lips to welcome him.

    Sonia felt beautiful and desirable . . . and wanted.

Chapter 12

The door opened and a beam of light bathed Sonia and Dave in its bright glow. Slowly they pulled apart, but her gaze remained locked on his. This wasn't the same man who had made wisecracks about her clothes, or the man who had been wallowing in self-pity, or the man who had originally knocked back her offer to help him. This was the man that she had fallen in love with after one kiss.

Sonia shook her head and stepped back, and her skin cooled where Dave's hands had held her close, as he let her go.

No. It couldn't happen. She wasn't going to open herself up for any more hurt.

'Hi, guys.' Taj ignored the fact that he'd opened the door to a couple in a hot clinch, although his grin was wide. 'Son, before you go up, Rosie and I wanted to have a quick word.'

'Go up?' she thought blankly before she nodded. 'Oh, yes, Sally told me you wanted a word. I'll be inside in a few minutes.'

The door closed behind him, and as she looked down, wondering if she had imagined that glorious feeling when Dave had held her, a fleeting shadow caught her eye

'Oh, quick,' she yelled. The moment along with the glorious feeling fled in a couple of tiny footsteps.

Dave looked at her, his expression as bemused as hers had been before Taj had opened the door.

'What?' he said as Sonia took off down the path to the gate. 'What's wrong?'

'Muggins,' she screeched as a car went flying past. Sally's cat had sneaked past Taj's foot when the front door was open. 'He got outside. He can't be out here. He's an inside cat.'

Dave hurried along behind her and another car zoomed along the road as the cat evaded them zigzagging across the small patch of lawn.

The little rag doll ran along the inside of the brick front fence, but all Sally could think of was the gap beneath the wrought iron gate, leading out to the busy road. Even though the house was at the end of a cul-de-sac, the traffic was busy as drivers used the short road to turn around and head back down past the beach. It was almost a part of the iconic tourist beach drive just like the beach walk they often used.

'Muggins!' She leaned down, stretched out and just caught the tip of his tail but he pranced away in the other direction.

Dave looked around at the small enclosed garden. 'You go and stand near the gate and I'll catch him when he heads to you.'

Sonia did as he asked and crouched down on the path. She looked at the gap under the gate. If she put her legs across the gap, it blocked the way out. Biting back a giggle, she watched as Muggins led Dave on a merry chase. To the left, to the right, back to the door, and then to the left again. Every time the kitten stopped, Dave lunged and finally with a triumphant cry, he flung himself to the ground in a tackle worthy of Jonathon Thurston. As his hands closed gently around the small kitten, Muggins turned around and sank his sharp little teeth into Dave's finger and he let go.

'Ouch that hurt, you little bugger.'

Sonia giggled again as the cat strolled up to her and nonchalantly settled into her lap and began purring. Dave lifted his head and pushed himself up on his arms and stared.

'He thinks he's in charge,' Sonia said with a shrug.

Dave slid over the small space and sat beside her with

his back against the brick wall. 'Obviously,' he said, sucking on his finger.

Sonia was quiet, not knowing how to act, and thankfully the door opened breaking the silence. Sally ran out and put her hand to her chest as she hurried up the path. 'You naughty little puss.' Sonia held the cat up and after Sally took him, she pushed herself to her feet and looked down at Dave.

'Thanks for dinner, Dave. It was fun.' She began to walk along the path to the door conscious of his eyes on her.

She knew she was being a coward, but she didn't know how to react. He was probably used to casual relationships and casual sex and had been expecting her to go upstairs with him. Sonia's experience lately was non-existent, along with her confidence.

Maybe she could—

No. She shook her head. She didn't know what to think.

'Sally, have you got a room ready for Dave?' That would make her intentions clear.

'Yes, up next to Aunt Aggie's suite.'

Sonia stood at the door. 'I'll see you in the morning and we'll talk more about the plan.'

Before he could answer, she fled inside and up the stairs to her room. She'd catch up with Taj tomorrow.

Why did every damn wall in the house look pink?

Or was the pink glow a product of two auras connecting?

Chapter 13

The sun was streaming through the two glass panels on each side of the front door as Sonia walked down the steps late the next morning. Muggins was lying in a pool of sunshine, looking innocent, but no doubt keeping an eye out for the door to open and provide an escape route to the world outside again. Low conversation filtered in from the kitchen at the back of the huge house, and Sonia strained to hear who was talking, but as soon as she started to listen all fell quiet apart from the clinking of cups and dishes.

She pushed the door open carefully and peeked around and expelled a sigh of relief—although a tiny bit of disappointment was mixed in there somewhere. Rosie and Sally were stacking the dishwasher and the kids were sitting up at the table eating cereal.

They all looked up as Sonia walked in.

'You slept late, Son,' Sally said nudging Rosie. 'Big night on the town?'

Sonia rolled her eyes. 'More like a big night chasing that cat of yours.' She looked around innocently. 'Where is everyone?'

'Everyone as in the cute Dave Walker?' Sally said.

Sonia folded her arms and leaned against the fridge, but she knew her cheeks were pink. 'No, just everyone,' she said airily.

'Taj has gone for a surf, he'll be back soon, and Sol walked to the car park with Dave,' Rosie replied as she closed the door of the dishwasher. 'You want some pancakes?'

Sonia shook her head. 'No. I'm not hungry, thanks.'

Sally and Rosie looked at each other and then high-fived right in front of Sonia.

'What's all that about?' she asked suspiciously.

'Not like you to be off your food,' Rosie said with a smile.

'I'm not off my food,' she said crossly. 'I'm just . . . just not hungry. We had a huge dinner of fish and chips. I'm still full.'

'Whatever.' Sally shrugged but she still had a bit of a smirk on her face.

'Anyway, I'll just grab a cuppa. I've got a lot to do today.' Sonia opened the fridge and took out the milk.

'Lots of appointments?' Sally asked. 'Mine have dropped right off.'

'I wish I did,' Sonia replied as she switched the kettle on. 'I've barely got anything booked for the next week. 'No. I'm helping Dave organise a fashion show. That's why I was hoping he was still here.' She crossed her fingers behind her back. She hadn't been hoping that at all. Sonia still didn't know how to react to him after that sweet kiss last night. She was dying to see him again, but at the same time, she didn't want to see him. 'I don't have his mobile number.'

'Sol's got it. And his landline at the farm.' Sally said as she passed a coffee mug to Sonia.

'When Taj gets back, we wanted to talk to you both together, seeing we didn't get a chance last night.' Rosie looked at the sisters.

'I'll be around all morning,' Sally said.

'Me too.' Sonia nodded. 'Just give me a yell. I'll be making some calls up in my room.'

Sonia took the coffee mug, and headed back to her room, scooping Muggins up in one hand on the way to the staircase.

She looked around at the beautiful cornices and ceiling roses. She was going to miss this old house. When she came down to talk to Taj and Rosie, she was going to try to convince them to let her stay until it was sold. Although she thought wryly, it was sure to be snapped up as soon as it hit the market. The beach house had been home to her and Sally for a long time now, and it was going to be hard to move on, especially to the sort of unit she'd be able to afford.

##

'That's the six, Sonia,'

'Thanks, Brigitte. I'll be in touch when I've got more details.' Sonia ended the call and entered the last of the details on her laptop. Dave should be pleased; she doubted if he'd realised the contacts she still had from the time she'd studied at Ultimo TAFE. The business skills she'd learned there—she grinned, including her business plan—had set her up in her current business.

Plus a wealth of contacts in the fashion industry.

If Sally and Rosie hadn't wanted to start up the Divine Soul Sisters, she probably would have finished the degree course there. It was a fabulous place to study and Brigitte had just told her it had been named the top fashion school in Australia.

Now with her connections, she had a venue, and six models and had already organised the hospitality school to do the catering as a work experience initiative.

She couldn't wait to tell Dave. Hopefully, it would be part of the solution to his problem. If he sold his stock and got enough money to get to the interview in Honolulu, he'd be set. All he needed then was for the police to catch the woman who'd taken all his money and helped blacken his name.

Although she wondered if he was worrying too much about that.

Brigitte had almost screamed when Sonia had said she was organising it for Dave Walker.

'The Dave Walker?' she'd asked.

'Um, the only one I know,' Sonia had replied.

'The one who's made it big in Japan?'

'I think he's one and the same.' Sonia remembered the kimono coat that Dave had worn to Christmas lunch.

'I'll bend over backwards to do whatever we can. And I'll get the college on board too. Sonia, you are a gem!'

As she closed her laptop, feeling pretty chuffed, there was a tap on the door, and Rosie poked her head around. 'Taj is back, and he's just having a shower. Meet in the kitchen in five?'

'I'm on my way down now.'

Rosie waited on the landing and they walked down together.

'I already know what you want to talk to me about,' Sonia admitted.

'Yeah, Sally said you'd both discussed it. Don't worry, Son we're not going to throw you out on the street. I won't go into any details; I'll let Taj tell you what's happening. I just feel bad.'

Sonia put her arm around Rosie's shoulder. 'No need to. We've had a pretty good run living in the old house.

Sally and Sol were in the kitchen when they walked in. Taj came in through the laundry door rubbing his long wet curls with a towel.

'Sol, can you text me Dave's numbers please.' Sonia walked behind Sally and pulled out a chair next to her twin.

Sol nodded and Sonia's phone pinged with an incoming message almost immediately.

'Thanks.' She nodded and pulled out her phone. A text would be better at this stage; she still wasn't very confident talking to Dave. And now that Brigitte had sung his praises so highly, she was feeling a little bit in awe of him too.

Sonia bit her lip as she stared at the text message box. What to say?

Finally just as Taj sat across from her, and Rosie

placed a pot of tea on the table, her fingers flew over the keys.

Great news. Fabulous response. No costs. All we need is a date.

As she pressed send Taj cleared his throat. 'The time has come.'

'To talk of many things,' Sally chimed in with a wide smile.

Sonia smiled at her sister. 'But not, of shoes — and ships — and sealing-wax —

Of cabbages — and kings —'

Taj frowned and looked at them with a peculiar expression. 'What?'

They both laughed and Rosie joined in. 'Don't worry, darling. It was an Aunt Aggie thing.'

'And one that was often said around this table,' Sally added.

'Okay.' He cleared his throat again. 'It's time that we have to sell the house. I'm sorry, girls, and I know what it means to you all—' he glanced at Rosie and she reached out and squeezed his hand— 'but for a few reasons, it has to go.'

Sonia leaned forward. 'You don't have to explain anything, Taj. The house belongs to you and Rosie, and it's yours to sell. Sally and I are just so grateful that we got to live here for such a long time.'

'And run our business from here too.'

'Phew.' Taj wiped his brow. 'We'll let you get settled before we put it on the market, so there's no rush.' He turned to Sol. 'When are you starting up at the vet practice at Peats Ridge?'

Sonia's hopes for a longer interim period fizzled when Sol replied. 'I got a call this morning. Sooner than I'd thought. Monday week.'

'But I'm going to stay for a month or so and wind up my business,' Sally added. 'If that's okay?'

'That's fine.' Taj looked very relieved and panic started to build in Sonia's chest. She had some savings put away, but not a huge amount.

'Son, if you want, there's room up at Peat's Ridge until you find something local.' Sally glanced up at Sol. 'We talked about that last night.'

'No, it's all good. That's a bit far away for me' Sonia hid her fears behind her usual out-there bravado. 'It's exciting. Finding somewhere new to live. I'm thinking about moving further north.'

Sally frowned. 'How far north?'

'Maybe Byron Bay. Maybe even to Brisbane or the Sunshine Coast.'

Rosie's eyes widened and her bottom lip trembled. 'You can't do that.'

Sonia folded her arms and Sally sent her a warning glance. 'Why not? You're going back to Hawaii. I'm going to find a nice little place with no clairvoyant in town and set myself up.' She smiled. 'Maybe even a little "tea shoppe" where I do the readings for the customers. You can all come and visit me. I'll become the local identity.'

Chapter 14

As Dave drove into the driveway and turned the engine off, his phone beeped with an incoming text. He climbed out, grabbed his bag from the back seat and headed for the house.

'Good boy.'

Otis was still in the large backyard and as far as he could see there was no collateral damage, nor any sign of hi-jinks with visiting wombats. The silver Weimaraner stood on his back legs, lifted his head and howled with delight when Dave headed for the gate.

'A very good boy.' Dave reached out and rubbed the soft silky fur before he unlatched the high gate. As he crossed the yard, his eyes widened.

'What the f—' He stood at the back porch and observed the post. Or more correctly the post that once held up the southern corner of the small roof. The bottom of the post was about a third of the size it had been two days ago. It was pitted and the teeth marks were very familiar.

'Jeez, Otis.' Dave sighed and shook his head and turned around, but Otis had slunk back to the gate with his tail between his legs.

Another thing to fix before Sol and Sally moved in. At least it wouldn't cost, there was enough timber and paint in the shed to renovate the whole house. His father—may he rest in peace—had obviously had good intentions.

'I suppose I can't be cross. I left you home alone, didn't I, mate?'

The dog bounded back and barked happily as Dave unlocked the back door. He put his bag on the kitchen table and pulled out the phone.

'You bloody beauty.' The grin on his face was wide as he read Sonia's message.

It had been hard leaving the house this morning, and

he'd hung around, had a second cup of coffee and waited for her to surface. By the time eight o'clock rolled around, he had no reason to stay any longer, so he'd left reluctantly.

Last night had been really interesting. The more time he spent in Sonia's company, the more she fascinated him. When she'd spoken of her childhood, and the death of her parents, his heart had gone out to her, and he'd wanted to reach over and hug her in the bar, but he'd held back.

When he'd finally kissed her outside the front door, it had rocked him to the core. He'd reeled from the feeling that had hit him right in the chest. Who knows what would have happened if Taj hadn't opened the door, and the damn kitten hadn't escaped?

Awesome news. Will call later, he texted back.

He crossed to the sink and filled the kettle. It was a shame that the timing was off. He had no time to start up a relationship now.

Not that he wanted to, of course.

Even if he had money behind him, he wasn't ready to settle down for a long time yet.

If ever.

And that reminded him. He needed to find a job. He pulled out his phone again and dialled.

It picked up almost immediately. 'You're home. That dog stay in okay?' Uncle Mac's voice boomed down the phone.

'Yeah. He was here.' Dave switched off the kettle as it boiled. 'I need a favour, Mac. You know of any jobs going up here?'

'Who for?'

'Ah, me. I just need something to tide me over until my . . . er . . . my next cheque arrives.'

Technically true.

'I could use you. Bloomin' Ted's gone on a bender

again and I could do with a second pair of hands in the workshop.'

'You're on.'

'No mechanical stuff, mind you. I know what you're like.' His laugh boomed out again. 'Unless it's a sewing machine, I know what you're like with motors.'

'So there's a job?'

'Yeah, keeping the workshop tidy, operating the hoist when I yell, answering the phone, pumping fuel, and doing some deliveries. Ya reckon you can handle that?'

'No problem. I can handle that.' Dave let the sewing machine comment go. He knew that his uncle thought he had a sissy job.

'And it's only till Ted gets his act together. Couple of weeks at most,' Mac said.

'You're on. See you in the morning bright and early.'

Excitement rushed through Dave as he pulled out the business card that Taj had given him. Knowing he had two weeks' work with Mac was enough for him to pre-book a flight to Honolulu. He'd call—he glanced down at the card—Mark— and check if two weeks away would suit for an interview.

'Whenever it suits you, buddy. Anytime in the next month suits me.' The conversation with Mark was brief and positive, and as soon as he disconnected, Dave went online and booked a flight for three weekends away.

Things were looking up.

He made himself a coffee and opened the front door and settled in the chair on the porch. He didn't need Otis distracting him right now. He saved Sonia as a new contact and pressed the call button.

'Hello?' The voice at the other end was tentative. A totally different person from the Sonia he'd first met a couple of weeks ago.

'Hi, it's Dave. Thanks for the text. You are one awesome organiser. Tell me all.' He settled back in the chair and put his feet up on the low wall of the porch. There was no breeze up here like there was down at the beach, and he still hadn't got around to adding an air conditioning unit to the house. No point when he was away so much.

'Well, have you thought about a date?'

'Yep. The sooner the better. How about just over two weeks away? Can you get the venue that soon?'

'Yes, it's free right through the holidays. TAFE has broken up till the end of January. So what day of the week is best?'

'Probably a Wednesday night. As soon as you check you can get it done then, I'll send you a spreadsheet with the buyers from the DDS and the—'

'DDS?' she interrupted. 'Where is that?'

'Sorry discount department stores. I'll send you them and about forty boutiques in the city.' He took a breath. 'Sonia, I can't begin to tell you what a favour you're doing for me.'

'Don't worry. It's going to fill in some time for me. It's pretty quiet here at the moment.'

'I'll pay you back somehow. There's only one problem. I've picked up a job up here for the next couple of weeks, so I won't be able to come down until next weekend. So any questions you'll have to ring me.'

'Okay. I've got your number now.' Her husky voice sent a shiver down his spine. He closed his eyes and conjured up an image of Sonia.

'And can you text me your email too? Just in case I need to send any big files. I've got six models, and the hospitality school are going to do the catering. For no cost.'

Dave shook his head. 'Like I said you are awesome.' There was silence at the other end and for a second, he wondered if he was being foolish in trusting the show to someone he barely knew.

Not a wise move on recent past history.

But he remembered the feel of Sonia's soft lips under his last night and the little soft moan that she'd let out just before Taj had opened the door.

'Sonia?' He lowered his voice. 'I really enjoyed last night. I was disappointed when I had to leave without seeing you this morning.'

Again silence and then she spoke so softly, he could barely hear her. 'I enjoyed myself too.'

'Maybe we can do it again next weekend.'

'Maybe.'

'Okay, I'd better let you go. Give me a call if there's anything you need, and I'll come down on Saturday. Have you got anything planned?'

'Not really.'

'Good, consider yourself busy.'

As he walked through the living room after he disconnected, he caught sight of himself in the mirror above the fireplace and was surprised by the goofy smile on his face.

Chapter 15

The first week he worked at the garage flew by, and Dave was pleased when Mac closed up on Friday afternoon. He caught the pay packet that his uncle threw his way and smiled when Mac said gruffly, 'You did okay. Maybe I'll keep you on instead of that useless Ted. Better for you too, than prancing round the world selling women's clothes. Your father would roll in his grave, I tell you.'

'No, but thanks, Mac. I appreciate the work. You've got me out of a tight spot, but I'm heading to Hawaii in a couple of weeks.'

'Oh la de da. Alright for some!'

'See you Monday.' Dave pocketed the pay packet, stretched and rubbed his back as he headed for his car. His muscles were sore from lugging heavy equipment all week. He smelled like petrol, and there was diesel ingrained in the skin of his hands. Not the sort of job he'd like for more than a couple of weeks. At least he had enough to pay for a one-way ticket to Honolulu now. With a bit of luck, he could stay at Taj and Rosie's place. If not, he could find a cheap backpackers' hostel. As he started the car, he thought of the change in his circumstances. In a way, he'd enjoyed the week. He'd talked to a lot of the old timers who often came into the garage for a yarn, and he'd rediscovered the beauty of a small community. The lights and lure of the big city fashion world had quickly receded into the past.

He shook his head and laughed.

God, what am I doing? Thinking about coming home and being a farmer?

He hadn't heard from Sonia all week, so he assumed that everything was going to plan, Dave was looking forward to seeing her tomorrow. He was thoughtful as he drove home.

He pulled out his phone and called Sol as soon as he turned into the drive.

'Hey, mate. I was wondering if I came down tonight if I could cadge a bed?'

'Sure. I'll check with Sally, but I can't see why not. It's just the two of us.'

Dave frowned. 'The two of you?'

'Yeah, Taj and Rosie and the kids flew home yesterday, and Sonia went to Byron Bay.'

'Oh.' All of a sudden Dave felt flat. 'When's Sonia coming home? Ah, I wanted to talk to her about the parade.'

'I'm not sure. Hang on.'

Dave waited for a few minutes until Sol came back. 'All good to stay. We might not be here when you get here. Sally said Sonia's coming home tonight and we're picking her up from Central Station at about eight.'

'Listen, I'll be coming through that way. To save you a run into town, I'm happy to pick Sonia up.'

'Great. Sounds like a plan. We'll have dinner ready for you when you get here. Thanks, mate. Look forward to catching up.'

***

As the train hit the outer suburbs of northern Sydney, Sonia relaxed. If she'd known how long the trip up to the north coast had been going to take, she doubted if she even would have set out. But in her usual way, she decided on a whim, booked a train ticket to Casino, and then caught the bus to Byron Bay. It had all stemmed from going over to Ultimo on Monday.

Now that she had Dave's go-ahead, and a date, the organisation of the event was flying.

'Give me the rest of this week,' Brigitte had said. 'Once I get the logistics sorted and the function locked in, you can start the invites early next week. A short lead time is good. Enough to garner interest—and trust me there will be huge interest. It's a long time since Dave Walker has had a show in his town.'

Sonia had frowned, wondering why Dave had thought his career was over. Or dead in the water, he'd said after a few drinks last Friday night.

But it had been time to think of her life ahead. A move, a change of scenery would do her good.

Restlessness had set her heading north. Checking out the work situation at Byron Bay had been depressing. Everywhere she'd turned; there had been wellness centres, psychic healing, clairvoyants and spiritual offerings of one sort or another.

It had taken all day Wednesday to get there, and then she'd spent Thursday wandering around and then travelled home on Friday. Half disillusioned, and half thoughtful.

Byron Bay hadn't been the right choice for moving her business, but she'd been meant to come there. The events of the day had shown her that.

The universe had been looking after her.

No one knew her up there so she'd ditched the tents, and worn jeans and a T-shirt up on the train and a loose cream cheesecloth dress as she'd wandered around town. A few times, she'd noticed people looking at her and commenting as she walked the main street.

As she stood outside a small alternative shop near the beach, enjoying the fragrance of the incense and the small bells of a wind chime tinkling in the breeze, the wind lifted her hair. She'd left it loose and the humidity had coiled her curls into a tangle to her waist.

As she stood staring at the surf, a pretty teenage girl had come up to her and spoke shyly.

'Excuse me?'

Sonia had turned with a smile. 'Yes?'

'Can I –I mean, may I—have your autograph?' The girl's cheeks blushed pink.

'Me?' Sonia looked around, embarrassed, and thinking she had been talking to someone else, but there was no one else nearby. Across the road a couple—obviously her parents— smiled as they watched the young girl.

'Yes.' The young girl dropped her gaze and her voice was soft.

'Why me?' Sonia was bemused.

'Aren't you the star of "House at the Beach?" It's my favourite show.'

Sonia laughed gently. 'Sorry, sweetie, it's not me, but you've made my day. Fancy thinking I was a TV star!'

'You should be,' the young girl said. 'You're beautiful.'

Sonia's mouth dropped open and she touched the girl's shoulder lightly. 'Thank you. You don't know what you've done for me. I'm going to have to watch that show now.'

'It's on Netflix. You could be Emily's double.' She smiled again as she turned to cross the road. 'Sorry I bothered you. Have a good holiday!'

The smile had stayed on Sonia's face for a few hours. After looking through the shops and buying a couple of dresses—her confidence buoyed by the mistaken identity conversation— she'd wandered into a café and ordered tea automatically. As she was sitting there, she noticed the sign pointing to a small curtained alcove.

Tea Leaf Reading: Book at the Counter.

When the waitress brought her tea over, she pointed to the sign. 'Do you know if there are any appointments today?'

'You're in luck, sweet. Willow was about to go home because her last appointment was cancelled. Are you interested? A hundred dollars for a half-hour reading.'

She nodded.

Why not!

Chapter 16

As the train chugged into Central Station, Sonia stood and straightened her dress. She'd fallen in love with the floral sprigged cheesecloth as soon as she'd seen it. It had reminded her of the pattern on Aunt Aggie's swim dress and had fitted her perfectly, although a little bit more fitted than she usually wore. Below the sweetheart neckline, the fabric clung to her breasts before falling into a gentle drop to her ankles. The air conditioning on the train was cool so she left her hair loose. Despite the long train trip home, she felt calm and had thought a lot about her future on the way home. The reading of her leaves had been worth every cent of the hundred dollars spent.

She'd been undercharging her clients, but maybe being a tourist destination made it okay. Then she chuckled at the direction of her thoughts.

You live at Bondi Beach, you goose. What was more of a tourist icon than that?

But it wasn't going to matter from now on. Sonia had come to a decision, and thanks to Willow, the tea leaf reader, she had big plans for her future.

The train eased to a stop, and she glanced at her phone before she picked up her bag.

Right on time.

The platform was crowded as the train disgorged its passengers, and she had to stand behind a large group of Asian tourists for a couple of minutes while they consulted their maps. Sally had said they would wait for her in Eddy Street near the coach terminal, so she set off in that direction.

'Sonia!'

She looked ahead, and a shaky rush of feeling warmed her chest as she spotted Dave walking towards her.

'Dave. Hello.' She frowned and looked past him. 'No Sally? Is everything okay?'

'Yes. All good.' He reached out and took her small bag. 'I was coming through town, so I offered to collect you. I'm staying at the beach house tonight.'

As soon as he mentioned the house, the memory of last Friday night rushed back in and her cheeks heated. But it was okay, here they were walking along together, acting naturally, and he hadn't greeted her with a kiss.

'Thank you. That was kind.'

He glanced at her and held out his arm, and she only hesitated a second before she slipped her hand through the crook of his elbow. 'So how's your week been?' he asked.

She nodded. 'Really, really good.'

'Sally said you're thinking about moving north once the house is sold.'

'I was, but I've got a better plan now. I had my tea leaves read.'

The look on Dave's face was sceptical. 'And that's enough to affect a big decision about where you're going to live?'

Sonia refused to be cross. She was feeling too calm and serene to let a comment like that upset her, but before she could reply he apologised. 'I'm sorry, that was rude. Closed-minded.'

'It's okay. I'm feeling good about my decision.'

His voice was low as he murmured a reply, and Sonia had to lean closer to hear what he said.

'You look good too.' He lifted his arm from hers and put it around her shoulders pulling her closer.

Sonia moved with him. His skin was warm against her bare arm.

'Drop-dead gorgeous actually. I love the dress and it matches the pink sneakers perfectly.'

'It was a good find.' She grinned up at him. 'Doesn't need a fruit basket?'

'You're never going to let me forget that comment, are you?'

'Nope.' She grinned back, but before she realised what he was going to do, Dave leaned over and dropped a quick kiss on her lips.

'Come out for dinner with me? To a real restaurant? We can't waste that dress on fish and chips.

'Why not? I have some news that needs celebrating.'

##

Sonia called Sally and told her that they would be late, while Dave rang his mate to see if they could get a table at short notice.

'For you my man, anytime!'

The saké bar and restaurant in Woollahra was busy, but Dave and Sonia were shown straight to a table. Dave waited at the table while Sonia headed off to the ladies' room.

'I've been on a train for ten hours, I need a wash.'

As she walked away, he let his eyes linger on her curves. The dress was stunning and he was pleased to see that her self-confidence seemed to have improved. He ordered two glasses of wine and waited for her to come back. He'd only have one drink, and then he could still drive them back to Bondi.

As Sonia sat down across from him, the light caught her hair. Golden curls fell over her shoulders, and his breath caught. He'd only spent a small amount of time with her, but he'd found her popping into his head at different times throughout the week, and he'd even dreamed about her one night.

He lifted his glass in a toast. 'So tell me what your news is?'

A sweet smile spread across her face, and he stared as

something hit him in the chest. Something warm and hard; something he didn't want to let go of.

'I'm going back to Ultimo. I'm going to finish the last year of my fashion degree.'

Chapter 17

By the time they parked the car in the car park at Bondi, and walked up the hill, Dave had his arm firmly around Sonia. They'd laughed over dinner, and he'd watched her face light up as she talked about her plans.

'And where will you live?' he asked as they approached the house. The night was cool; a southerly change had roared up the coast as they'd left the restaurant, and the temperature at the beach had dropped from the high thirties to the low twenties in a matter of minutes.

Sonia shivered as she answered, and Dave pulled her closer. 'Who knows? But something will happen. You have to trust.'

He shook his head. 'You are an amazing woman.'

Almost in an exact replay of last week, he pulled her close after he shut the gate.

'May I?' he asked quietly, tucking a stray curl behind her ear.

She didn't reply but she lifted her lips to his. They stood there, Sonia cocooned in his arms, as she opened her mouth beneath his. Heat rushed through him, and he closed his eyes as she ran her tongue lightly over his lips.

'You make me feel so good,' she whispered, slipping her hands beneath his shirt.

'You make me feel incredible,' he murmured against those soft lips. 'When I'm with you, all my worries disappear, and you make me realise I don't need anything else to feel good.'

The house was in darkness; Sol and Sally must have gone to bed early.

Sonia's voice was hesitant as she stepped back a little bit.

'Dave, can I ask you something that might sound silly?'

He nodded and held her beautiful eyes with his. He was lost.

'Do you want to come to my room?'

'Silly? I don't think that's one bit silly. I think it's an excellent idea.' The feeling of her fingers caressing his back was driving the need higher.

She brushed her lips against his. 'The silly bit is . . . um. . . can we leave the light turned off.'

'Sweetheart, whatever you want is fine by me.' He lifted his hands and held her hair away from her neck and lowered his lips to her throat.

'Maybe some candles and some massage oil,' she said and then sighed as his lips went lower.

Dave groaned when his tongue traced a path to the swell of her breast. As he caressed her skin with his lips, her fingers moved to the waistband of his jeans.

A car drove past, and the horn tooted. Dave lifted his head. 'Maybe we'd better go and light those candles.'

##

Sonia woke just before dawn. She rolled over and propped her head on her elbow. Dave was sleeping peacefully beside her, his broad chest rising gently with his breathing. The candle had burned down to the base and snuffed out, but there was enough light coming through the window facing east to let her watch him. His hair had grown a little in the last week, and the purple tips were almost gone. His face was composed, and the worry lines that she'd noticed had eased. She gently ran her fingers down the side of his face but quickly lifted them before he could stir. Her confidence might have come back, and it had come back in bucket loads as they'd pleasured each other for most of the night, but she still wasn't going to let anyone see her naked.

She didn't want to scare him off. Slipping quietly from the bed she picked up her pants and T-shirt from the chair near the window and headed for the bathroom up the hall. As she shut the bedroom door behind her, a series of bangs sounded from above.

'No, Aggie, I'm not going to stay in there. I'm going for a walk.'

Sonia shook her head with a sigh, remembering what Sally had said.

It wasn't Aggie. It was only the southerly wind lifting the roof tiles.

Chapter 18

The two couples headed down to the café at the beach for breakfast. It suited Sonia; she still wasn't sure of the protocols of the morning after. Sally, she could deal with—the raised eyebrows and the wide grin and the knowing nod—had brought a smile to Sonia's face.

Dave had been casual and relaxed and held her hand as they walked down the hill. He didn't even say anything about waking up alone in her bed.

Over breakfast, she told Sally and Sol of her plans to go back to college, and Dave sat there quietly with a satisfied look on his face.

Dave and Sonia lingered after the other couple left, heading into town to look at wedding rings, Sol said with a wide smile.

Dave sat back with a grin as she finished her tea. 'No readings today?'

'No need to. I think we're both sorted.' They'd discussed the upcoming show and he was happy with what had been organised so far. 'I'm going over to the TAFE on Monday, and then I'll start the invites.'

'And then we're set,' he said.

'You'll be set.' Sonia nodded. 'You'll have your reputation back, and then you'll get that fabulous job in Hawaii.' She bit her lip, the thought of Dave moving on made her feel sad, but she pushed the feeling away. Being with him was fun, and she was helping him out, and she'd make the most of that.

'The cool change didn't last long,' he commented as they watched a continuous line of cars dropping off beachgoers. 'Want to go for a swim?'

Heat rushed up into her face and she shook her head. 'Oh no. No. I'm fine.'

Dave's eyes narrowed and suspicion laced his voice. 'Sonia. It's a lovely day, and we have nothing else planned, so tell me exactly why you won't go for a swim.'

She lifted her chin. 'Because I don't want to.'

'Be honest with me.'

Sonia couldn't help it when her eyes swam with tears at his soft tone. He reached over and took her hand.

'Look, Sonia. You have to overcome this ridiculous inferiority complex you have. You are gorgeous. One very attractive, sexy woman.'

'Don't be silly I'm not. I'm huge and ungainly. I mightn't be overweight but I'm big.'

'You are tall, and in proportion, and you have a stunning body.' He lowered his voice and his eyes danced. 'Trust me, I know it very well.'

She couldn't help the smile that tugged at her lips. 'Thank you. And it was dark.'

Dave put on a fake leer. 'I snuck the light on when you were asleep.'

She widened her eyes and her mouth dropped open before she realised he was teasing her. 'You did not!'

'I didn't need to. I know how beautiful you are. In your tent dresses, in your bike clothes, in that gorgeous swimsuit, or lying naked next to me by candlelight.'

'Whoa, you go, girlfriend.'

Sonia swivelled her head around, horrified to see Mitch listening unashamedly to their conversation.

He crouched down between them. 'That's the best conversation I've overheard for a long time. Mate, I've been telling this gorgeous lady that for the last three years.' He wagged his finger at her. 'Now Sonia, go home, get your cossies and go for a swim with this equally gorgeous man you've found.'

Mitch winked at Dave as he stood and cleared the

table, and Sonia giggled. 'Mitch, you are incorrigible.'

'Sonia, you are beautiful,' Mitch called back as he walked away.

Half an hour later, when they were floating behind the break at North Bondi, and Dave's hands were in some naughty places, she felt even more beautiful.

Chapter 19
Two weeks later...the show

The call came at the beginning of the fashion parade. Sonia was behind the scenes and Dave was standing at the side of the stage when his mobile buzzed.

'Dave Walker,' he said brightly, one eye on the crowd that was building in the auditorium of the college. This idea of Sonia's was brilliant. He waved as he recognised the buyers from two of the top boutiques in the Pitt Street mall.

'Mr Walker, it's Detective Inspector Johnson. I've got some good news for you. We've got her.'

'Mitzi?'

'Yes, and she's confessed to everything. I suggest you get your lawyer involved because she's agreed to write a letter absolving you of any knowledge of the cancellations, and the failure to pay a deposit in Japan.'

'That is bloody brilliant!' Dave gave the detective his solicitor's number and said he would follow up with the detective later in the day.

The lights dimmed and he stepped to the side as the music began. Sonia had the idea of Robert Palmer's 'Simply Irresistible' to burst in at full volume as the first models hit the stage.

It was the beginning of a spectacular show. The models were amazing, for non-professionals, the lighting and the music were better than any shows he'd paid thousands to set up, and by the half-time interval when the champagne and canapés came out, he knew the show was a winner.

The compliments flowed and the two young women who Sonia had sitting at the back with order books were kept busy. He looked around after exchanging air kisses with the David Jones and Myers buyers, but there was no sign of

Sonia.

'Fabulous, darling.'

'What a unique idea to give the upcoming fashion people a demonstration of how a show is run using the college.'

He searched around but still couldn't find her. Sally and Sol were in the front row, but they shook their heads when he asked if they'd seen Sonia. 'Only at the very beginning, I saw her peek around the curtain, and she waved to us,' Sally said.

The music for the second half of the show started with a crash of guitar riffs and some of his more "out there" creations appeared. Dave sat on the spare seat at the end of the row, hugging the good news to his chest, eager to tell Sonia, and loving every minute of what she'd done for him.

Finally, it was time for the last set of clothes, and the emcee took the microphone again. He lifted a card and waited till the music stopped.

'I'm under strict instructions to read this word for word, but before I do I want to offer my congratulations to our brilliant designer. Dave Walker was a student at Ultimo and we love seeing his success. And buyers, what a brilliant venue for a show. What do you think, ladies and gentlemen?'

Dave lifted his hand in acknowledgment as applause filled the room.

The emcee continued. 'Our last category is swimwear, and we know how "out there" our Dave can be, but today, he's softened his line. What I have to say is from a lady he knows very well, I believe. She says: Thank you, Dave. You have opened my world and opened my heart, and given me confidence. Congratulations on a very special show. I hope you don't mind my addition.'

He frowned as the music started. Sonia had run it by him when she'd seen the swimwear line, and he'd agreed to her choice of music from the nineteen forties.

It worked like a charm. The crowd roared and applauded as each model strutted the stage—for beginners, their strutting was top-class.

The lights dimmed a little and he held his breath as the last model paused by the curtains. His eyes widened, and his heart pounded as nerves kicked in for the very first time. He'd designed a strapless one-piece suit with a boy-leg. A silk cape attached to the back of the swimsuit was designed to billow out behind the model.

Sonia stepped out into the light and the specially placed fans picked up the silk. It billowed behind her in a myriad of sea greens and aqua blues. She strode confidently down the catwalk one hand on her hip, the other holding the basket of fruit on her head. A sea-green turban hid all of her curls, and her beautiful strong features glowed as she smiled at him.

Dave couldn't help himself. He ran up the steps and by the time, Sonia had turned and was about to leave the stage, he reached over and took her arm.

'Can you do it one more time?'

She nodded. Her eyes were brilliant, and he could see in them what he hoped for.

Together they walked to the end of the catwalk. He put his other hand on her arm so that she stopped beside him. Tumultuous applause filled the room as he leaned over and kissed her, before gesturing to the emcee for the microphone.

He waited until the applause had died down. Keeping his voice even, he looked at Sonia, but couldn't help the love shining in his eyes.

'I'd like to introduce you to Sonia Smith, folks. Hold that name in your head, because I'm sure you'll hear a lot more of her when she starts her own label very soon.

'I owe this beautiful lady the world. She organised this

show, but more than that Sonia taught me how to trust again. She taught me how to laugh, and most importantly, she made me believe in love at first sight. Please show her your appreciation.'

The crowd went wild, as Sonia wound her arms around his neck and kissed him.

'I love you,' he said against her lips. 'And I love the fruit basket.'

Epilogue

Sonia wiped her eyes as Dave carried the last suitcase out to his car. He'd parked illegally at the end of the cul-de-sac because it was the only way they could get all her luggage to the car. Sally stood beside her, and she too lifted a tissue to her eyes as they stood at the gate. The real estate agent had done a fabulous job of the photography and the for sale sign in the front garden was so large it hid the front entry.

"I'm pleased we're not going to see everyone traipsing through,' Sally said. The first open house had been organised for the following weekend, when Sonia and Dave were in Hawaii, and Sol and Sally had moved to the farm at Peat's Ridge.

'Me too. 'Sonia dabbed at her eyes. 'Did you get on to that vintage shop to go through Aggie's trunks?'

Sally nodded. 'And Taj has organised for the furniture to go into storage later in the week.'

The sisters stood with their arms linked and stared at the old house. The sun was dazzling and the day was still. The sounds from Bondi Beach below faded as they both were lost in their memories.

'Rosie should be here too,' Sonia whispered.

'We'll all come back together and say good—' Sally looked up and broke with a gasp.

Sonia smiled. 'Just wind and creaks, you reckon, Sal?'

A tall graceful lady in a long purple dress stood on the narrow balcony at the top of the house on the hill. As they watched, she faded and shimmered and disappeared into the bright blue sky.

'Bye, Aunt Aggie,' they whispered together before they both turned to Sol and Dave.

Sol closed the boot and he stood with Sal, looking out

over the beach.

Dave held his arms open and Sonia stepped into them, resting her head on his shoulder as he held her close.

'Are you ready for the next step of our adventure?' he whispered. 'Who knows where we'll end up?'

'I am.' Sonia lifted her head and held his eyes. 'And as long as I'm with you, I'm happy.'

Ginny's story

Beach Dreams

Annie Seaton

Chapter One

Ginny Silver waited on the footpath outside the big house on the hill above Bondi Beach while her client took a call.

'Hello? No, I'm sorry, we're closed.' Sally Brown's voice held exasperation. She shook her head and rolled her eyes as Ginny stood quietly beside her, anxious to go inside the house and see the promised treasures. Sally had been late for their appointment and she mouthed another apology to Ginny before turning back to her phone.

The faded grey paint of the old mansion softened to a silvery hue in the dying sunlight of a perfect spring afternoon and a wave of nostalgia settled in Ginny's chest. The house was of a similar vintage to her grandparents' house on the ridge overlooking the paddocks in central western Queensland. She shut down that line of thought quickly; those happy days were long gone.

'Sonia is at the coffee shop opposite the beach doing readings, but she only works Mondays and Wednesdays. Yes, Bondi Beach.'

Ginny turned away and watched the surfers catching the waves on the point as Sally continued to answer her caller. She had high hopes for this visit; her shop desperately needed new stock. The last three "collections" in the deceased estates that she'd been invited to view had been disappointing; they had been more appropriate for the tip and had been barely suitable for St Vinnie's, let alone her upmarket vintage store.

Sally tapped her hand against her hip as she tried to wind up the call. 'I'm sorry I have to— no, the yoga classes aren't at the house anymore either. We're closed for good. The house has been sold. Thank you for your interest. Bye.'

Ginny turned back to her as Sally slipped the phone into her handbag.

'Sorry about that. And sorry I was late. My husband had a vet emergency with a horse up at Peats Ridge, and then the traffic on the motorway was awful.' Sally glanced at her watch. 'And I'm going to have to apologise again because I only have about ten minutes to show you around. My sister and I have an appointment with the solicitor about the sale of the house at five.'

'That's fine. I closed the shop early because I had another couple of houses to look at, so the wait didn't matter. You're my last appointment.' Ginny looked out over the water. 'And I was enjoying the view. It's such a beautiful afternoon.'

The afternoon light was fading to a pearly dusk and the slight westerly wind blew a fine mist of spray above the crest of the waves before they broke in a gentle arc of white foam. The last of the sunlight danced on the waves and Ginny smiled as serenity flooded through her. She could have stayed there watching the waves all afternoon. She took very little time to enjoy Sydney. Her time was spent in the shop or in her tiny apartment scouring the papers, and Gumtree and eBay online, for opportunities to buy stock. She let out a soft sigh; not that you should see someone's death as an opportunity.

'It's beautiful, isn't it? I do miss the sound of the ocean since we moved to the country. There's nothing like the sound of the waves to lull you to sleep at night.' Sally laughed as she opened the gate and led Ginny towards the front porch of the old house. 'At the moment, all I hear at Peats Ridge is the mooing of cows and the dogs barking!'

'That's a big change. Moving from Bondi to the country.' Ginny said but didn't mention that she had done the opposite; no one in Sydney knew of her outback background and she was happy to leave it that way. It was safer for her emotional well-being.

She shut down those thoughts as the too-familiar anxiety tugged at her chest. She swallowed and was pleased when Sally kept talking.

'Yes, it was a change. I've always been a city girl, and I've lived most of my life close to the beach.' Sally hoisted her handbag onto her shoulder.' My husband has just started a new vet practice up at Peat's Ridge. We've been so busy getting settled that I haven't had time to think to miss the beach or my yoga business yet.'

How wonderful would it be to live in a house overlooking the water? Ginny's tiny one-bedroom apartment looked over the footpath outside a Vietnamese bakery in Randwick; it was all Ginny had been able to afford when she'd moved to Sydney and she'd put what money she had left into setting up the shop.

One day, she promised herself. One day she'd move to a place near the water, and she'd take the time to smell the salt air. One day, when she made enough money to be independent and leave the past behind for good. Now all her energy and finances were going into her business. A glimmer of guilt ran through her; she really shouldn't have closed the shop early today. Who knew what sales she'd missed; every cent and every dollar counted towards her goal. Working in the shop alone was the most difficult part of running a business alone because it meant it was so hard to spare the time to visit properties and source the goods. Even though she preferred nights and weekends for visiting houses, most people wanted to meet during the day.

Every hour the shop was closed impacted her income. Hopefully, soon she'd be able to increase Jo's hours. Now, her part-time shop assistant came in two afternoons a week

'You've sold your house to move?' Ginny stared up at

the front of the elegant mansion and then followed Sally along the path to the front porch.

'Long story, but yes the house is on the market. And it looks like it's finally sold. That's what this afternoon's meeting is for.' Sally nodded as she put the key in the front door and wriggled it. 'But it's not my house. It's complicated. My friends, the owners, are in Hawaii and my sister and I are meeting the solicitor representing Rosie and Taj while the sale goes through.' Sally rubbed her hand over her very pregnant stomach.

'So, you think it has been sold?' Ginny asked as Sally pushed the door. 'If we are going to work together, I'd need to know the time frame for collecting anything suitable. That is if there is anything here that suits.'

'The house is almost sold, I think. It's been a long and difficult process.'

Ginny frowned. 'I thought a house in this location would have been snapped up?'

'Oh, yes. But none of us wanted to sell it. You know memories, nostalgia, family and all that?'

Ginny nodded even though she had no time for memories or nostalgia. Family, well, she wouldn't go there either.

'Rosie and Taj could have sold it a hundred times over, but one of their conditions of sale was that the house wouldn't be demolished to make way for a modern apartment block,' Sally said. 'So there'll be no new box of modern apartments on the hill. That was all the interest that was shown by the first buyers interested.'

Satisfaction filled Ginny. 'That's good to hear. It would be so sad to see a beautiful home like this demolished. Although I suppose it would be out of the price range for someone just looking for a family home.'

'Yes. It is a fabulous place to live and such a gorgeous

old house. They thought long and hard about keeping it because of'— Sally cleared her throat — 'because of Aunt Aggie, but when Sol and I moved, and then my sister and her partner moved out, it was easier for them to sell it. Taj, the owner, is a surfer on the pro circuit and he and Rosie and the kids are based in Hawaii. But they finally found someone who suited them. The purchaser is a builder who has agreed to develop apartments within the existing shell, so it was a bit of a compromise.' Sally looked up at the house. Her voice was quiet and her words held a tinge of sadness. 'It's so hard to see the house go. I worry about—' She broke off and shook her head. 'Come on, let's show you this Aladdin's Cave my sister tells me is upstairs. We need to get a move on. I've spent too much time yabbering on about the house and us, sorry. Is it okay with you if I show you the rooms where everything is, and then leave you to it?'

Ginny nodded. 'If you show me how to lock up, that's fine. It will be dark soon. Is the power still on?'

'Yes, it is. Stay as long as you need to. I'm just sorry that I can't show you everything.' Sally shook her head. 'Mind you, there's so much here, I haven't seen it all myself even though I lived in the house for a few years. Aggie was a hoarder, but I know it's all quality.'

The heavy door opened with a creak and Ginny followed Sally into a large foyer. A sweeping timber staircase curving to the floor above filled the space. Light filtered in through a large glass pane high above the front door. Dust motes danced in the late afternoon sunlight and the dark wood of the polished bannister shone with a warm glow. Ginny wrinkled her nose and inhaled with pleasure. The smell of beeswax mingled with the sweet fragrance of spring flowers and she looked around expecting to see a vase of freesias or jonquils in the foyer. She frowned as the fragrance disappeared; there was nothing there. No hallstand or table to hold a vase; in fact, there was no furniture at all.

And no flowers in sight. She sniffed again but the fragrance had gone.

'It's really sad to see the house like this.' Sally glanced across at Ginny and gestured towards the stairs. 'Downstairs has been emptied out. We all took some of the furniture, but most of it went to the second-hand shop. It was old, but not good enough for the antique dealers.'

Ginny frowned. Despite what Sally had said about the clothes being good quality that didn't bode well for what was upstairs; she hoped she hadn't wasted an afternoon. But the house was old, and Sally had assured her that there were wardrobes full of old clothes and shoes there. A niggle of excitement settled in her tummy. She never knew what she was going to discover in these old houses of a past Sydney.

The carpet runner in the centre of the stairs muffled their footsteps as they climbed to the first floor. Sally paused on a landing that led to a long wide hallway and at least half a dozen closed doors. The hallway was dark and quiet but as they stood there was a loud thud from the floor above.

'What was that?' Ginny asked looking up the stairs. 'Is there someone else here?'

Sally waved her hand dismissively and shook her head, but there was an evasive note in her voice. 'No, just the usual creaks and groans of an old house. We're used to them.' She set off up the next flight of stairs and then paused on the next landing. Inhaling deeply, she rubbed her stomach again. 'This baby is getting bigger by the day.'

'Take it easy. Just point me in the right direction and I'll be fine. When are you due?'

'Six weeks to go yet.' Sally reached over and opened the door to the right of the stairs. 'Most of the clothes are in the wardrobes on this floor. Behind the other door, there's a small flight of stairs up to the attic on the top floor—you don't need to go back to the main staircase— and Sonia told me there are bags and shoes, and lots of other bits and pieces up there. I've never been up there. I've got no idea if they'll be of interest to you, or if they're only good enough for the tip.'

'One way to find out,' Ginny replied. 'It sounds interesting from what you described to me so far. And if I find anything personal, or anything jewellery that looks valuable I'll refer it to you immediately.'

'Thank you. Apparently, Aunt Aggie was a bit of a socialite in her young days. We never knew the whole story but there was some family tragedy and she changed her lifestyle and fostered children for a long time. Rosie was her last foster child.'

Ginny smothered a grin. Sally was talking about the family again; it sounded as though they were very close. She glanced at her watch. 'It's almost five. Do you have far to go?'

'Oh heck, yes. Mr Pepper is over at Bondi Junction. But he's a dear old soul. He won't mind if I'm a teensy bit late. He loves Sonia, and they'll be chatting.' Sally hurried down the hall and opened the last door. 'Aunt Aggie lived on the middle floor for most of her life, but she stored all of her clothes up here. Take as long as you like. I'll leave you to it. I'll set the latch on the front door when I go and all you'll have to do is pull it shut behind you when you leave.'

Ginny's face heated and she turned to Sally. 'I feel silly asking, but would you mind locking the door while I'm up here?'

'No problem at all. Probably wise. You never know who's hanging around these days, and the last thing we need is squatters in the house. Oh, and turn the light out please when you leave. I'll give you a call to see what you think.'

Sally stood back and ushered Ginny into the room.

Ginny nodded, paying scant attention to the other woman. Her eyes widened, and her mouth dropped open as she looked around. 'Oh my God.'

Chapter Two

Greg Tindall pulled the tape from the pocket of his work shorts. As he crouched in front of the fence and put one hand against the bricks to steady himself, he admired the intricate herringbone pattern of the bricks along the top.

The fence would have to go. Even if he was keeping the façade of the house the same, the burnished colour of the bricks didn't match the colours he had in mind for the development.

A shame, he thought. The setting sun gave the bricks a deep reddish glow and the contrast with the silver blue of the water in the background was stunning.

Maybe I could work it in somehow? Maybe he could change the colour plan he had in mind.

Greg shook his head and secured the spring steel tape to the corner of the fence where it joined the modern Colorbond fence of the new apartment block next door. He was getting ahead of himself; if this measurement was less than he thought there would be no development, and no need to be worrying about colour plans.

He'd asked his solicitor to hold back on the final exchange of contracts that had been scheduled for this afternoon because he wanted to be sure there was enough room at the side of the house to access the new parking area that he would build behind the house. That was one of the things that the council had insisted upon before the DA could be approved. If his plan came to fruition, he should be able to get at least six, maybe seven apartments in the old house. Two on each level and hopefully a luxury penthouse on the top floor to take in the views. Greg grunted with satisfaction as he stretched the tape and walked to the other end of the fence.

Perfect. The access was wide enough. Once he'd called Johnno, he'd go up and look at the top floor; he wanted to take some measurements up there too. He pulled out his mobile and hit the speed dial for his solicitor.

'Greg. How did it go?'

He and Johnno had gone to school together, and although their careers—and their lives—had gone in very different directions, they had stayed good mates.

'She's a goer, mate. So we can go ahead with the paperwork. I'm happy to exchange and pay the ten percent deposit.'

'O…kay.'

Greg frowned. 'What do you mean with the "o…kay" tone? Don't tell me you're against this development too. Don't worry, it'll look the same as it does now.' Greg was very protective of this project; the thought of working on the beautiful house filled him with enthusiasm—and there hadn't been a lot of that lately.

'No. Nothing like that. I think it's a great idea.'

'So what's with the hesitation?'

'I know what you're like, mate. I know you've got a lot of work contracted for the next few months, and as well as not knowing what delegate means, you're trying to please two masters.'

Greg put the tape back in his pocket and dug for the key that the owners had allowed him to have for the past week. 'No need to worry. I can handle it. Dad's eased off me now. I'm my own boss these days.'

'You're a bloody workaholic. You need to ease back a bit. It's not as though you need the money. Honestly, mate, I worry about you. Life's too short to spend all your time working. I know what motivates you, but it's time you pulled back. It's time we had a drink or three . . . and a catch-up.

What do you think? This weekend?''

Greg stared at the water as he listened to Johnno. The sun had dropped below the horizon and the surfers were heading towards the beach.

How good would it be to be out there, riding the waves, with nothing to worry about? He hadn't had a surf for the past couple of summers. Greg knew the pressure he was under was his own doing. It was time to reconsider his workload. Years of trying to prove himself hadn't left much time for any social outings or leisure stuff. Johnno knew him too well, so he tried to reassure him.

'I told you I'm fine. This development is going to be a hit. And I might even take a holiday after it's done. A long one.'

Johnno's laugh spluttered down the phone. 'I'll take a bet on that. If you take a holiday, I'll—'

'You'll buy the first apartment. Kitty would love that.'

'I'm sure she would but we already have a very suitable apartment. I'll donate a thousand dollars to the charity of your choice if you take a holiday.'

Greg laughed. 'You're on, mate. And ditto if I don't.'

'See, you're already thinking about the next job.'

'Yep, but right now I've gotta go work. I'm not on office hours like you.'

'Okay, thanks for the call. I'll let the vendors' solicitor know you're happy to exchange. I've got another appointment before I can leave.

Greg glanced at his watch; it was heading for five-thirty. 'Overtime on a Friday, hey mate? I'm impressed.'

'I'll call you over the weekend. Kitty was talking barbeques this morning. Can I tempt you? I just took delivery of some good reds. Tomorrow night about six?'

'Sounds like a plan. See ya.'

'Whoa, hang on. Anyone you want to bring, feel free.'

'Jeez, don't you start. It's enough that I have to put up with my mother.' Greg injected lightness into his voice to soften his words.

'Okay, I won't nag. See you tomorrow.'

'Look forward to it. Now, I'm going to go work.' Greg disconnected the call and put the phone in the pocket of his work shirt. He opened the gate and looked up at the house that towered over him and a frown creased his brow.

Bloody hell.

There was a damn light on at the top of the house. As he watched a shadow passed across the window.

He shrugged. Maybe the light had been left on to make it look as though someone was there. But the memory of squatters and the difficulty of getting them offsite on one of his developments last year had him walking up the path and trying the front door.

Bloody squatters. He strode up the path and dug into his pocket for the house keys that the vendor's solicitor had passed on to his solicitor. Once he'd agreed –to most—of their conditions, they'd been very accommodating in letting him have access to the house.

As he went to put the key in the lock, the door pushed open beneath his hand. The loud creak of the hinges echoed through the cavernous foyer and a whoosh of cold air sent a shiver down his back. Greg put the keys back into his pocket and frowned as he headed for the stairs. He sat on the bottom step and quietly removed his work boots. The last thing he wanted to do was warn them he was coming up. He'd been on every floor and in every room of the old mansion over the past couple of weeks, and there were heaps of cupboards and nooks and crannies that could hide a horde of house squatters. He knew what would happen; once they got into a vacant building it was hell's own trouble to get them out. The last time he'd had squatters in one of his buildings at Cremorne, it had been a long and drawn-out process to move them on and had put the building of the new apartment block back by over six months. He put his boots to the side of the steps in the dark corridor leading to the back of the house and counted the steps as he started up the stairs. There was a creaky step on the left, halfway up the first flight, so he stayed on the right-hand side. Pausing on the middle landing Greg put his head to the side and listened, but all was quiet. Setting off again, he ran through the layout of the house in his head, working out which floor he'd seen the light on. It had been on the floor underneath the widow's walk. He knew that the owners still had stuff on that floor—some old wardrobes and beds, and clothes draped over everything. As soon as contracts were exchanged, he'd organise for them to remove the last of their possessions. The sooner he could get in here and start measuring up properly, without anything in the way and surveying the site, the faster he could get to work. Legally, they didn't have to vacate the premises until settlement, but he was happy to pay some rent to get access.

Time was money.

And despite Johnno's words that he didn't have to prove himself, Greg needed this project to be successful. Not so he could take the holiday he and Johnno had talked about, but to put him in a position to cut ties with his family. Financially . . . and maybe more.

Life wasn't all about making your first million. But when he did, he had some plans. Exciting plans that would mean a total lifestyle change.

As he walked past the first floor, he quietly switched a light on. The timber that skirted the floor along the edge of the polished floorboards held a mellow glow in the soft light. Above the archways that split the long hall into sections, the whorls in the timber created patterns of sunlight on the butter-yellow walls. For a moment Greg regretted the work that was ahead. The original timber would be removed when the walls of the graceful old hallways were knocked out and widened into the common areas that would lead to the apartments on each floor. Modern square-cut plaster mouldings would modernise the space and open it up to the light from the ocean. He looked up to the open space above the second floor. He'd asked Johnno to discuss the removal of the widow's walk with the vendor's solicitor today. You couldn't see it from the street and the removal of the small room and landing wouldn't impact the look of the house. It would make room for a large skylight in the room that would stream light onto the stairwell. Greg had a feeling that he was going to lose that one, but this afternoon's meeting would tell.

    He'd agreed to keep the façade of the old house and that was the thing that had secured the deal for him. It was an exciting project and one that would make him a lot of money. Hopefully, enough profit to keep his father off his back.

    Greg frowned as soft whispering came from the door ahead; maybe they'd seen him come up the path. There was somebody there, and he'd be putting the skids under them quick smart. If he had trouble getting them out it would put a hold on his development, and even worse, delay his plans for the future.

Chapter Three

Ginny sat on the floor under the window in a sea of silk. Ruby red, emerald green, deep violet and all shades of the rainbow between. She could still hear Mrs Beynon, her primary school teacher teaching the class how to remember the colours of the rainbow.

'Mr Roy G. Biv, children,' she would say when there was a storm and the rainbow arched across the playground after the rain.

'Red, orange, yellow, blue, indigo, violet,' the children would chant, and Mrs Beynon would nod as she ushered them outside to look at the sky.

Ginny stared down as the smooth, cool fabric silk slipped through her fingers. Those early days with Gran and Poppy had been happy. She so wished she could have them back in her life. She jumped as a soft whisper seemed to surround her.

'Wish. Wish. Wish.'

Straightening her back, she focused back on the task at hand. Yes, wishes were for dreamers, Gran would have said, but resolve filled Ginny.

Yes, yes, yes. The words filled her mind and she imagined they echoed in the warm air around her. That whiff of freesias lightened the air again, and she looked up in surprise. It must be the perfume embedded in the fabric.

As she sorted through the dresses that she'd found in a large chest beneath the window, Ginny stretched her legs out in front of her, and wriggled her toes. It had been easier to sit on the rug-covered floor and sort through the clothes than carry them over to the large old brass bed against the far wall, but she'd been sitting there for so long, she had pins and needles in her feet.

Excitement filled her, and she had to concentrate on slowing down. She'd had a quick look in the two wardrobes and emptied one of the three chests, and already there were enough clothes to stock her store for months.

And, oh my God, Sally had been right. What an Aladdin's Cave of treasures this old house held.

The first wardrobe Ginny had opened had been disappointing and her spirits had sunk. A solid cupboard lined with narrow shelves held a variety of undergarments. Bombay bloomers in navy blue, white and beige, as well as a few corsets. A delightful fragrance of lavender permeated the garments, and even though they wouldn't sell in her shop, Ginny was sure they would be of interest to someone who was looking at the history of fashion.

Maybe the local TAFE would be interested again? She'd put them on to a few things over the past year since she'd started up her shop. These undergarments were old; she was sure some of them had to be at least fifty years old. Not the type of thing her trendy customers would be looking for.

Or be prepared to pay for. That was the bottom line.

She'd opened the door of the second wardrobe expecting the same and held her breath as she caught sight of the rows of dresses on crocheted padded coat hangers.

For a moment it was like being back in Gran's bedroom, the smell, the colourful dresses and the hats that were on the shelf above the silk dresses. There were snoods, boaters, upturned sailors' hats, pancake berets, and turbans knitted in silk—they would be worth a fortune.

She smiled; this time the memory was a happy one. Her skin tingled, and the room seemed to get warmer as she sat there. When she'd been a small girl, Gran had let her dress up in some of her older clothes and it was then that Ginny had learned to appreciate vintage fashion. She'd moved on from playing dress ups with her dolls and making Brent play with her—

Ginny cut that thought dead before it took hold.

'It was after the war.' Gran had smiled when Ginny had appeared in the kitchen wearing one of the hats, a veil of lace covering one ten-year-old eye. Ginny had squinted at her grandmother through the lace and listened to Gran's stories as she'd wielded her massive rolling pin over the pastry she was rolling out. 'Our hats had a purpose back then. A new hat was something to brighten a worried face, cheer a broken heart and there were a lot of those when the boys came back—or in many cases—didn't come back from the war.'

Ginny had loved hats ever since Gran had let her play dress ups in those happy days. She put her hand to her head and touched the small hat that matched her tangerine patent leather shoes, and her small handbag; she loved dressing up when she came out to look at the old clothes. She shook her head and pulled her thoughts back to the present. Those days with her grandparents were long gone.

I'll never go back there.

That was a closed chapter of her life and she didn't want to think about it. Her recovery had been slow, and she had made a new life for herself. A life that she was happy with, a life where she didn't need anybody. A life where nobody knew her. What was wrong with her this afternoon?

If I don't get a move on, I'll be here all night.

The next dress in the pile was buttercup yellow, and Ginny spread it out on the patterned rug beside her, shaking her head as she examined it, piece by piece. The fabric was in perfect condition, the covered buttons were intact, and there was no discoloration in the fabric. She'd turned the light on a while back when it got too dark to see. Her tummy grumbled, and she glanced down at her watch.

She wanted to stay and explore the rest of the rooms, but common sense kicked in; she couldn't stay here much longer. Her car was parked a couple of streets away and it was dark already. Walking back down the deserted streets in the dark was not something that appealed.

'Five more minutes,' she whispered as she reached for the next dress on the pile on the floor beside her. Her soft words echoed around the room and the whisper of the silk seemed to amplify it. Goose bumps ran up her arms and the hair on the back of her neck rose as the temperature dropped again, and a chill breeze touched her skin before it fluttered through the dresses on the floor beside her. As Ginny looked up, she caught her breath and froze as the door handle began to turn slowly. She lowered the dress to her lap with shaking hands and waited.

***

Greg stood outside the closed door. A sliver of light shone through the gap on one side of the door frame, and he paused with his hand on the doorknob. There was more than one person in there; he could hear them whispering. For a fleeting moment, he wondered if he'd been wise to come up here; maybe he should have just called the police and then he realised how stupid he would have sounded if he had.

'Um, there's a light on in a house I'm about to buy.'

He would have sounded like a fool, and the police had their hands full with more concerning issues than the possibility of house squatters.

He would be confident and use authority as he ordered them to leave the premises; that's all that was needed. They didn't have to know he wasn't the owner.

Yet.

Greg took a breath, turned the knob and pushed the door open quickly and stepped into the room.

'What do you think you're doing here?' he demanded in a loud voice as he quickly scanned the room, but it wasn't until he looked over at the window that he saw the woman sitting on the floor in a rippling sea of colour. He blinked, and a shadow flitted across the wall beside him. He turned to stop whoever it was heading for the door.

'Stop right there,' he called out as he swung around, but he was too slow. Before he could stop the person, they had slammed the door shut behind them. The house shook, the windows rattled, and the loud bang reverberated around the room before it faded away to silence. He turned slowly, and his mouth dropped open as he stared at the woman sitting on the floor.

She shrank back away from him, her dark eyes wide as she stared at him.

Greg cleared his throat and tried to stay focused. A very attractive woman—scrap that, a stunningly beautiful woman dressed to the nines—stared back at him, her dark eyes wide. For a moment he thought he was hallucinating or seeing a ghost. She looked like someone from another time.

He blinked a couple of times, and she was still there. Pointing at her he jutted his chin out. 'Just want the hell do you think you're doing? In my house. And how many of you are there?'

When she took in a sharp breath and paled, he regretted his tone.

'Well?' he said, his voice less harsh this time.

She finally spoke; her voice was quiet but cultured, and Greg flinched when he heard the tremor in her words.

'There's only m—' She shook her head and lifted her chin. 'Um, there's three of us. The owners are upstairs. And didn't anyone teach you it is very rude to point?''

'I own this house, and you and whoever was here with you, and whoever is upstairs have no right to be here.' He took a step forward trying to be firm, but his voice was more bemused as he looked at her. 'What on earth are you doing?'

As he watched, she tipped her head to the side and put

one hand to her mouth to cover the O-shape of her lips. Her back was straight, and her posture and movements were graceful. Greg dropped his gaze from the small square orange hat thing on her head, and back down to the pretty mouth painted in the same bright orange. Her lips were pursed now, and she frowned as she answered him.

'You do *not* own this house.' Her voice was much firmer now. 'Sally and her sister—
They're upstairs—they own it, and I think whoever you are, you'd better leave right now. How did you get in? The door was locked.'

Greg took a step towards her, but sympathy kicked in when she leaned away from him. Her eyes were huge, and the fingers held to her mouth were shaking; he realised she was terrified.

Of him.

He put his hands up in front of him to reassure her. 'Please, calm down. There's no need to be frightened.'

'You don't own the house,' she repeated. 'Why are you here? And what do you want?' She lifted a small handbag the same bright orange colour as the hat and shoes and held it up. 'You can take my purse, but there's very little money in there.' She put her head back and called out loudly. 'Sally, come down here… quickly!'

Greg took a step closer and lowered his voice. 'Please don't be frightened. I don't want anything except for you and your friends to leave my house.'

'It's not your house.'

'Technically not yet, but it almost is.' He moved forward again, and this time she pushed aside the fabric that was on her lap and crabbed back along the floor away from him, using her hands to balance herself. 'It will be.'

Her long dark brown hair lay in a twisted curl over one shoulder, underneath the quirky hat, and she reached up a hand and pushed it away from her face. Greg couldn't stop staring at her.

Whoever she was, she was beautiful. One of the most gorgeous women he had ever seen. Her lips were full and rosy, and her fair skin held a pretty flush at the edge of high cheekbones. As she reached up to push her hair back, her movements were languid and graceful, but he could still see the slight tremor in her hands.

'Don't come any closer.' Her voice was a little steadier now, and she put her hand on the window sill and pulled herself to her feet—without taking her eyes off him. Greg couldn't help his gaze raking down to her feet and up again as she stood there, her chin lifted and her eyes wary.

She was wearing a suit in a pale apricot, a quirky little jacket with a sideways neckline and a knee length skirt that hugged her hips. He could see the shine of flesh-coloured stockings on her slim legs. Shapely legs.

Her shoes were the same orange as everything else and she looked as though she had stepped from a fashion magazine. He began to think he had a made a mistake. This was no house squatter in front of him, but what the hell was she doing her surrounded by clothes that had obviously come from the wardrobes in the room?

He reached into his pocket and pulled out his wallet and retrieved a business card before holding it out to her. The fear in her eyes had receded a little and the tilt of her head was haughty now.

'This'll prove to you that I'm not a burglar.'

She took his card and glanced down at it before bending and picking up the bag that she had left on the floor. It opened with a click, and she reached inside. A business card was held in his direction.

'And this will prove to you I have every right to be here.'

Their fingers brushed as he took it and the woman pulled her hand back quickly as though she still didn't trust him.

Greg looked down at the card and turned it over.

'Ginny Silver of Shabby-Chic,' he read aloud.

'Greg Tindall of GT developments,' she replied as she read his card.

He nodded. 'That would be me, and I think I owe you an apology.'

Chapter Four

Ginny stood, one hand on the windowsill, and the other clutching the business card of the man standing in the middle of the room. Greg Tindall, if he *was* who the card said he was.

'Perhaps you do. But I can understand why you challenged me. It is a strange time for me to be doing a house visit.'

'A house visit?' His voice was deep and strong, and matched the masculinity that oozed from him. It was his size and his strength that had frightened her more than anything when he'd burst into the room.

Ginny nodded slowly and gestured to the clothes on the floor and the bed. 'Sally offered me first look at the clothes for my shop. Shabby-Chic is a retro shop.'

'Retro?' His face was screwed up in a frown.

'Vintage. You know, old clothes and accessories. My shop is in Paddington, and it's the only time I could come and look at what she had. Friday afternoons are a quiet time.'

'Ah. I see. And I guess Sally isn't really upstairs?'

She nodded. 'No, but I wasn't prepared to let a loud hulking stranger know that.'

His face flushed and that surprised her.

'Hulking. Hmm. I really am sorry. I was a bit over the top, but I've had some bad experiences with squatters on some of my other sites.' He looked at her sheepishly. 'And as soon as you said Sally Brown was upstairs, I knew that wasn't true because she's currently at a meeting with my solicitor. In fact, if all's gone well, contracts may have been exchanged already, and I could actually be the owner.

Ginny nodded again. 'She had to rush away. You have a key then? She said she was going to lock the door.'

Greg shook his head. 'No, it was unlocked and open actually.'

'She must have forgotten to lock it.'

'Or it could have blown off the latch. It was cold downstairs.'

There was an awkward silence for a moment, and Ginny clasped her hands in front of her.

'I guess I had better put all this away, and head home,' she said finally. 'I didn't realise how late it was.' She looked at him curiously. 'Why were you here anyway?'

'I had to measure the width of the driveway, and I looked up and saw the light on. Then I made the wrong assumption. I'm really sorry I frightened you barging in like I did.' He cleared his throat, and she sensed that he was out of his comfort zone, as he stared at her and then dropped his gaze and fumbled with the business card before he looked up and continued. 'Maybe I could take you out for dinner to say sorry.'

She stared at him, and a dark flush tinged his cheeks, and then he rushed on before she could decline politely.

'That is, if there's no one waiting for you at home, or if you already have plans.'

He ran a hand through his already tousled, sun-tipped brown hair. 'Of course, you will have plans. I'm sorry. Once again, let me apologise for my rudeness. Now, let me help you with this lot.' He was babbling, and Ginny sensed he was embarrassed.

Not that she'd had much to do with the opposite sex over the past few years and was certainly no expert in reading moods or sub-text.

She glanced down at his hands and shook her head 'Thank you, but no. I can't afford to damage this fabric. I don't have any gloves on myself and I was being super careful.'

'Okay, fair enough. But I'll wait here with you, and then walk you to your car.'

She looked at him surprised again by this thoughtfulness. It appeared that the belligerent man had all been an act. 'Thank you, that would be very kind of you.'

She reached down and picked up the dresses and laid them on the bed one by one as Greg crossed to the window and looked outside. He turned to her after a few minutes. 'I use a few old stores to source old building materials for my renovations, so I guess that's a similar field to what you're in. You know, windows and stuff like that.'

He sounded as though he was trying to be friendly and make an effort, but even though his words were friendly enough his tone was awkward.

'It is. I don't chase windows'—she smiled for the first time— 'but I probably know some of those places you use. I keep in touch with a few of them if I see something that is suitable for them, and they do the same for me.'

She spoke quietly as she picked up the ruby red dress and laid it out carefully on the bed. 'When I moved to Sydney a few people told me what a cold and unfriendly place it was, but I haven't found that.'

"How long have you had your shop?'

Ginny reached across and picked up her bag. 'Ten months.'

'And it's going okay?'

'It is. I've been lucky. I've had access to some fabulous estates, and this—' she spread her arms wide— 'is an exciting find. This will get me into the black before the end of the financial year, I hope.'

The look he gave her was curious, but before Greg could answer, there was a loud bang from above. He frowned. 'Have you been upstairs this afternoon? There must be a window open up there, making a door bang.'

Ginny shook her head with a frown. 'No, I haven't, but there were some noises before and Sally said it is just the usual noises of the old house.'

'Settling timbers don't make a huge bang like that. I'll go up and check.' As he passed her to walk to the door, Greg stopped and looked at her curiously. 'I forgot to ask. Who was with you when I first came in?'

'Nobody. Why?' Ginny looked back at him with a frown. 'I was here by myself after Sally left.'

'But someone ran past me when my back was turned and slammed the door shut. I saw their shadow on the wall, and then the door slammed before I could turn around.'

She shook her head. 'No. There was no one with me. I thought *you* slammed the door. That's why I was so scared of you for a minute.'

Greg looked from Ginny to the shut door. 'I could have sworn there was someone here. Strange.' He headed across the room to the door and paused. 'Come on, we'll go and check upstairs, and then after I lock up I'll walk you to your car.'

Ginny swallowed. 'Um, about what you said before.'

'What I said before?'

Nerves rushed through her and her fingers tingled. 'About dinner. Um, I have to eat and um—' *oh for goodness sake, you're a city woman now, act like one*—'and there's no one waiting, so dinner would be nice. Thank you.' She expelled a deep breath, entirely out of her comfort zone and wondering why she had said that at all.

The smile that lit up Greg's face reassured her. 'Sweet! Come on. Let's get out of here.' He paused and looked down at his work clothes and heavy boots. 'Jeez, look at me, about the only place I'll get into is a pub, and you look far too nice for that.'

'A pub would be fine,' she reassured him. 'But just a

quick meal, I do have to be home early because I open my shop early on Saturdays and Sundays to catch everyone going past to the markets.

'Sounds good to me. I have a big day planned too.'

Greg waited until she crossed the room to the door beside him before he reached for the door knob. She watched as he tried to turn the old brass knob, but it didn't budge.

'Looks like the mechanism jammed when it slammed shut.' Greg put both hands to the knob and wrenched it to the left, and then to the right, but it didn't move. 'It's stuck fast.'

'There's another door to the hall.' Ginny looked around and pointed to the door on the other the side of the bed. 'There's an interconnecting door there, that leads to another bedroom. I noticed a door from that room out to the hall when I first went in there. Might be easier than fiddling with this lock.'

'Good, come on then, we'll go out that way. I'll leave the light on in here and try and come back from the hall side to turn it off.'

Ginny followed Greg around the bed and to the interconnecting door. He turned the knob and jiggled it, but the door didn't open.

'This is the door you went through before?'

'Yes, it goes to the next bedroom and a small bathroom.' Ginny frowned as Greg jiggled the knob and was pleased when the door opened, and he chuckled.

'That's a relief. I was starting to think I was going to have to climb out the window.'

Another loud thud reverberated from the floor above them.

'It does sound like there is somebody up there, doesn't it?' Ginny rubbed her arms as goose bumps lifted on her arms, despite the warmth of the room.

'It's a door banging. But I want to lock up and close

any windows before we go.'

She followed him into the smaller room, relieved when he switched the light on and the shadowy corners disappeared.

'Bloody hell.' Greg cursed as he tried to turn the knob of the door to the hall. 'You're not going to believe this, but this one is jammed too.'

'It can't be. Here let me try. Maybe it needs a light touch. I saw Sally open the other one and she did jiggle that one a little bit.'

Greg stepped back as Ginny grasped the door knob with both hands and tried to turn it. The brass knob was cold beneath her fingers, but he was right, it was jammed tight and didn't move.

'That's really strange. Unless they've been key locked?'

Greg put his hand over hers, and tried to move it, but again it didn't budge. 'Come on, we'll go back to the other room. At least we know that one's not locked. We both came in that way.'

The first quiver of unease twanged in Ginny's tummy and she swallowed. Right on cue, her stomach gave out a loud grumble, but it broke the tension when Greg laughed. 'I'm a bit the same. It's been a long time since lunch.'

They tried the door knob for a full five minutes, each of them having a go at trying to open it.

'Well, it looks like we're going to have to call for help.' Greg scratched his head. 'It's going to have to be the owners, or someone with a key because I locked the front door behind me. Do you have Sally's number? I don't have it in my phone. My solicitor has been our method of communication.'

'I do.' Ginny crossed to the bed and sat down and opened her handbag, before sliding out her iPhone. She pushed the button to wake it, but the screen didn't light up. With a frown, she pressed it again, but it stayed stubbornly black.

She wrinkled her nose as she looked up at Greg. 'That's strange. My phone's gone flat. It was fully charged when I got out of the car. I charged it on the way over.'

'Try turning it off, and then on again. My iPhone plays up like that occasionally.'

Ginny did as he instructed but shook her head again. 'Nope, dead as a doornail.'

'It's okay. I'll ring my solicitor and get Sally's number.'

'It's late. Will he still be there?'

'I've got his mobile number. He was at the office when I arrived here. With a bit of luck Sally might still be there too.'

'Maybe, but I think she was heading straight back to Peat's Ridge. She was in a rush. Maybe the solicitor will have a spare key?' Ginny tipped her head to the side. 'Wait a minute. I think her sister lives close to here, or at least she works locally. Maybe Sally could call her if she's already left. Her name's Sonia.'

'Sounds like a plan. I'll give Johnno a call and get us out of here somehow.' As he pulled the phone from his pocket, Greg walked back to the door, and jiggled the knob again, but as before, he had no luck.

***

Greg was pleased that Ginny seemed to have relaxed with him and didn't think he was trying something on with them being locked in the room. Hell, she'd even agreed to go out for dinner with him, much to his disbelief—and pleasure. He'd mumbled like a schoolboy when he'd mentioned dinner. Halfway through asking her, he'd changed his mind, and he knew he'd sounded like an idiot. But she'd been kind, and then to Greg's utmost surprise, she'd said she'd go out with him. The way they were going, it would be too late to go anywhere.

Although it was Friday night, but the sorts of places that would be open and buzzing weren't exactly what he'd had in mind. Ginny must have read his mind because, as he hit the button on his phone, she crossed to the window and looked out into the dark.

'By the time we get out of here, it will probably be late, so I might pass on the dinner now,' she said softly.

Disappointment ran through him, but he nodded with a smile as he hit the speed dial for Johnno 'You're probably right. But how about a rain check? To make up for this I'll take you somewhere nice one night.'

Her nod was non-committal, and Greg tried not to frown as he waited for the call to connect.

What the hell am I doing? He needed to get out of here and start acting like a rational human being again.

After a few more seconds, the call still hadn't dialled out; he lowered the phone and looked at the screen. Johnno's number was there but the phone was still trying to connect the call. He lowered his brows as he stared at the service. There were no bars at all.

'What the f—' He glanced across at Ginny at the window. 'Sorry. I'm used to working with men all day.'

'What's the problem?'

He walked over to the window, keeping his eye on the service bars. 'The network must be down. There's no service. Look.' He handed her the phone in case she thought he was up to something. 'There's not even the usual SOS call option that's there when the network's down.'

'Oh dear,' she said softly. 'What do we do now?'

'The window. It's our only option.' he said and looked up as there was another loud thud from upstairs. 'Maybe I can get up to the next floor.' Greg unlocked the window and tried to push the sash window on the left up, but it was jammed. He moved to the one beside it but again, there was no movement even though it was unlocked. 'I can't believe it. It doesn't bode well for this project. Maybe I should have scoped it out a bit more before I signed the contract.'

'Maybe it means the house should be left as it is?' Ginny tilted her head and stared at him. 'It's a beautiful old home that just needs some TLC.'

Greg stilled with his hand on the window as regret shot through him. 'So you're another one who doesn't think old houses shouldn't be refreshed?' His words came out more harshly than he'd intended as his patience was being sorely tested by being locked in this room. 'I'm sorry, I didn't mean to snap at you.'

'I suppose it depends on what you mean by refreshed,' she said slowly.

Greg looked down at his phone and shoved it back in his pocket, without answering her. 'I'll give it a few minutes and try again. I can't believe this.'

'Actually, I'm glad you came up when you saw the light on. I don't know how I would have fancied being locked in here by myself.'

Greg crossed to the bed and stood beside Ginny. 'So, what did I mean by refreshed? It's a bit like what you do, I guess. It's valuing old things and working with them and making them suitable for today.' He pointed to the door and the window in turn. 'So, this is a graceful old house, but I imagine living in it as it is would be quite challenging. Sticky doors and windows, leaking hot water systems, thuds and groans in the night, nowhere to park on the block or outside . . . and the list goes on.'

Ginny's hat wobbled as she shook her head, and Greg almost reached out to catch it, certain it was going to slide off her hair. She was sitting up straight on the bed, her handbag grasped firmly in her lap and her legs crossed demurely at the ankles.

She was an unusual woman. The way she spoke and the way she carried herself was quite old fashioned, and her confidence seemed to come and go. She intrigued him, and that was different for him. For the past few years, he'd been too tied up in his business to take an interest in socialising.

'So what are we going to do until we get phone service?' she asked.

The bed dipped as he sat next to her, and there was another loud thud from upstairs.

Chapter Five

'Do you think there *is* someone up there? Or is it just the house settling?' Ginny asked. Considering the situation she and Greg were in, she was feeling remarkably calm. Greg sat beside her on the bed, tapping his fingers on his thigh, a frown creasing his forehead.

'Maybe we could bang on the door and if there is someone up there they might come to see what's wrong, do you think?' Ginny persisted. It was a strange situation. She'd forgotten all about the clothes and was trying to get used to being confined in a room with a man she had only met an hour or so ago.

He was a *nice* man. No, she shook her head. Nice was such a weak word, and one that Mrs Beynon had taught them never to use in the stories that they had written every Friday afternoon at primary school.

'Worth a try, I suppose.' Greg shook his head. 'But if there is, they're more likely to take off than come and help us. And I think this house probably settled about eighty years ago.'

The wide smile on his face lightened his face for the first time since he'd burst into the room.

'Maybe it's the aunty,' Ginny said with a little smile. Her tummy let out another loud gurgle and heat ran up her neck. Feeling self-conscious, she placed her hand bag carefully on the floor, and fiddled with the catch. Anything to divert Greg's attention from her digestive juices.

'The aunty?'

'Aunt Agatha.' She nodded. 'Sally told me on the phone the other day that they didn't want to sell the house or empty out her belongings in case it upset her.'

'Is she in a home? It's the first mention I've heard.

They must have power of attorney to act on her behalf. I thought the house was owned by Taj Brown, the surfer.'

'No, she's passed.'

Greg's forehead wrinkled in a frown. 'So what do you mean upset her?'

Ginny waved a hand and the light from the bare electric bulb in the ceiling above caught the iridescent orange glow of her manicured nails. 'I was being silly. All those thuds and creaks and groans set my imagination running rampant. I grew up in a haunted house.'

His eyebrows rose. 'Interesting.'

Ginny felt a bit silly and hurried on. 'I mean I imagined it was haunted. I had a couple of imaginary friends and sometimes when I was going to sleep I'd swear I'd see them next to my bed.'

'Sounds like a fun childhood.' He stared past her at the door, and then pulled his phone out and checked it again

'Not really. It was pretty lonely.'

'Okay.' Greg's eyes crinkled at the corners with a bright smile, but Ginny wondered if he was being polite after her talk of haunted houses. He probably thought she was a fruit loop. She'd seen the way he looked at her orange hat and shoes when he'd first burst in.

'I'm going to get a few thuds going down here, just in case there is someone up there.' He glanced at his phone and shook his head. 'The network is still down. Hopefully it won't be too much longer.' Greg crossed to the door and tried the knob again as though it may have fixed itself. He glanced back at her as he formed a fist and pounded on the door six times in succession.

Ginny jumped as there was one answering thud from above. 'Do you think there really is someone up there?' A shiver ran down her back at the thought that there'd been someone else in the house with her the whole time she'd been looking at the clothes and talking to herself.

'I think it's just a door banging. If there was someone up there, they wouldn't want us to know. They wouldn't be banging about, or they'd come down to see what we were doing.' Greg said.

'True.' She grinned as his stomach gurgled. 'It's past dinnertime. '

'It is. I'm starving.'

Ginny smiled as she flipped open the top of her square patent leather handbag. She reached in and held up a muesli bar with a flourish. 'This has been in here for a while, but I guess we can have dinner together after all.'

Greg shook his head. 'No. You have it. I'll survive.'

The plastic crackled as she unwrapped the bar and she held it up. 'No. We're stranded together, we'll share.'

He sat there quietly as she snapped the bar in two and passed half to him. 'I didn't bring a water bottle this afternoon, because I didn't think I'd be here long.'

'The water's still on, and there's a bathroom next door.'

'A veritable feast,' she said with a laugh. Despite the strangeness of the situation and being locked in a bedroom with a man she hadn't known an hour ago, Ginny felt comfortable.

'As long as we're not in here for too long, I think we'll survive.' Greg looked across at her as he bit into the oat bar. 'Shame I can't put my boy scout skills to good use.'

'Boy scout skills?'

'You know. How to make a fire, build a raft, all those sorts of handy tricks. I can tie a damn fine knot too.' His grin was wide. 'If I could get the window open, I could knot the sheets together and climb down.'

Ginny giggled. 'I used to love the story of Rapunzel.'

'What's that? I didn't learn that one in boy scouts.'

'Really? You haven't heard of "Rapunzel, let your hair down?"'

'What, she was a party animal?' Greg held her gaze and a funny warm shimmer ran down Ginny's back.

Honestly, this was the strangest night.

'No, she let her hair down so her prince could climb up to the tower where she'd been locked away.'

He glanced at her hair with a smile. 'Well, I don't think that's going to happen unless we're stuck in here for a long time.'

'We'd starve before my hair grew long enough,' she replied.

'It's all academic anyway, because I can't get the window open.' Greg stretched and put his hands behind his head.

'And I don't have a prince.' Ginny neatly folded the wrapper from the muesli bar and put it back in her bag. 'I could make the most of the time and keep sorting these clothes.' She stifled a yawn.

Greg reached into his pocket and checked his phone again. 'God, there's still no service. It must be a big outage. I wonder what's happened.'

Ginny's heels clicked on the timber floor as she stood and walked over to the window. She looked down; the street below was deserted. The only movement was a scrap of paper being blown along by the stiff breeze. In the distance she could see the white caps of the waves where the lights across the front of the beach reflected on the white foam as they curled and pushed up to the sand. 'There's not even anyone down on the beach.'

'Even if there was, we'd be too far away to be seen up here.'

'This is crazy.' She clenched her hands together as helplessness flooded through her. 'I have to open the shop early tomorrow. I wonder how long before the phone comes on?'

'Soon, I hope.' Greg checked it again as though staring at it might make it work. He put it back in his pocket and stood. Pulling his keys out he crossed to the recalcitrant door and crouched down.

'What are you doing?' she asked curiously, walking over to stand beside him. Ginny looked down at the top of his head as he peered at the hinges on the door. She put her hands behind her back because she had the silliest urge to run her fingers through his sun-tipped short hair.

'I thought maybe I could use my key to undo the hinge and lift the door off it, but…' He leaned forward, and a whiff of a pleasant, woodsy cologne reached Ginny. She took a step closer and leaned over to look at what he was doing.

'But?'

'It's jammed tight and the hinge is different to any I've ever seen. A real historical piece. He turned his face up to her and his expression was cheeky. 'Just the sort of thing that you'd see in a vintage shop.'

Ginny smiled back. 'I'll have to see if there is a demand for them.'

Greg pushed himself up to his feet and looked down at her before holding out his hand. She looked down at it with a slight frown before slipping her hand into his. His fingers were firm and cool.

Greg led her over to the bed and she frowned when he spoke.

'Let's try and fill the time.'

'How?' She pulled her hand from his and the bed creaked as he sat down, avoiding the clothes that she had spread on the end.

'Conversation. Come and sit down. Pacing the room isn't going to help. We're going to be here until the phone service comes back on. At best.' He patted the bed beside him. 'Kick your shoes off, get comfortable and tell me about Ginny Silver. Start at the beginning and tell me about this lonely childhood in a haunted house. I'm fascinated.'

'Not very fascinating. I had a good imagination.' Ginny reached down and unbuckled her shoes, before slipping them off and moving across to the other side of the bed. Greg had moved up near the wall and was leaning against the brass bed head. She sat with her legs tucked to one side beneath her and smoothed her skirt over her knees demurely.

'What about the hat?' Greg pointed to her head. 'It's a bit disconcerting. I'm used to looking at blokes in baseball caps on the building site all day.'

'Oh, I forgot I had it on.' Ginny reached up and touched it. She must look silly sitting here with the pillbox hat on.

'You dress the part for your shop?' he asked. 'Not that there's anything wrong with wearing a hat, of course.' The cheeky grin belied his words.

She pointed to his work shirt and boots. 'You dress the part for your job.'

'I do.' He folded his arms and watched as she removed the hat and placed it carefully next to her bag and shoes. 'But I'm not as colour co-ordinated as you are.'

'I couldn't resist this hat and shoes when I found them. They're genuine sixties, you know.'

'Probably wouldn't suit me.'

'Probably not.' Ginny screwed up her nose and pulled a face at him.

***

Greg was enjoying himself. The light banter between them had eased the tension of the situation. Being in enforced intimacy with someone he didn't know had been off-putting for the first few minutes after he'd realised they were stuck in this bedroom together. Ginny had relaxed now and the little grin that played around her pretty lips after she'd pulled the disapproving face at him when she'd removed the hat was cute.

She was very particular in her movements. The way she'd folded the wrapper, and the neat way she'd placed her shoes and hat on the floor pointed to a very organised person, and he liked that. Kitty had set him up on a couple of dates last year and he hadn't enjoyed himself at all. The women had all been late, full of inane chatter and self-centred.

'Greg, you have to move on.' Kitty had chastised him softly after she'd demanded a report after the second disastrous date. 'It's been three years.'

'Four actually.' He'd lifted the beer that Johnno had handed him and crossed the deck that overlooked the harbour. He'd seen the glance that Kitty and Johnno exchanged. Sometimes it was harder to deal with the expectations of friends than deal with what had happened.

The bed cover moved as Ginny settled onto the bed and Greg pulled his thoughts back to the present. 'Okay, so time to tell me about this lonely child.'

As soon as the words were out of his mouth her expression closed again. 'There's not a lot to tell,' she said slowly. 'I lived in Mt Isa with my grandparents. They died. I moved to Sydney.'

It was what she wasn't saying that put the sad look in her eyes. Her words were sparse but there was a lot of feeling underneath them. He wondered why she had lived with her grandparents.

'Life can be tough.' He glanced down at his phone for the hundredth time. 'I had you pegged as a North Shore girl.'

'Oh?' Her pretty eyebrows lifted.

'Shouldn't make assumptions, should we?'

'No, *you* shouldn't.'

'So you lived in the town or out on the land?'

'Both.' But that was all she said. Didn't tell him much about her. Greg was fascinated by her; she was such a mix, but he couldn't put his finger on why he was so interested in what she had to say.

'Boarding school?'

She shook her head. 'Public school. Why do you ask?'

He shook his head sheepishly. 'Should I be honest?"

She nodded. 'Yes, please.'

'The way you speak, and the way you dress. Pure private school. The posh accent. Where did that come from?'

As he waited, Ginny stared at the wall behind him. Finally, she let out a deep sigh, looked back and held his gaze. She had the prettiest eyes; he could see the gold flecks in the green as she leaned forward.

'Gran was from England. Central London, from a well-to-do family. She came to Australia when she was in her twenties and fell in love and stayed. She never lost her accent. I guess it rubbed off on me.' Her eyes lit up as a smile tilted her lips. 'I have such good memories. One of the funniest things you'd ever seen. Gran on horseback, a string of profanities being directed at a beast, but always in the most cultured voice. Ginny giggled. 'She'd be sitting up straight in the saddle—she was a brilliant horsewoman and she used to play polo too and she'd yell out. "Get back, you bastard," at the top of her voice and the cattle would always jump to her command. We all loved her so much.'

'We?' Greg couldn't take his eyes off Ginny's face. Her eyes were bright, her smile was wide, and her voice was full of enthusiasm. As he watched, her eyes closed briefly, and the smile disappeared. It was like a shutter had been pulled down over her face and the joy of her memories extinguished in one breath.

'My parents, and my brother. Mum and Dad passed before Gran and Poppy.'

When her eyes met his again, they were bleak and a ripple of sympathy ran through him. He knew exactly how she felt. She didn't mention what had happened to her brother, and he didn't ask.

'But that was a long time ago. So I guess, all that remains is my *posh* accent, as you call it.'

Greg held up both his hands. 'I wasn't having a go or anything. I like the way you speak. So tell me why Sydney? It's a long way from the central west of Queensland. Why did you move here?'

She didn't speak for a full minute, but Greg sat there waiting, wondering if he'd overstepped some line that he couldn't see.

Finally, with a gentle sigh, Ginny answered. 'Life changes. Poppy died, and Gran went the very next week. She loved him so much, her heart broke and she just couldn't go on.' She turned her face to his. 'I was always so jealous when I was a child. I wanted someone to love me so much that they couldn't live without me, but when you grow up, you realise it's too much of a risk. People die or leave you, and you lose them. I think it's better off not having anybody.'

Greg nodded and his reply was soft. Now that she was talking he didn't want her to pull back into her shell. 'I understand exactly what you're saying.'

'So, I had no one else, and very little money, and no prospects of a job… and I gathered up all the things that Gran left to me and moved to Sydney. I had enough money to rent a fairly decent shop, I had stock, and I have a work ethic.' She folded her arms and her eyes challenged him to disagree.

'And you've settled here?' he said carefully.

She nodded slowly. I've got somewhere to live, I've got my shop, and I'm slowly building my business up.' His voice was firm, but Greg sensed there was a lot she wasn't saying.

'Did you already have friends or family down here? Is that why you came to Sydney?

She shook her head. 'No. I just thought it would be a good place to open a retro shop. Lots of customers, from all over the world.' She sat up straighter as though pulling her thoughts together and pointed one manicured finger in his direction. 'Okay, so you know my entire life history. Now it's your turn. And when you get to the end, I'm interested in why you're buying this gorgeous old house, and turning it into a block of apartments?'

She bit her lip as she looked back at him, and a warm, but long-lost feeling of awareness settled in Greg's chest.

Chapter Six

Greg watched as Ginny's orange-painted nails picked at the tufts of balled cotton on the floral bedspread. What a strange night this was turning into. He had planned to finish measuring up here, pick up a burger and chips and head back to the study in his apartment and do some more work on the plans of this house.

But if he was honest, it was much more interesting being locked in a bedroom with Ginny Silver. Everything about her fascinated him, including her comment about being alone being better than losing someone.

'So, me?' He looked up and held her gaze, again taken aback by how pretty she was. Even though her features were delicate there was a strength in her face, and after listening to her, he had more of an idea about what a strong woman she was.

She nodded. 'Yes, you.'

'Well, I hate to say it, but I come from a well-to-do family on the harbour. My father is an architect.' He looked away. 'If you ask him, he is *the* architect in the city. My mother is a socialite, who lunches.' He turned his head back to look at her. 'I had a brother, but he died a few years back.'

'I'm sorry,' she said softly, looking back at him. He lowered his eyes to her mouth. She had a habit of biting her bottom lip when she was uncomfortable; he'd noticed it several times already.

'Thank you. I've moved on now, but my fiancée was with him in the car when it crashed. According to the post mortems, they'd both been drinking and to this day I still don't know why they were out together at lunchtime on a working day.' Greg put his hands together and tapped his chin. 'I know exactly what you mean by better to be alone, than lose someone. A lot less angst.'

Ginny put her head down and didn't speak for a moment. 'It must have been very hard for your family,' she said after a few minutes had passed.

'Not really.' Greg knew his voice was cold, but the memory of those weeks and months was not pleasant, and one he hadn't revisited for a long time. It was amazing how working hard could keep your mind occupied. 'My mother dismissed it as an innocent lunch, and all my father wanted was for me to step into the business and take over Ryan's role.'

'He was a builder?'

'No, he was an architect too. The same as me. It's the profession that our father wanted us both to follow.' Greg put his hands down and spread them out. 'I did my degree in architecture, just like he wanted, but I also got a building apprenticeship at the same time, much to my parents' disgust. Very Western Suburbs, I was told.' He grinned as he remembered winding his mother up and putting on her plummy tones. 'Or at best *lower* North Shore.'

'I'm still learning the geography of Sydney. I haven't ventured far from Paddington and Randwick.'

'Randwick?'

'Yes, that's where I live in a tiny shoebox.' She looked up and gestured to the ceiling and Greg looked up too. 'One day I am going to be able to afford a beautiful house like this near the beach, and I'll do all the things I want to do.'

Greg hadn't noticed the ornate ceiling rose detailed in pale pink and green to match the carpet when he'd first looked at the rooms. He let his eyes sweep around the room, the plaster cornice was ornate too and the flowers and leaves had been hand-painted. He shook his head; hours and hours of painting with your head tipped back.

What a huge job.

He frowned. What a shame it was all going to be pulled out. 'I wonder how many of the other rooms are like this,' he wondered aloud.

'Like what? With dodgy doors?' Ginny's giggle lifted his spirits.

'No, with such detailed painting. It's in very good condition for its age.'

'Having second thoughts?" She lifted her beautiful arched eyebrows and another unfamiliar feeling consumed Greg, but this time it headed south, and he pulled his knees up to his chest self-consciously.

'No. This is the last development I'm doing before I leave.'

'Leaving?' The fleeting disappointment that crossed her face was gratifying. Where are you going?'

Greg shrugged. 'Sounds crazy, but I don't know. Just somewhere else.'

'As I did,' Ginny muttered half under her breath. She lifted her head again and this time he let his eyes hold hers without looking away. 'So what's your goal?' she asked.

'My goal? I guess I really don't have one.'

'Well, Greg, for someone who works with plans and makes things beautiful, that is really stupid.'

Stupid? Greg frowned. The idea of making enough money and leaving Sydney behind had been with him for a long time.

Ever since the accident. No thought of where he was going, or what he was going to do with his life. When he'd put it into words he realised it was exactly like he'd described it to Ginny. Not only did it sound crazy, his plan—or lack thereof— *was* crazy.

He spoke slowly 'Maybe it is. Maybe I should give it more thought.'

'That sounds sensible. So where do you think you'll

go? This place where you're going, to do you don't know what.' Her eyes still held his, and they were full of disbelief. He realised she was dead serious and horrified that he was intending to just leave.

Greg shrugged again and watched, surprised when she pulled her legs from beneath her and crawled up the bed to sit beside him. She reached over and took his hands between hers. She looked intently into his eyes, and he knew that she had done what he was planning, but Ginny had a goal. As she gripped his hands, he sensed her inner strength. This woman, in her quirky clothes, had a backbone of steel. He could take a lesson in coping with life from her experience.

'You really have to have a plan. Otherwise, how will you know if you're happy?'

'You had a plan? When you left your old life and came to Sydney'

'I did.' She nodded.

'And that makes you happy?'

This time the lip-biting happened again before she answered. 'Sort of, I guess. My plan is still only just being put into practice though, so I can't do a real analysis yet.'

'Do you ever do anything without planning?' Greg looked down at their joined hands and rubbed his thumb along the back of her soft skin.

She jumped and looked embarrassed that she was holding his hand, and tried to pull it away, but he held firm.

'No. I'm not very brave.' She looked at him intently.

'I think you are a very strong woman.'

'What do they say? What doesn't kill you makes you stronger?'

He laughed, but it held bitterness. 'Yeah.'

'What about your business?'

'I'll close it down.'

'Um, what will you do for money?' She tipped her

head to the side and damn if she didn't nibble on that sexy lip again. 'Sorry, that was rude of me. That's one thing Gran taught me not to do. You should never talk about money.'

He let go of one of her hands and waved dismissively. 'Very different to my upbringing. Money was the most important thing in my household. That's why I'm trying to get myself in a position where it's not important.' Greg suddenly realised how loose his plans for the future had been. He hadn't been able to see past getting away from his father's expectations. 'I had a conversation the other night, about taking a holiday. Maybe that's what I need to do first.'

'Take off and bum on a beach somewhere where it doesn't cost much to live?' She let out a gentle sigh. 'You know, that doesn't sound too bad.'

'Or too stupid?'

'I'm sorry that was rude of me. And judgmental. Being alone most of the time has made me more direct than perhaps I should be. I'm sorry. What you went through was tough. I can't blame you for wanting a change of scene.'

'Okay. I'll act on your sage advice. A holiday first. A travel buddy would be good.' Again, the banter was light and put a smile on his face.

'I'll give it my due consideration.' Another bright smile lifted those gorgeous lips and Greg looked away.

Ginny pulled her hand out of his. 'So tell me now about this house. Tell me what your big plans are.'

The hours passed quickly, as Greg told Ginny more about himself than he'd ever shared with anyone. She was a good listener, and he could sense the empathy that she shared with him. It was a bit of a wake-up call for him. Here he was unsettled and dissatisfied with his life.

He had a family—of sorts, and he had no money worries, plus he had a good mate in Johnno.

A couple of times, she closed her eyes and he'd

wondered if his talking had put her to sleep. He stopped talking but Ginny opened her eyes and yawned.

'What time is it?

Greg glanced at his watch. 'It's three o'clock. I can't believe I haven't been able to get us out of here.'

'The witching hour,' she said with another wide yawn. Ginny put her hands up to her mouth. 'We need to summon up a ghost or some magic to open the door for us.'

'I thought midnight was the witching hour?'

She smiled, and he watched her pretty eyes crinkle.

'No. I wrote an essay on it once. Interesting stuff.'

'If you believe in that sort of thing.' He shook his head. 'But I guess if you grew up in a haunted house, you do.'

'I don't dismiss the possibility.'

They both jumped when his phone dinged.

Ginny laughed. 'See, it worked. You just have to believe.'

'Yes.' Greg fist-pumped the air so hard that the bed bounced beneath them and caught Ginny off balance. Before he could reach for his phone she had fallen sideways into his lap. He looked around surprised; he could have sworn he heard a soft chuckle come from the shadows on the other side of the wardrobe. Goosebumps lifted on his arms and he frowned as he reached over to help her sit up. All this talk about witching hours was creeping him out. His fingers held her shoulders lightly and her mouth dropped open as she stared up at him.

For the life of him, he couldn't help himself and leaned forward and touched his lips to hers, waiting for her to tense and pull away, but her soft lips clung to his. Warm ripples of excitement rushed through every nerve ending when she lifted her arms and put them around his neck. All was quiet for a minute or so, as her lips opened beneath his mouth and she returned his kiss.

Eventually, he pulled back, reluctant to break the contact. He stared at her flushed cheeks and wide eyes and was pleased when she smiled at him

'Sorry. I got a bit excited. About the phone, I mean' He pulled out his phone as she slipped off the bed, stood straight and smoothed her dress down over her thighs.

'It's okay. Do you have service?' Her voice was hopeful. 'I'm really hungry.'

Greg couldn't help the laugh that bubbled up from his chest. 'You do wonders for a guy's ego. I just shared the nicest kiss I've had for a long time and all you can think about is food?'

'And you do wonders for a girl's ego. Nice? Didn't I tell you before what Mrs Beynon used to say about nice?'

'No?' He shook his head with a grin. He hadn't had this much fun in years. 'Who's Mrs Beynon?'

'My primary school teacher. Nice is not a good word to use. Anyway, forget all that. Check your phone.'

Greg looked down at the screen and groaned.

Chapter Seven

'What's wrong?' Ginny peered over at the screen.

'A couple of messages came in, but there's no service again. It must have come on for a couple of seconds.' Greg crossed to the window and held the phone up high and kept his eyes on the screen. Ginny followed him over, but he shook his head.

'Damn and blast, I can't believe it.' He put his hand on her arm. 'I'm sorry, Ginny. I'm going to do my best to get us out of here. Listen, will anyone wonder where you are if you don't go home?'

Ginny bit her lip. 'No one will miss me until the shop doesn't open. And I suppose no one would even miss me then. Not until my part-timer, Jo, goes to work on Tuesday afternoon.'

'Friends who might try to call or visit?'

Ginny shook her head slowly and dropped her head. 'I haven't had time to make friends yet.'

God, how pathetic did she sound!

She lifted her chin. 'Lee down in the bakery beneath my unit would miss me after a while... maybe. But what about you? Will anyone wonder where you are tonight?'

Embarrassment crawled up her spine. Maybe he thought she was digging to see if there was anyone else in his life.

'Nope. Sounds like we're a pair of loners, doesn't it?' Greg leaned against the wall. The atmosphere was a little bit tense since they'd shared that kiss, and Ginny dropped her gaze to the floor. Her lips were still tingling. It was the first time she'd kissed anyone in about five years.

'No, just busy, independent modern people.'

'Still sad though, when you think about it.' He pushed

himself away from the wall. 'When we get out of here, and I'm going to do my best to sort that out now, we are going to be friends. Then if one of us disappears, someone will notice!'

'Sounds like a plan to me, but there's only one problem?'

His brow wrinkled as he looked at her, but his eyes were bright. 'What?'

'How the heck are we going to get out?'

Greg strode across to the door and ran his hands along the plaster wall. He reached into his pocket. 'I'm going to cut a hole in the plaster with my key, and then push it out. There should be a big enough space for you to get through.'

'And then what? How will you get out?'

'You can go down and get some tools from my ute, and I'll take that lock out of the door, or take the hinges off.' Greg tapped on the wall and it sounded hollow.

Ginny stepped back and leaned on the door as he pulled his keys out.

The door creaked, and she stumbled as it opened beneath her weight. Greg's mouth dropped open and his eyes widened.

'What the f—'

Ginny stepped out into the hallway, and Greg pushed himself to his feet and followed her.

'The door swings both ways! I've never seen that before on those hinges,' he muttered as she stood there staring at the open door. 'How the heck did the door open?'

'It must have been my weight on it.'

It couldn't be,' Greg said with a frown. 'I put all of my strength against it several times.'

'Well, whatever it was, we're free.' Her knees were trembling with the relief of getting out. *Not* because Greg was standing close to her.

'We are and I'm not going to risk getting stuck again. I'll hold it open. You go back in and get your bag and shoes. And your hat. Don't forget your hat.'

Ginny stepped past him, and the warmth from his body, and that lovely woodsy fragrance sent a little frisson of something down her back. It was a wonder he couldn't hear her knees knocking. As she stepped into the room, Greg's phone jangled, and he shook his head again as he lifted it to his ear.

'Greg Tindall,' he answered with a frown. 'Who the heck would be calling at this time of the morning?'

Ginny sat on the edge of the bed and reached down and slipped her shoes on as he took the call.

'Johnno. I know. My phone's been out of service, the blasted network went down.' Greg ran his hand through his hair. 'What the heck are you doing calling at this time of the night anyway?'

Ginny picked up her bag and carried her hat and glanced at the bed before she walked back to the door. The clothes could stay there. She'd have to come back a few times to finish sorting and take them to the shop anyway.

'Fair enough. You know me well.' Greg looked across at her and his warm brown gaze held hers. 'I'm still at the house. Long story. But a good story,' he added softly.

Ginny waited as Greg finished his call. 'Great news. I guess I can celebrate. Yes, we will tomorrow night.' He nodded. 'And mate... I'd like to bring a friend with me if that's okay.' Disconnecting the call, he put the phone into his pocket. He pushed the door open and walked into the room and picked up a small footstool that was in front of the dressing table. Placing it securely against the door to hold it open, Greg stepped into the hall where Ginny was waiting.

'Is everything okay?' she asked quietly.

'Yes, my crazy solicitor mate. He knows me well. He

said he knew I'd been up working.'

'And he was too? At this time of night?'

'He was. But he had good news.'

'Yes?'

'Welcome to my house... almost. The contracts have been exchanged and settlement is in two weeks.' Greg reached across and placed his hands loosely on her waist. 'I've been invited to a barbeque at their place tomorrow night. I'd love to take you out. What do you say? Can you put up with the crazies?'

Chapter Eight

Ginny stood in front of the clothes rack at Shabby-Chic just before closing the following afternoon. She couldn't believe she'd agreed to go out with Greg. The whole episode last night was like a dream, and when she'd woken up in the apartment this morning to the smell of baking bread and croissants, she'd wondered if she had dreamed it.

The text that she'd received from Greg—her new friend—mid-morning, had dispelled that notion quickly.

Thanks for a fun night. See you at five.

It *had* been fun, surreal, but fun. Ginny looked at the clothes in front of her, she put her fingers to her lips and remembered that gentle kiss they had shared. It had turned into such a strange day.

When he'd taken the call from his 'mate' after telling her that, like Ginny, he had no friends, a glimmer of suspicion had run through her, but he'd quickly explained that Johnno was his solicitor and they had been mates since school.

As he'd walked her to her car—after checking that the front door was securely locked—she had agreed to go out with him.

Now she was regretting it. What was she going to wear? She rifled through the rack, pulling out dresses, suits, trousers and frilly blouses and discarding them. Finally, her gaze settled on a red dress that she'd found at a garage sale last week.

She'd arranged for Greg to pick her up at the shop and had left her car in the alley around the back of the bakery, and then caught a bus to the shop. Lee, whose family lived in the unit at the back of the bakery, had said he would keep an eye on it until she came home.

Since she and Greg had been locked in the house

together, Ginny had thought about what would happen if she had gone missing. No one would have known.

No one would care.

The quick three hours of sleep she'd snatched when she'd arrived had been restless, and she'd had to put extra concealer beneath her eyes when she'd dressed for work.

A decision had been made; she was going to make an effort to let Lee know when she was coming and going. His wife, Hong, was a sweetie and had tried to be friendly since Ginny had moved in upstairs, but Ginny had deliberately kept her distance.

Trying to keep her life private was well and good, but last night had been a wake-up call. She'd ended up sitting down there this morning with Hong before she'd left for the shop, and they'd had a long chat.

Ginny had caught the bus with a smile on her face. How strange that being locked in a room with someone for a few hours could bring such a change.

Now she locked the shop door, turned the "Sorry We're Closed" sign over, and carried the dress to the small room at the back of her shop. She slipped off her hot pink fifties suit, had a quick wash, and then pulled the red dress over her head, before turning to the long mirror beside the fitting room. The dress left her shoulders bare but for the narrow straps holding it up, a straight-edged neckline sat above her breasts and then fitted snugly down to her waist before it flared out to a slight gather. The gaily patterned dress—watermelon red, green and dark blue—sat just above her knees and was a perfect match for her red sandals with the green bows.

A fresh application of make-up, a swish of cherry-red lipstick, a pair of red earrings with a matching necklace and she was ready.

Well, she was dressed and ready to go, but her nerves

kicked in and for the hundredth time that day, she wondered what on earth she was doing. Going to a barbeque at a stranger's house, with a man she barely knew. What had she been thinking to agree to go with Greg?

But he was the man who had kissed her and brought her to life.

A bit like Rapunzel's prince. She smiled as she looked in the mirror and brushed her loose hair so that it sat on one shoulder. Not spun gold like Rapunzel's, but dark and shiny with the hint of a curl. Brent had been the one with the curls. Ginny closed her eyes and pushed that thought away

Slipping her lipstick, purse and hair brush into the small shiny leather bag, she sat in the chair by the shop entrance and waited for Greg. She crossed her legs at the ankles and focused on keeping calm.

***

Greg couldn't help singing along with the radio as he navigated the car through the heavy Saturday early evening traffic in Surry Hills. His current apartment was in a block he'd just finished renovating at Erskineville, so it wasn't far across from Ginny's shop at Paddington.

He smiled as he mouthed the words.

What a crazy night last night had turned into, and what a strange way to meet someone. He knew more about Ginny—and she knew more about him—after one night than any of the women he'd dated over the past couple of years. Mind you, he did know a bit about some of them, because they hadn't stopped talking about themselves the whole night he'd sat opposite them in a restaurant.

Enough to turn him off dating for life.

But Ginny had been different.

Her story had tugged at his heartstrings. Despite her obvious inner strength, her vulnerability had him wanting to protect her. He wanted to make her smile and hear her laugh again like she had last night. When she'd finally relaxed with him, her face had come alive. Her life sounded lonely, and the thought of no one missing her had given him a bit of a wake-up call too.

Ginny Silver was someone he'd like to spend more time with—as a friend of course—and tonight at Johnno and Kitty's was a good start.

There was a parking spot outside the shop, and Greg pulled his work ute into the spare space and turned the engine off before reaching across to the passenger seat and picking up the flowers he'd bought on the way over.

Ginny was sitting near the doorway, but the closed sign was facing the street. As he walked across the footpath, she looked up and smiled, and something hit Greg in the chest. For a minute, he thought he'd actually bumped into something, and then he knew, that hadn't happened. It was the sight of Ginny's smile that had sent his heart thudding. His smile grew wide and anticipation tickled at him.

She opened the door and ushered him in. When he handed her the flowers, her cheeks blushed a pretty pink and she buried her face into the sweet-smelling blossoms.

'Thank you, they're gorgeous.'

So are you, he wanted to say, but held the words back. She looked fresh and cool and pretty in her red dress. 'Are you ready?' he asked instead.

'I am. I'll just put the flowers into a vase, and the shop will smell sweet tomorrow.'

Greg waited while she picked up an old-fashioned vase from the shelf near the counter and disappeared into the back of the small shop. Pipes creaked and clanged as water ran and he smiled. A bit like the old house on the hill.

She quickly arranged the flowers and then picked up her bag and turned with that sweet smile. 'Ready to go.'

Greg took Ginny's arm and led her outside and waited

while she locked the shop door. She brought out the gentleman in him. Even in small ways, he wanted to make sure she was okay. Opening the passenger door, he waited until she was settled inside and hurried around to the driver's side.

Chapter Nine

They talked nonstop, through the inner city, across the bridge and into Mosman. Ginny was surprised when Greg pulled up in a quiet leafy street overlooking the harbour. The trip had gone by in a flash.

'This is where Johnno and his wife, Kitty, live,' he said as undid his seatbelt. Ginny waited until he came around and opened her door. Her nerves had kicked in big time, and she wished she was at home, sitting in her tiny living room listening to Lee bang around in the bakery downstairs.

'Um, I didn't get a chance today, but maybe I should have bought some wine or something?' She swallowed; she even sounded scared.

Pull yourself together, she chastised herself. *It's about time you got back into life.*

'All under control.' Greg helped her out and, leaving her waiting on the footpath, went to the back of the ute and with a flourish, produced a bottle of wine, and another bunch of flowers. 'Voila!'

'That's lovely. You're very thoughtful'

'Come on, come and meet my friends. And please don't be nervous, but best to be prepared. Kitty will put you through the twenty questions spiel.'

He held out his arm, and Ginny tucked her hand into the crook of his elbow as they walked up the path, and into a modern foyer.

The wall facing the harbour was made of glass, and the lights twinkling on the boats below bounced off the walls in rainbow colours. Ginny looked around fascinated by the light play.

'This is amazing, so pretty,' she said.

'I like it too. This is one of my apartment blocks.

Johnno and Kitty bought the penthouse when I did it a couple of years ago.'

Ginny was surprised; it was a very upmarket complex in a posh area.

'It's very swish,' she said. 'And modern.'

Greg shrugged. 'I like nice things. A bit of colour makes all the difference.'

She looked at him curiously as they waited for the lift. 'So this is the sort of thing you'd do with the house at the beach?'

'Maybe. I haven't got my head around that interior yet. It's a hard one. I'd like to keep as much of the interior as I can. After noticing that fancy ceiling rose last night, I've had a few different ideas.'

The lift arrived with a ding, and Greg stepped back and let her step in first. They were quiet as it raced smoothly up to the top floor. Ginny was trying to push away the nerves that were dancing in her tummy and resist the urge to hang onto Greg. All too soon the doors opened, and this time Greg took her hand as he led her along a wide corridor with a skylight in the middle. He paused underneath and pointed up. 'You can see the stars at night, and in the daytime, it brings in beautiful light.'

Ginny looked up at the stars that were appearing in the early evening sky, and then back to Greg as he led her towards the end of the corridor. 'You're more than a simple builder, aren't you? You add beauty to everything. It gives me more hope for the house at the beach.'

'What do you mean hope?'

'I don't have a right to an opinion, because the house is nothing to do with me, but the thought of those lovely rooms being turned into modern apartments is …'

'Is what?' Greg's tone was a bit cool.

'Unappealing I suppose. But you know me. I love old

things, and like I said, it isn't any of my business.'

'I'm always happy to listen to opinions.' He pressed the bell on the door of the apartment they had reached. 'I'm going to put a couple of apartments on each floor, but I'm still trying to get a feel for the place. Now that I know the sale's going through, I'll give it a lot more thought.'

Ginny nodded slowly. 'That's good.' She waved a hand as the door opened. 'It's nothing to do with me.'

A petite blonde woman pulled the door open and ushered them in. Greg handed over the flowers and received a kiss on the cheek in return before the woman stepped forward and took Ginny's hand in hers.

'I'm so pleased to meet you. I'm Kitty.'

Greg intervened. 'And this is Ginny if you'd give me a chance to do the introductions, Kit.'

'Oh, don't be a grouchy pants, Gregory. Come in, both of you. Ginny, it's so good to have you here.'

Ginny drew a breath but couldn't get a word in as Kitty chattered on. 'John's out on the deck, checking the Weber.' She lowered her voice and put her hand to her lips. 'He watched a home and garden show on TV the other night, and now he thinks he's Jamie Oliver. He's been in the kitchen all afternoon, mushing herbs in the mortal thingo.' Her laugh tinkled across the huge living room as she led them to the glass sliding door. A tall man came out of the kitchen.

'Not a mortal thingo. A mortar and pestle, darling.' He dropped a kiss on the top of his wife's head before he turned to Ginny. 'Hi, I'm John. Welcome. It's good to meet you. Any friend of Greg's is welcome in our house. Now what would you like to drink?'

Ginny was a little overwhelmed by the nonstop talk. Living alone, the only conversation she heard was on television. All of a sudden everyone was quiet, and she looked up as each of them looked at her.

'Sorry, I wasn't listening.'

'Greg and I are having a beer, Kitty will have a wine, what would you like, Ginny?'

'A wine would be good. Thank you.'

Kitty looked at her with a frown as they walked out to the balcony. 'Have we met before, Ginny? What school did you go to?

Greg smiled and shook his head, answering before Ginny could reply. 'Kitty, poor Ginny has already been through the whole school thing with me.'

'I've only been in Sydney for a few months.' Ginny crossed to the balcony with Kitty and they looked over at the water. Greg lifted the lid on the Weber and gave an appreciative sniff.

'Smells pretty damn good, Jamie' he called to Johnno through the open kitchen window.

'I think you might have been in my shop,' Ginny said. She thought Kitty had looked familiar when they'd walked in.

'What sort of shop?'

'Shabby-Chic at Paddington.'

'Yes,' Kitty exclaimed. 'That's where it was. I love the shop. I was there with my sisters a couple of weekends ago. And now that I know that, I bet that gorgeous dress you're wearing is vintage.'

Ginny nodded, but before she could speak Kitty was off again.

'So where on earth did you meet Gregory? I noticed your shop hours, and I know he never goes out anywhere. Don't tell me he was in there buying a present for his mum?'

'No, we um… we met out on a job.'

Kitty looked across at Greg and beamed. 'Wherever it was it's wonderful to see Greg here with someone. We've been worried about him.'

'Kitty.' Greg's voice held a note of warning, but Kitty

waved a dismissive hand.

'Don't worry about him, Ginny. Greg knows I'm a stickybeak so come and sit down and tell me all about yourself.'

Ginny caught Greg's gaze on her, and he rolled his eyes.

'Go and help John, Greg, and leave us to some girls' talk.'

Chapter Ten

Greg left the balcony reluctantly and headed back into the kitchen. Johnno was about to head outside with two wines, but he handed them to Greg.

'Here, take these out to the girls, and then come back for your drink. I've got a couple of finishing touches to put to the salad, and you can keep me company.'

Greg took the two glasses and made a disparaging noise. 'You could at least be honest, mate, and say you're going to grill me about where I met Ginny.'

Johnno's grin was wide and innocent. '*Moi?* Never. Now hurry up and get back here. You can peel the avocado.'

After he'd delivered the drinks, Greg wandered back into the kitchen. The girls had barely noticed him as he'd put the drinks in front of them, and he was pleased to see that Ginny seemed relaxed. He worried about her; she had such an air of fragility and vulnerability, but if he was honest, he guessed that was just what the world saw.

Anyone who moved to Sydney with no family, or friends to support them, and started up a business, had to be tough.

Greg stood at the sink and stared outside as Johnno bustled about. The view from the penthouse over the harbour to the city was incredible, and he wondered if his friends would stay here after they started a family. Lights lit up the water ruffled by the constant water traffic on a Saturday night. Ferries, charter and party boats, and even small fishing boats dotted the harbour.

It wasn't as good as the view from the house at Bondi Beach, though. He wouldn't mind living there for a while when he finished the development. A niggle of doubt tugged at him. Ginny had been vocal about leaving the house as it was.

Maybe he could refurbish it as a house, and not turn it into apartments? It would be less expensive to do that, but the long-term returns wouldn't be there.

He could do a total period renovation—and his mind kicked in—he could get Ginny to help him with the interiors. They could scour the markets together, looking for suitable fittings, and that way he could spend more time with her.

'What are you mulling over, mate?' Johnno walked over to join him and leaned back against the marble bench top.

'Thinking about the development at Bondi.'

'I knew you'd be up working when I rang you.'

'Yeah, sort of. Did you get any sleep last night?' Greg took a sip of his beer.

'No, but Kitty and I had a long sleep this afternoon.' He winked.

'Too much information, mate.'

'You should try it sometime. Although it's good to see you with someone finally. Where did you guys meet? I didn't think you were out and about on the social scene.'

Greg chuckled. 'At the house on the hill. We were actually there when you called at three a.m. I'll tell you one day.'

Another wink. 'Too much information? You have me intrigued.'

'You'll have to stay intrigued.' Greg lifted his beer and held it out to Johnno. 'Anyway, mate, cheers. Thanks for your work on the Bondi deal. I know it was a complicated one.'

Johnno clinked glasses and shook his head. 'It was a different one, that's for sure. They were reluctant to do the proxy signing even at the last minute. I've never seen anyone so attached to a house in all the conveyancing I've done.'

'I got that impression.' Greg frowned. 'With that, and

Ginny's ideas, I'm having second thoughts about the apartments.'

'What, you're not going to do the development?'

'I don't know. I've got some ideas rattling around in my head.'

'Whatever you do with it, you have a prime piece of real estate.' Johnno's voice was curious. 'What happened to your plan of doing this and then taking a holiday? Sounds like my bet is pretty safe?'

'Could be, mate.' Greg couldn't help his wide grin. 'Sydney is looking pretty damn good all of a sudden.'

'I'm really pleased to hear that, and not just because of losing a bet either.'

A timer on the bench dinged and Johnno moved away towards the door. 'Meat's ready. You grab that salad and bring it out.'

Greg appreciated the affectionate tap on the shoulder from his mate as they walked out to join the women.

***

Ginny was enjoying herself. The meal had been superb, Greg's friends were welcoming, and she smiled as contentment filled her. Her limbs were relaxed, and the peculiar feeling that hit her tummy every time Greg caught her eye was unfamiliar, but pleasant. Kitty had organised to come and have coffee with her at the shop one day next week and she was going to bring a few friends over as well. Business was looking good.

And her social life was looking up.

She leaned back and inhaled deeply. Jasmine tumbled down from a pot high on the wall at the side of the balcony. The sweet smell took her back to her childhood in Brisbane, when her mother was alive. She'd only been small when Mum got sick, and she and Brent had been shipped off to their grandparents, but she could still remember crouching next to the garden beds with Mum, and how happy Mum had been when the jasmine had first flowered each spring.

There had been happy times before she and Brent had been orphaned. Like his father, Dad hadn't coped when Mum had passed. Poppy had died from a broken heart, but Dad drank himself to an early grave.

She'd coped, but Brent hadn't been able to and he'd taken off and had never come back. Somewhere, Ginny had a brother who was lost to her as well. It had all left Ginny feeling unloved. No one had loved her another to stay.

'Are you ready to go?' Greg's warm breath brushed her cheek as he leaned over to her, and she looked up, pulled out of her thoughts. Cross that she had let her thoughts take a maudlin turn, she forced a brilliant smile to her face.

'Yes, whenever you are.'

'We both have to work tomorrow, so I guess an early night is in order.' Greg turned brick red and she loved the way he tried to get over what he'd said.

'An early night for each of us, in our own places, I mean...'

Johnno stood and pushed his chair in and then held his hand out to Kitty. 'It's okay, mate, you're all grown up now and you don't have to explain anything.' His words were innocent but the wink he directed at Greg had him spluttering again.

'I-I...we.'

Ginny took pity on him. He was such a good guy. 'Don't stress, Greg. You can drop me home and still be home in time for a not too late night tonight. Where are you working tomorrow?'

'Now that contracts have been exchanged'—he had recovered his equilibrium, but Ginny caught the dirty look he directed towards his mate— 'I'm going back to Bondi and have a really good look at the structure.'

They said their farewells, and Kitty hugged her and extracted a promise that Ginny would come back and visit again.

Ginny was touched when Johnno took her hand and kissed her cheek.

'Any time, Ginny. A friend of Greg's is a rare thing, and you are most welcome here. We're having a bit of a do on Saturday week, and would love you to come.'

'Thank you. I'll check my diary and let you know.' She didn't want to seem too keen. Even though it had been a good night, she was not going to rush in and risk getting hurt.

Greg pushed the button for the lift, and Ginny rubbed her stomach. 'After that meal, I feel as though I should jog home.'

'I don't think your shoes would be up to it.'

'Maybe not.' She loved how easy it was to talk to Greg. Even after only knowing him — she glanced at her delicate rose gold watch— just over twenty-four hours, she felt as though she'd known him for much longer. She knew instinctively he was a good person, and from what he'd told her last night he'd done it tough too.

'I liked Kitty and Johnno,' she said quietly as the lift descended.

'They're good people and they were there for me when I needed friends. I've been slack, I don't see them as much as I should. But that is going to change now that I have three friends!'

'I guess I do too. We've had a big social week.'

Greg took her hand as they stepped out of the lift and headed towards the ute. The silence was comfortable, and even the mournful hoot of the ferry crossing the harbour didn't make her feel sad like it usually did.

'One day I'm going to get the ferry across to Manly, and have fish and chips on the beach,' she said.

'You've never been there?' He sounded surprised.

'I haven't had time. I only take a half day off on Sundays and I'm usually doing my accounts then.' She slowed her pace. 'Speaking of which, would it be okay if I came back to the house tomorrow if you're going to be there. It would give me a chance to go through some more of the rooms.'

For a moment, she was worried that he was going to say no, and awkwardness filled her. Letting go of Greg's hand as they approached his ute, she folded her arms across her chest.

'On two conditions,' he said slowly.

'Yes?' She tipped her head to the side and her earring tinkled.

'You come early enough, and we'll have a fish and chip picnic on the beach. It mightn't be Manly, but Bondi fish and chips are good.'

'Sounds good to me. What's your second condition?'

'That we prop open every door with something, in case that mysterious wind blows the doors shut again. I'm going to have a good look at that lock tomorrow.'

'You be careful before I get there. I'd hate you to get locked in alone and not be able to let me in.'

'If I'm going to get locked in again, I'd much prefer to have your company.' Greg leaned past her to open the door of the car, but when he stepped back, he reached up and took her chin gently in his hand. 'Thank you for a lovely night. I'm really pleased you came with me. If I ask you nicely, will you come out with me again? As friends, of course.'

Ginny trembled as Greg's thumb caressed her lips. That wasn't the sort of things that friends did, but she was helpless in his hands. Not willing to trust her voice, she nodded as she held his gaze.

He dropped his hand and smiled. 'Good, we'll have to

check that diary of yours.'

Chapter Eleven

Ginny hummed as she rearranged the dresses on the rack. She was going to call Sally after she chose what she wanted at the house today and then she'd have to make room for a heap of new stock. And she would be reasonable; this was going to fill her shop with new stock. Everything was in perfect condition, and she would make a good offer for it. Business slowed about eleven-thirty when the market up the road got into full swing, with the aroma of different foods enticing market-goers out of the shop, as well as the lively music coming from the park, catching everyone's attention.

'Right,' she said to herself. 'Early closing for you today, Ginny Silver. It had been a good morning and closing an hour early wouldn't hurt. Not that she was in a rush to get to the beach. It was past time she relaxed. Spending some of her hours out of the shop in the company of a new friend was a bonus. Greg was expecting her at one; he'd offered to come over and collect her, but she had insisted on driving her own car.

Last night, she'd wondered what she would do, and what Greg's expectations would be if she'd invited him in, but he had simply walked her to the bottom of the steps, kissed her cheek, and waited while she walked up the stairs and unlocked the door of her apartment. As much as she gave off a sophisticated demeanour, her experience in relationships—or encounters—was sadly lacking. The last time she'd slept with a man—scrap that, you couldn't call Darrell Hampton a man— make that a *young* man was a long time ago. They'd got together after the year twelve formal, and even though it hadn't been an unpleasant encounter, it hadn't been an experience that Ginny had sought out again. Darrell married Jenny James a few months later. Five years on, Ginny hadn't been tempted again. She had kept her distance from people in all parts of her life.

With a wave, Greg had headed out to the street, and she'd rushed across to the window and watched him walk to the ute. Her fingers lingered on her cheek where his lips had brushed a moment earlier.

But he was only a friend. These warm tingles attacking her tummy were to be ignored.

Now the thought of seeing Greg again in an hour or so made her smile and damn if those silly tingles didn't start up again. Maybe she was coming down with something.

Today she was going to surprise him by going casual. It was a cool spring day, and she'd brought a pair of jeans and a T-shirt and her Converse sneakers with her from home. She had still bowed to her fashion sense and picked up a light red jacket that was like a Japanese kimono, with black swirls of dragons and pink cherry blossoms patterned down the back.

After she had changed Ginny touched up her lips with a swipe of lip gloss, and after slipping on her sneakers, she headed to the door with a jauntiness in her step that hadn't been there for a long time.

Several people smiled at her as she walked to her car, and she smiled back, feeling content and happy with the world. The lightness that flowed through her limbs was unfamiliar, and the worry that normally sat in her chest like a stone wasn't there today.

The universe was with her, she didn't get a red light all the way to Bondi and jagged a parking spot only two doors down from the house on the hill.

As she walked up the footpath, the sound of the crashing surf and the squawking of the seagulls put her in a holiday mood.

She paused outside the house and looked up at the room where they had been trapped on Friday night.

Greg was standing at the window, and she waved with a big smile, and pointed across the road; she'd wait for him on one of the seats above the beach.

She crossed the road and chose a double seat on the grass above the rock wall and waited for him to join her. After a few minutes, when he hadn't come across, Ginny turned and was surprised to see him walking up the street from the bottom of the hill.

'You're early.' He took her hand in his and brushed her cheeks with warm lips. 'Let's go eat, I'm starving,' He gestured back the way he had come. 'There's a fish and chip shop on the corner.'

Ginny frowned. 'Greg … were you just up in the room in the house. The one where we were on Friday night?'

'No. I haven't been to the house yet. I got held up by a few calls. I figured I could do my looking around while you're working upstairs.

She tugged her hand out of his and pointed to the top floor of the house. 'Look, I'm sure there's still someone at the window.'

He followed her gaze and shook his head. 'I can't see anyone. Maybe it was a reflection on the glass.'

Ginny wasn't convinced. 'I'm sure I saw someone. I even waved.'

'Do you want to go for lunch, or will we go up and have a look first?' Greg seemed to take her seriously.

Ginny paused and then shook her head. 'No. Let's go eat. It must have been a reflection.'

Greg kept hold of her hand as they walked down the hill. The street was crowded and a couple of times they had to step to the side to make room for children on bicycles riding beside their parents. Once Greg put his arm around her and held her tucked into his side as three children on bikes preceded their parents.

Ginny swallowed as he held her close. A flutter of warmth ran from her tummy right down to her toes, and her knees actually trembled. She gripped his hand tightly and he looked at her curiously.

'Okay?'

She nodded as her cheeks heated. God, anyone would think she was fifteen, not twenty-three. 'Yes, all good.'

'I didn't tell you how nice'—Greg grinned— 'whoops, there's that word again. You look nicer than nice.'

Ginny giggled and relaxed.

'You look lovely,' he said. 'Is that word allowed?'

'Thank you. Old fashioned, but um… nice.'

Greg chuckled and bumped her lightly with his shoulder. 'Come on, I'll shout you a *nice* lunch.'

Ginny groaned but her lips twitched. 'That would be very *nice*.'

They reached the shop and Greg rolled his eyes when he saw the crowd. 'A bit of a wait, by the look of things.'

'That generally means the food is good. It smells yummy.' Ginny said. 'Can you survive the wait? I've got a muesli bar in my bag.' She grinned up at him.

'How about I order, and you go over and nab us a patch of grass?'

Ginny looked up at the menu board, told Greg what she wanted and wandered out of the shop.'

As she walked along the path looking for a spare spot on the grass, a loud scream reached her.

'Oh my God. Virginia!'

She turned slowly, and her eyes widened as a pair of hands grabbed her shoulders.

'It is you, isn't it? I've been trying to find out where you disappeared for years! Oh my God, Virginia, I can't believe it's you.'

Ginny put her hand over her mouth. 'Margie?' Margie

Holmes had been her best friend right through high school until her family had moved to Brisbane at the end of year ten.

'Margie Wright now. That's my husband over there, and our little boy. I've been looking for you everywhere. I went back to the school reunion last year, and you weren't there, and no one knew where you were. And you're not on Facebook or Instagram unless you've got one of those crazy made-up profile names.'

'Shabby-Chic,' Ginny said with a smile. 'And I go by Ginny now.'

'No wonder I couldn't find you. It was as though you disappeared off the face of the earth. I even put your school photo into Google and did a reverse image search, but nothing came up. Only that movie star I used to say you looked like. Are you on holiday at Bondi?'

Ginny shook her head. 'I live here now. How about you?'

Margie's shriek was full of excitement. 'We've just moved here too. We don't even have anywhere to live yet. Ryan just got transferred to an investment firm in the city. And I don't know anyone, I can't believe we've bumped into each other. It was meant to be. Just like your lovely Gran used to say.'

'It is, isn't it?' Ginny shook her head. It was funny to see someone from her old life, but she and Margie had always been close friends. When she'd moved to Sydney, Ginny had deliberately cut ties with her life in Mt Isa. It had been easier to cope when there was no one else to lose. Maybe she would have stayed in touch with Margie if she'd still lived there, but when Margie and her family had moved, they'd lost touch.

Seeing Margie was strange but good.

As they chatted, Ginny spotted Greg walking up the path, his arms loaded with three white cardboard boxes of fish and chips. He spotted her and crossed to the grass where she and Margie had moved to, so Margie could watch her husband and little boy down on the sand.

'Greg, this is a friend of mine from Mt Isa. Margie, this is Greg.'

Ginny blushed when she saw Margie glance down at her ring finger.

'Pleased to meet you.' Greg tried to juggle the boxes of food and hold out his hand at the same time, but Margie waved him away.

'No. You guys go and eat. I'll go down to the beach and when you're finished we'll do some more catching up. Virginia… Ginny … don't you dare disappear again.' She pulled out her phone. Give me your number just in case.'

Ginny obediently recited her mobile number. 'But we will catch up before we go. Greg and I have work to do after lunch, but I'll make some time.'

Margie headed to the beach with a wave, and Greg put the boxes on the grass.

'Virginia?' he said with a smile.

'Ginny is Sydney. The new me,' she said.

'I like the new you.' Before she could answer Greg leaned over and brushed his lips over hers.

Heat rushed into her face, into her tummy, down her legs and into every part of her.

Every part.

Her face got even hotter and she fanned herself.

'Summer's not far off,' Greg said with a little smile.

Ginny sat still and quiet as he unwrapped the food, determined to put some space between them. Things were moving a bit too fast for her.

Her voice was bright when she finally spoke. 'It's nice that I've made some new friends and found an old one all within a couple of days.'

Greg passed her a box of chips and put his head to the

side. 'I'm shattered.'

Ginny froze, and the box fell unheeded to her lap. 'What's wrong?'

'I've been relegated to *nice*?' His grin belied his words, and Ginny couldn't help herself. She leaned over and bumped him with her shoulder.

'Yes, but you are *very* nice.'

'Very is better.'

They sat close to each other and made their way through the pile of chips, and two huge pieces of fish. A strange feeling overtook Ginny; it was as though she'd known Greg for a long time. She was comfortable in his presence and she felt good about herself when she was with him.

'Penny for them?' Somehow Greg had got close and before she knew it, he had turned her around and pulled her back against his chest.

'I've got greasy fingers,' she said trying not to touch his jean. As she leaned back against him she could feel the slow thud of his heart against her back.

'No, don't answer that. I want to tell you something. 'I feel as though I've known you for a long time, Ginny.' His words echoed her thoughts.

'I know. I guess it's because we talked so much when we were in the house together.' She twisted her head and looked up at him; at the same time, he lifted his hand and gently brushed her hair back from her forehead. 'I don't usually feel this comfortable with people.'

'I don't usually need to *be* with people, I'm usually happy in my own company, but I don't know.' He shook his head, but his eyes stayed on hers 'I'll be honest. Since Friday night I can't get you out of my head.' His voice dropped as he lowered his head closer to hers 'You've bewitched me, Ginny Silver.'

Warm lips, still with a taste of salt, brushed against

hers and Ginny stretched up to meet them. The pressure increased, and she closed her eyes and Greg's lips teased backwards and forward against hers. A warm rush settled down low, and she almost purred with contentment. Greg's hand cupped the back of her head and the pressure of his lips increased.

'Mummy is that your friend? Is she feeling sick? Is he kissing her better?'

Ginny leaned back away from those magical lips and tried to pull herself back to the present.

'Sorry to interrupt, but we have to go and look at an apartment.' Margie stood above them, and Ginny pushed away from Greg and scrambled to her feet.

'Oh, um, er, it's fine. We were just about to leave anyway.'

'To work?' Margie's smile and raised eyebrows showed her disbelief. 'I didn't want to leave without seeing you again, and promising that I'll call you this week.'

Ginny nodded trying to bring herself back to the present. 'That would be great. Make sure you do.' She bent over and pulled a business card from her bag and handed it to Margie. 'This is where you can find me through the day.'

'Shabby-Chic. I love it,' Margie said as she read the card. 'I'll definitely call in.'

Greg stood beside her as she waved her friend off, and they watched as Margie and the little boy caught up to a tall man who was waiting on the footpath.

'Are you okay?' Greg wrapped his arms around her protectively. 'You look a bit shaken.'

'I'm fine.' Ginny plastered a smile on her face, feeling anything but fine. Knowing she was heading off to a whole empty house with Greg for the afternoon was sending those warm thrills crazy.

Chapter Twelve

Greg was determined to pull back. Every good intention he'd had, and every vow that he's made that he would keep his hands off Ginny, had disappeared as they sat there on the grass together.

Ginny had set his feelings on fire. Like he'd said, it was as though she'd bewitched him. He'd been in a long-term relationship before the accident, and he'd taken other women out, but never in his life had he felt such a strong pull to a woman. It scared him.

In one way he wanted to go to the house with Ginny this afternoon, but Greg was worried about his self-control. In another way, he wanted to run a mile, be alone, and get his head immersed in work and plans, to see if he could get her out of his head. It was ridiculous; he hadn't even known her for forty-eight hours.

'So are you ready to go to work?' Her voice was low and held a note of something he hadn't heard before. A teasing husky note.

He swallowed and nodded. 'I am.'

Greg gathered the rubbish and put it in the bin, and they walked slowly up to the house. There was a subtle tension between them, and he knew that Ginny was as aware of it as much as he was. She kept a good distance between them. They walked through the gate, and he pulled out the keys to open the front door.

'It's locked today. That's a good sign,' he said.

They stepped into the foyer together and Ginny's eyes were wide as she looked up. 'Can you feel it, Greg?' She sighed and put her hand on his arm. Her fingers were warm on his skin. He lifted his hand and put it on hers.

'This house has memories.' Ginny's voice sounded as

though she was far away. 'No matter what happens to it, the memories of people living here, and children growing up, will always be a part of it.'

She reached for him, and he closed his eyes as her arms went around his neck. Ginny's lips were against his, and he used one foot to close the door behind them.

'Happy times, and sad times. It's like life.' Her soft lips vibrated against his.' No matter what happens, the memories are there to help us get through. It's a lesson in life. One that I need to take heed of.'

She lifted her head and her eyes drilled into his. 'It's time I took risks. I've been too scared of getting hurt, and I've only been half alive. Kidding myself that a shop full of old clothes would be enough to keep me happy for the rest of my life. If you want to be my friend, Greg, that would be good. If you want to try being more, well'—her gaze dropped, and her cheeks flushed—' that would be alright with me too.'

***

Greg took her hand and led her up to the room they had been in together on Friday night. She waited as he propped the footstool against the door and turned to her. He brushed her hair back from his face, and his fingers were gentle.

'I would like to make love to you,' he said softly, her lips warm beneath his. 'But only if that's what you want.'

'Oh, yes,' she whispered back. 'But I'm nervous. I'm not very… very experienced.' Shyness brought heat to her cheeks, but he tilted her chin up with his fingers. She lifted her hand and ran one finger across his lower lip, her lip caught nervously between her teeth.

But Greg's kisses were slow and leisurely, and before she knew it, they were lying together on the old brass bed. Her breath caught as he dropped kisses on her eyelids, then slid his lips slowly down her cheek to the corner of her mouth. As she sighed, he took her hand and pressed it against his heart.

'Can you feel what you do to me, Ginny?'

The air hummed as she stared up at him. 'I can. Can you feel how happy you make me?'

The house stayed quiet as Greg reached for her T-shirt and gently pulled it over her head. His contented smile made Ginny pleased that she had worn her pretty lacy bra, but it soon joined her T-shirt on the floor.

##

Ginny woke a couple of hours later to the sound of the door closing gently. She stretched and searched the floor for her clothes. She took them into the bathroom, and had a quick wash, listening for Greg's return. The thought of the door being closed sent a shiver through her, but she quickly pushed it away. Nothing was going to take away from how wonderful she felt. Once she was dressed, she went back into the bedroom, and with a rueful smile, she gathered up the clothes from the floor. The rainbow silks that she'd placed carefully on the bed the other night had ended up in a pile of colour on the floor at the end of the bed.

She looked at the closed door and listened, but the house was quiet.

No thuds, no creaks, no sense of someone else being here. Something was missing; the house felt different.

She stood and walked to the door, but the knob began to turn slowly before she reached it. The door opened with a slow creak and Ginny held her breath, letting it out in a loud whoosh as Greg's head appeared around the door.

She put her hand against her chest, her heart thudding.

'Oh sweetheart, I'm so sorry. I didn't mean to scare you. I just went down for my phone. I left it in the car. And then I realised when I was at the front door, that I closed the bedroom door behind me. I hope you weren't scared?'

'No. I wasn't scared. I knew you'd come back.' She frowned as she looked around.

'But where did the stool go?

Greg followed the direction of her gaze and shook his head. 'I thought you'd moved it?'

Epilogue
Six months later.

'I'm pleased that you could all be here today.' Greg looked around the small group assembled in the foyer of the old house. Ginny followed his gaze and smiled. The smell of beeswax mingled with the sweet fragrance of flowers that she had filled the vases with. 'It's an occasion that we wanted to share. Ginny smiled as Kitty looked down at her left hand. They had spent a lot of happy times with Greg's friends over the past months. She shook her head slightly. No, they were her friends too

The last months had been incredible. In between working at Shabby-Chic, and carting over all the wonderful treasures from the house, getting to know Margie all over again, her days, and many of her nights—had been spent with Greg.

Sally and her husband, Sol, were standing beside an old-fashioned pram where a contented baby boy slept peacefully. Sonia, Sally's sister, and her partner, Dave, stood beside them.

'You have us all intrigued.' Taj Brown, a world-famous surfer, and his wife Rosie who was peering into the pram, had sold the house to Greg. 'It was lucky we were in town for the tournament.'

Greg reached over and put his arm around Ginny's shoulders. 'We wanted to tell you personally. As we've worked in the house, we've gotten to know it very well, and I've—we've—decided that this house needs to be a home.'

The smiles of the three girls lightened Ginny's heart. It had been Greg's idea, and even though she agreed with his decision, it had been one he'd come to alone and of his own accord.

'I'm not going to turn the house into apartments.'

Ginny nestled into his chest as his voice broke a little bit.

'Up until I bought this house from you all, a building, to me, was a building, bricks and mortar, old pipes, and maybe sagging windows, and door locks that jammed of their own accord.' Ginny looked up and met Greg's loving gaze. She swallowed as a lump filled her throat. How was it possible to love another person so much?

'But this house brought Ginny to me, and I know now that a house is more than a pile of timbers, a frame and a roof. Even in years to come when the house is gone, the memories that have been made will stay here. It's been home to many people, and Ginny and I are going to live here, and hopefully, one day soon, raise a family in this gracious old house.'

The cries of delight were accompanied by a loud thud from above.

Ginny saw the look exchanged between the three women.

'We know someone else who's happy too,' Sally said with a smile.

Greg looked down at her and his grin was wide. 'I think that explains a lot of what's happened here. 'Are you happy to live in a haunted house?'

'It's not haunted; it's just the happy memories making themselves felt. And, Greg, wherever you are, I'm happy to be with you.'

Greg leaned down and kissed her. 'There's only one more thing to be done.

Ginny frowned. 'What's that?'

Greg's grin sent that ever-present warmth spiralling to her toes. 'We have to take a holiday, or I'm going to lose a bet with Johnno.'

'Just as well I've got Margie to work in the shop for

me.'

As Greg's lips met hers again, Ginny could have sworn she heard a contented sigh drift down from above.

THE END

OTHER BOOKS from ANNIE

Daughters of the Darling
From Across the Sea
Over the River (2024)

Porter Sisters Series
Kakadu Sunset
Daintree
Diamond Sky
Hidden Valley
Larapinta
Kakadu Dawn

Pentecost Island Series
Pippa
Eliza
Nell
Tamsin
Evie
Cherry
Odessa
Sienna
Tess
Isla

The Augathella Girls Series
Outback Roads
Outback Sky
Outback Escape
Outback Wind
Outback Dawn
Outback Moonlight
Outback Dust
Outback Hope

An Augathella Surprise
An Augathella Baby
An Augathella Spring
An Augathella Christmas

An Augathella Wedding

Sunshine Coast Series
Waiting for Ana
The Trouble with Jack
Healing His Heart
Sunshine Coast Boxed Set

The Richards Brothers Series
The Trouble with Paradise
Marry in Haste
Outback Sunrise
Richards Brothers Boxed Set

Bondi Beach Love Series
Beach House
Beach Music
Beach Walk
Beach Dreams

Second Chance Bay Series
Her Outback Playboy
Her Outback Protector
Her Outback Haven
Her Outback Paradise
The McDougalls of Second Chance Bay Boxed Set

Love Across Time Series
Come Back to Me
Follow Me
Finding Home
The Threads that Bind
Love Across Time 1-4 Boxed Set

Bindarra Creek
Worth the Wait
Full Circle
Secrets of River Cottage
A Clever Christmas
A Place to Belong

Others
Whitsunday Dawn
Undara
Osprey Reef
East of Alice
Four Seasons Short and Sweet
Follow the Sun
Ten Days in Paradise
Deadly Secrets
Adventures in Time
Silver Valley Witch
The Emerald Necklace
A Clever Christmas
Christmas with the Boss
Her Christmas Star

About the Author

Annie lives in Australia, on the beautiful north coast of New South Wales. She sits in her writing chair and looks out over the tranquil Pacific Ocean.

She writes contemporary romance and loves telling stories that always have a happily ever after. She lives with her very own hero of many years and they share their home with Barney, the ragdoll puss, who hides when the four grandchildren come to visit.

Stay up to date with her latest releases at her website: http://www.annieseaton.net

Awards

2023: Winner of the long contemporary RUBY award for Larapinta

Finalist for the NZ KORU Award 2018 and 2020.

Winner ...Best Established Author of the Year 2017 AUSROM

Longlisted for the Sisters in Crime Davitt Awards 2016, 2017, 2018, 2019,2022

Finalist in Book of the Year, Long Romance, RWA Ruby Awards 2016 Kakadu Sunset

Winner ...Best Established Author of the Year 2015 AUSROM

Winner ...Author of the Year 2014 AUSROM
Best Established Author, Ausrom Readers' Choice 2017

Printed in Great Britain
by Amazon